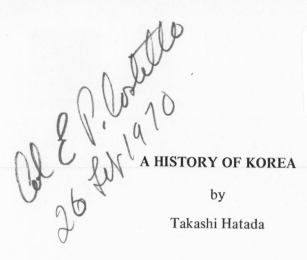

A HISTORY OF KOREA

by

Takashi Hatada

Translated and edited by:

Warren W. Smith, Jr.

and

Benjamin H. Hazard

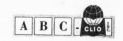

Santa Barbara, California
1969

©1969
by
ABC-CLIO, Inc.

Library of Congress Catalog Card No.
69-20450

SBN Paperbound Edition 87436-065-X
Clothbound Edition 87436-064-1

American Bibliographical Center — Clio Press

*Riviera Campus, 2010 Alameda Padre Serra
Santa Barbara, California 93103*

This translation is dedicated to the memory of

Joseph R. Levenson

W.W.S., Jr. & B.H.H.

CONTENTS

Chapter

Chapter

MAPS

TABLES

Translators' Preface

During 1952, when the translators were working on the compilation of a *Korean Studies Guide* (University of California Press, 1954), they received a copy of Hatada Takashi's then recently published *Chōsen-shi* (History of Korea) (Tokyo: Iwanami Shoten, 1951) and were impressed with its lucid interpretation of Korean history.[1] Since they had found, while compiling the *Korean Studies Guide* that there was no good survey history of Korea in a Western language, they decided it would be useful to translate Hatada's work.[2]

Unfortunately, for a number of reasons, almost two decades have passed since Hatada's book first appeared in print and the publication of this translation. Much work has been done during this time in studying Korea's past, particularly among Korean historians, and the *Korean Studies Guide* has become dated. However, there is still no adequate history of Korea in English or other European languages, a fact reconfirmed recently by Gregory Henderson in his book, *Korea: The Politics of the Vortex* (Cambridge: Harvard University Press, 1968), page 1. Henderson's perceptive work, which provides a stimulating analysis of the dynamics of Korean political activity, will be difficult for readers to judge, precisely because few will have the background in Korean history to evaluate his generalizations.

To be sure, we have had for years Homer Hulbert's *The History of Korea* (Seoul: The Methodist Publishing House, 1905), republished with editorial comment by Clarence N. Weems under the title of *Hulbert's History of Korea* (New York: Hillary House, 1962). But Hulbert's history, although replete with anecdotes, is largely a paraphrase of traditional Korean histories and shares their limitations. However much such histories may reflect of the praise or blame of rulers and their ministers through use of the Confucian "pruning pencil," they fail to provide the necessary framework for understanding the development of the past of the Korean people.

An unsatisfactory attempt to fill this lacuna was made in 1963 by the Center for East Asian Cultural Studies through the publication of *A Short History of Korea* (Honolulu: East West Center Press), with the assistance of UNESCO. It is a translation based on a Japanese work, *Chōsen-shi no shirube* (Introduction to Korean History), published in 1936 by the Government General of Chōsen, and it suffers from the defects implicit in an official Japanese history of Korea written at a time when Korea was still under Japanese rule. In addition, as was the case with the original Japanese work, it is lacking in historical interpretation; there is little correlation between political events and social and economic developments; and the chapters dealing with nineteenth and twentieth century Korea are woefully deficient.[3]

---

[1] For a book review of the *Chōsen-shi* by the translators in 1954, see *Far Eastern Quarterly*, XIII, 2 (February 1954), pp. 219-21. This review refers in turn to several other reviews of the *Chōsen-shi* by Japanese and Korean historians.

[2] Chapter 10 of Edwin O. Reischauer and John K. Fairbank, *History of East Asian Civilization: East Asia, the Great Tradition*, (Boston: Houghton-Mifflin Co., 1960) pp. 394-449, presents a good but very brief outline of Korean history. Of interest here is that this outline was largely based on Hatada's *Chōsen-shi*, with revision by Yi Pyŏngdo and Edward W. Wagner.

[3] For a lengthy criticism by three Korean historians, see "A Maliciously Distorted Book," *Korea Journal*, VII, 4 (April 1967), pp. 9-19. These reviews, though occasionally marred by patriotic fervor, justifiably attack the choice made by the East West Center Press and UNESCO for a survey of Korean history and should dispose of consideration of *A Short History of Korea* as a serious work. Another critical review by Wi Jo Kang may be found in *Journal of Asian Studies*, XXV, 1 (November 1965), p. 147.

At this point, a reader of this translation of Hatada is justified in asking whether it will satisfactorily fill the gap, recalling that it is still a history of Korea written by a Japanese and that Korean historians have made great advances in the study of their country since 1951.

There is no doubt that if one were to attempt to choose today among the available survey histories of Korea suitable for translation into English, there would be much more choice than faced the translators of Hatada in 1952. For example, we now have the monumental seven volume *Han'guk-sa* (History of Korea), written and edited by a group of Korea's outstanding historians, and published by the Chindan Society in Seoul between 1959 and 1965 with the assistance of the Rockefeller Foundation, which will undoubtedly be a standard reference for many years to come. There is also Professor Yi Pyŏngdo's *Kuksa taegam* (General Survey of National History), a good one volume work widely used in Korean high schools and colleges. Professor Yi Pyŏngdo, considered by many as the dean of Korean historians, has modified and expanded his history a number of times, the latest revision being in 1964. Another recent fine survey history, compact and including many useful up-to-date references, is Yi Kibaek's *Hanguk-sa sillon* (New View of Korean History), (Seoul: Ilchogak, 1967). Professor Yi Kibaek, one of the leading younger historians of Korea, based this work on an earlier history of his published in 1961, *Kuksa sillon*, (New View of National History), which he revised and amplified while at Harvard University in 1966 under the auspices of the Harvard-Yenching Institute.

Where, then, does Hatada's history fit into the spectrum of Korean studies? The characteristic of Hatada's book which most recommended itself to the translators was the skill with which the author revealed the interrelationship between political history and social and economic development. Western language accounts of Korea up to the present have stressed Korean political history and foreign affairs, and given little or no reference to internal economic conditions and social change. Hatada displays the close relationship of these factors, describing, for example, the conditions under which a surplus was produced in Korean society during the Silla period, which in turn made possible the means and the leisure for the development of such cultural achievements as the palaces, temples and artifacts of that time. For subsequent periods, Hatada continues to emphasize changing economic and social conditions, taking particular care to explain the interrelation between the structure of power and the control of land in each period, while the details of Korea's political and diplomatic history are not discussed unless they have a bearing on these.

The author seems to have a criterion for determining whether progress was made in the historical periods under consideration, for he speaks constantly of "advance," "growth," and "maturity" in characterizing the social and economic conditions of each period. The basis for this criterion is not clearly stated, but it appears from the context to mean a wider sharing by the Koreans in the fruits of their labor, and their increased participation in the political and cultural life of their nation. At times it is the method of land administration, taxation procedures, or the forms of political association in which Hatada finds evidence of progress, and although one may take exception to the author's point of view, it is consistent and stimulating.

A special characteristic of Hatada's book is its sympathetic attitude toward the Koreans, nowhere better expressed than in his analysis of Korean conditions under Japanese rule between 1910 and 1945. His candid evaluation of the benefits of Japanese rule in Korea is unusual for a Japanese and a tribute to his intellectual honesty.

Hatada's description of Korea between 1945 and 1950, however, was based on insufficient information, a fact pointed out by a fellow Japanese historian, Suematsu Yasukazu, in his review of Hatada's book in the third number of *Chōsen gakuhō* (Journal of the Academic Association of Koreanology in Japan) published in 1952. The translators have also noted a number of instances of misinformation. For example, Hatada states that there was no land reform in South Korea during this period, but in fact the land formerly owned by the Japanese in South Korea, which constituted much of the best land in the country, was distributed to small farmers by the American Military Government, and besides a land-reform program was instituted by the South Korean Government. The troubles on Cheju Island, which he attributed to popular discontent, were in fact organized and fomented by Communist agitators who came from North Korea, and the so-called rebellions at Yŏsu and Sunch'ŏn were Communist instigated. Hatada also was overly credulous of the figures and progress reports claimed by the authorities in North Korea. He should have pointed out, moreover, that it was the refusal of these same authorities in North Korea to allow the United Nations into the North in 1948 that prevented the holding of nationwide elections, which might have unified the country.

These few shortcomings noted above do not detract from the overall quality of Hatada's work, and would presumably be corrected if he were to rewrite his *Chōsen-shi* today. As a matter of fact, when queried in 1961 by the translators regarding a number of points and interpretations in the book, Hatada answered that they should translate the book as published, since if he were to begin modifying its contents, he would have to write another history of Korea. In other words, the *Chōsen-shi* represents the author's analysis of Korean history as it appeared to him in 1951.

We are fortunate in having a recent evaluation by Hatada himself of his 1951 history, in a book published by an association known as the Chōsen-shi Kenkyūkai, entitled *Chōsen-shi nyūmon* (A Guide to the Study of Korean History), (Tokyo: Taihei Shuppan-sha, 1966). This association was formed in 1959 by younger scholars in Japan, both Japanese and Korean, to encourage the study of Korean history along new lines and to promote a better understanding of Korea's past among the Japanese. Hatada, a founding member of the association, was the general editor of *Chōsen-shi nyūmon*, and he also wrote its first chapter which is an essay surveying the past, present and future of Korean studies. In this excellent essay, Hatada discusses the emphasis of the principal Japanese historians prior to 1945 and the hypothesis they supported. Because many of their theories are still current today and have affected the study of Korean history, it may be useful to summarize them and indicate some of their better known proponents.

The earliest theory developed by Japanese historians and scholars of other disciplines in the late nineteenth and early twentieth centuries regarding Korea was that both countries had the same origins and the same ancestors. According to this, Koreans were not basically different from the Japanese, which was of course a convenient point of view after Japan's annexation of Korea in 1910, it being claimed that Korea had often been under Japanese domination in ancient times, so that the unity was natural. Of more far reaching effect in the study of Korean history was that this theory negated any uniqueness or individuality to Korea's historical development. Many scholars and historians paid lip service to this theory, including such authorities as Kuroita Katsumi, Sekino Tadashi, Kanazawa Shōzaburō, Shidehara Taira, Tsuji Zennosuke and Yoshida Tōgo.

One of the most painstaking attempts to buttress this hypothesis, marshalling data from archeology, ethnology, etymology, and historical sources, was made by Kida Teikichi in 1921 in a long study published in the scholarly journal *Minzoku to rekishi* (Race and History), VI. Appearing as it did shortly after the Korean Independence Movement of March 1, 1919, it seemed like an effort to prove the pointlessness of any similar movements by the Koreans in view of their affinity with the Japanese. Kida's study, however, not only encompassed Korea, but also uncovered bonds between the Japanese and the peoples of Manchuria and Mongolia, and in this sense it was a prelude to the Greater Asia doctrines of Uchida Ryōhei in the 1930's when Japanese expansion spread into Manchuria and Inner Mongolia.

Not all Japanese scholars looked at Korea from the point of view of Japanese history. Japanese interest developed early in the techniques and methods of Western Sinology and Oriental studies, and study groups were formed to investigate Asiatic history, emphasizing Manchuria and Northeast Asia where Japanese commercial and political activities were strong. The South Manchurian Railway field study group is the best known of these and included such outstanding scholars as Shiratori Kurakichi, Ikeuchi Hiroshi, Matsui Hitoshi, Inaba Iwakichi and Tsuda Sōkichi, who have left a notable collection of historical, archeological and geographical studies of the area, including Korea. There developed among these men the attitude that Korean history was really not an independent field, but part of the larger history of Manchuria and Northeast Asia. This theory, similar in its effects to the "Korea and Japan as one" hypothesis, discouraged the investigation of the unique features of Korea's cultural history and her internal social development and sought rather to explain Korea's past in terms of endless waves of foreign incursions and influences from Manchuria and elsewhere on the Asiatic mainland. The historian, Inaba Iwakichi, was particularly known for his writings stressing this unity of Korean-Manchurian history and culture.

A theory regarding Korean history, which grew out of these earlier two and combined their common features, was the heteronomy theory. Heteronomy, which means growth dependent on forms imposed from without, as opposed to autonomy, was most notably applied to Korean history by Mishina Akihide in his popular *Chōsen-shi gaisetsu* (Outline of Korean History) first published in 1940. According to this theory, Korea's past can only be understood by appreciating the fact that her development has been dependent on both her close Japanese relationship and her association with Manchuria and the rest of East Asia. This explanation does recognize an individuality to Korean historical development, but it is on an inferior, almost parasitic, level.

As almost a corollary to these various theories was the theory of the stagnation of Korean society. In attempting to explain Korea's backwardness in the late nineteenth and early twentieth centuries, Japanese travellers and observers generally characterized Korean society as having stagnated on a level with society in

Japan during the Nara period (710-784) or the Heian period (794-1185). These characterizations received more detailed support from such men as Wada Ichirō, in charge of the extensive land survey carried out in Korea between 1910-1919. Wada found that the pattern of land ownership in Korea was along communal lines, typical of primitive societies. And the respected Japanese economic historian, Fukuda Tokuzō, wrote that Korea's stage in historical development was pre-feudal, which explained her backwardness and many of the apparent contradictions in her economic and social organization.

The backwardness of pre-modern Korea and its explanation through the stagnation theory became widely held with little variation among pre-war Japanese historians and economists. And from this premise, it followed that Korea did not have the seeds for modernization, which in turn served to justify Japan's annexation of Korea as a necessary means to reform its social structure and bring progress to the country.

When writing the *Chōsen-shi* in 1951, Hatada was aware of these theories and attempted to make a break with them in explaining Korea's past. In particular, he wished to stress the unique and individual character of Korean history as produced by the Koreans themselves, and as was mentioned earlier in this preface, he found evidence of progress in the course of Korea's history which would belie the stagnation theory referred to above.

The *Chōsen-shi* was an ambitious undertaking, and Hatada himself confessed in 1966 that it was daring and perhaps even foolhardy. He recognized that it had many failings, among the principal of which would be the unsatisfactory treatment given to cultural developments as evidence of the creative talent of the Korean people throughout their history.[4]

We may now conclude this consideration of Hatada's *Chōsen-shi* by saying it was a milestone, whose translation it is hoped will serve as an impetus to further the study of Korea's past. And while those who do not relish the social science approach to historical study may find fault in Hatada's generalizations, yet as Yi

----

[4]The unsatisfactory treatment given by the *Chōsen-shi* to the far-reaching cultural achievements of the Yi dynasty's creative first century is certainly a case in point. The sections on "culture" in the various volumes of the Chindan Society's *Han'guk-sa*, mentioned earlier in the Translators' Preface, can help fill this gap. Also, the recently published two volume *Chōsen bunka-shi* (Cultural History of Korea), (Tokyo: Atōsha, 1966), a Japanese translation of a cultural history which appeared in 1965 in North Korea, is of particular interest because it attempts to view culture broadly, including the physical sciences, technology and medicine, and to suggest the connection between cultural achievements and historical circumstances. A review by Hatada of the *Chōsen bunka-shi* may be found in *Chōsen gakuhō*, 43 (1967), pp. 172-176.

For coverage specifically of the cultural developments related to the revolutionary Korean language reform in the fifteenth century, there is the excellent unpublished PhD. dissertation by Gari K. Ledyard, *The Korean Language Reform of 1446: The Origin, Background, and Early History of the Korean Alphabet*, (University of California in Berkeley, 1966).

A useful survey emphasizing the fine arts of Korea is Evelyn McCune's *The Arts of Korea, An Illustrated History*, (Tokyo: Charles E. Tuttle Company, 1962). More specialized treatment of particular aspects of the fine arts may be found in G. St. G. M. Gompertz, *Korean Pottery and Porcelain of the Yi Period*, (New York: Frederick A. Praeger, 1968), and in the beautifully illustrated *Treasures of Korean Art: 2000 Years of Ceramics, Sculpture and Jeweled Arts*, (New York: Harry N. Abrams, Inc., 1966) by Chewon Kim and Won-yong Kim.

Kibaek told one of the translators in 1966 in Cambridge, one may disagree with Hatada but historians of Korea cannot ignore him.

In translating the *Chōsen-shi*, the following has been the general division of work between Benjamin H. Hazard and Warren W. Smith, Jr. The original literal translation of the first half of the book, through Koryŏ, was done by Benjamin Hazard; and the second half and the author's preface by Warren Smith. The rewriting from the literal translation and the editing of the whole book was entrusted to Warren Smith, who was generously assisted by Dr. Mary M. Street in the final English version. The checking of the proofs and preparation of the maps were the work of Benjamin Hazard. The drawing of the maps was done by Roger Mobley. The glossary was prepared by the translators and the index by Benjamin Hazard. The calligraphy was done by Mrs. Yoshimi Nakamura.

In translating the book, it was found desirable to eliminate some repetitous phrases and alter the wording in certain parts in order to make the text more readable. Also a limited amount of editing was deemed necessary, either through footnotes or amplification of the text, when it appeared that a reference made by Hatada needed clarification to be understood by English readers.

A recurring translation problem was to find adequate words in English for ranks and titles, concepts of land tenure, classification of slaves and unfree persons, and similar expressions. As a general rule, a direct literal translation and an explanation has been given for such terms when they first occur, and if they are important and often repeated, the romanized Korean has been included in the text of the translation in order for the reader to become acquainted with the Korean terms themselves. The author was consulted in cases where the translators were unable to find a suitable English expression equivalent to the Korean or were at a loss over the meaning of a term. An attempt has been made to avoid the use of words such as "feudalism," "fief," "serf," and related terms which are not properly applicable to Korean historical development. Although the word "feudalism" is often loosely applied today, in fact it refers to a particular type of political, economic, and social organization based on a complex system of ascending and descending rights and obligations among military men which never really developed in Korea.

The lists of references and suggested readings included in the Japanese original at the end of each section and at the end of the book have been omitted in the English translation since the translators felt it would be of little value except to those with a knowledge of Japanese, Korean, and Chinese, who could refer to Hatada's original text for this information. The chronology also has been omitted, but a list of rulers and their dates has been appended in the translation for the convenience of the reader. The translators used the first edition and first printing of the *Chōsen-shi* (Tokyo: Iwanami Shoten, 1951).

The translators have tried to mitigate language difficulties whenever possible. Standard Romanization has been used throughout: the McCune-Reischauer system for Korean, Wade-Giles for Chinese, and modified Hepburn for Japanese. Old Korean terms have been transliterated according to modern Korean phonetic equivalents, admittedly an imperfect method, but one which will have to suffice until a Karlgren of Korean comes along. Throughout the translation, old place names and geographical areas have been identified in reference to modern Korean provincial boundaries and the names of presently existing towns and landmarks. No Chinese characters appear in the text of the translation, but every Korean,

Chinese, or Japanese name, word, title, and so on occurring in the translation will be found listed alphabetically in the glossary with its corresponding Chinese characters or, where appropriate, with its Korean phonetic *(hangŭl)* equivalent.

In the names of Koreans, Chinese, and Japanese, the customary order of the family name first, followed by the personal name has been used, unless the individual is well known in the West by the Western style of personal name followed by family name. When dates are given following a person's name, they refer, for rulers, to the years of their reigns, and, for other persons, the dates refer to the years of birth and death.

Finally, acknowledgement for publication of the translation is due to the publisher, Dr. Eric H. Boehm, and the editor, Mr. Lloyd Garrison, of Clio Press of Santa Barbara, California, who have been most helpful in encouraging the translators in the completion of their task. Others to whom the translators are indebted for assistance at various stages of preparation of the book are Mrs. Elizabeth Evans, Mrs. Ruth Lee Smith, Mr. Larry Rogers, Professor Suematsu Yasukazu, the late Professor Joseph Levenson, Dr. Kim Chewon (Kim Chaewŏn), Director of the National Museum of Korea, and Professor Michael Rogers.

Professor Hatada Takashi was born in Korea in 1908. He graduated from Tokyo University (then Tokyo Imperial University) in 1931, majoring in the history of the Far East. He worked for a time with the distinguished Japanese scholars who comprised the South Manchurian Railway field study group. He is a specialist on Korean and modern Chinese history and is considered an authority on the Korean family system and Chinese rural society. He is presently professor of Far Eastern history at Tokyo Metropolitan University.

Berkeley, California   Warren W. Smith, Jr.
                                              Benjamin H. Hazard

Author's Preface

During the latter half of the nineteenth century, the pioneers in the study of Oriental history in Japan showed great interest in the history of Korea and often initiated their investigations with that country. In these early years, too, scholars specializing in ancient Japanese history, legal history, linguistics, and other fields frequently turned their attention to Korean history with the result that we can find studies and even heated debates on ancient Korean history in the early numbers of the Japanese historical journal *Shigaku zasshi* (The Journal of Historical Science), written by scholars such as Naka Michiyo, Tsuboi Kumezō, Yoshida Tōgo, Shiratori Kurakichi, Miyazaki Michisaburō, Nakata Kaoru, and Kanazawa Shōzaburō.

Then, as a Japanese policy of expansion toward the Asiatic mainland became formulated, with Korea as the starting point, the attention of the Japanese scholarly world was focused more on the country itself, and when the South Manchurian Railroad began the economic development of Korea and Manchuria, a research department to study the history of these countries was formed by the Company, composed of such scholars as Shiratori Kurakichi, Ikeuchi Hiroshi, Yanai Wataru, Tsuda Sōkichi, Inaba Iwakichi, and Matsui Hitoshi, who were to become the leading Orientalists in Japan. Among the results of their efforts were outstanding publications on historical geography including *Chōsen rekishi chiri* (Korean Historical Geography), *Manshū rekishi chiri* (Manchurian Historical Geography), and *Mansen chiri rekishi kenkyū hōkoku* (Study Reports on the Geography and History of Manchuria and Korea), which set a distinct pattern for Japanese Oriental studies.

After direct Japanese administration — the so-called Government General — was established in Korea, the study of the country was officially encouraged and made great strides. Beginning with the publication of the 35-volume *Chōsen-shi* (History of Korea), the 15-volume *Chōsen koseki zufu* (Album of Korean Antiquities), and the *Koseki chōsa hōkoku* (Archeological Investigation Reports), the study of Korean historical sources, ancient sites, and archeological remains progressed, far and away more vigorously than similar research in other areas of East Asia. The thoroughness of these studies of Korea gave Korean history the appearance of being a Japanese preserve, although the investigation by the Japanese of other areas of East Asia was probably inferior to that carried on by Western scholars.

As mentioned, Korean historical study was stimulated by the growth of Japan's policy of expansion in Asia, and yet its importance relative to the over-all historical research being done on Asia gradually declined. Aside from persons engaged in studies in one capacity or another for government agencies, the number of scholars dedicated to Korean history was small. This was especially true of the younger generation of Orientalists. The decrease in interest in Korean history can be attributed partially to the growing interest in China, and partly to the lack of research in this field by Koreans themselves, although the study of Korea progressed under government auspices. The policy followed under Japanese rule was not designed to produce Korean scholars of Korean history. I think that at a time when the word "Korea" invoked feelings painful to Koreans, they naturally felt little desire to explore the history of the country. Their attitude undoubtedly influenced that of young Japanese historians.

Moreover, the political situation under Japanese rule did not constitute the sole obstacle to Korean historical research. The content of such works as were compiled did not inspire young scholars. The major emphasis was placed on ancient history, and little attention was paid to recent events. Furthermore, the studies in ancient history specialized in textual exegesis, chronological tables, and verification of geographical place names. Such specialization may have served to break down old dogmas, but it was far removed from daily life and interests. No attempt was made to examine and study the kinds of people who had grown up under varying social conditions. Although the recording of events and of the sites where they took place is an important prerequisite to historical study, the detachment of such a presentation from human life and the disregard of human history made it uninteresting to the younger generation.

When Japan was defeated in the Second World War and her control over Korea ended, government-supported Korean historical research collapsed, and Korean studies active up to that time abruptly fell into stagnation.

The study of Korean history is now in a new phase. Although the findings of the old investigations must be used, a new kind of history must be written, a history of the Korean people as they lived it through the ages. The starting point for this history, I think, must be an appreciation of the hardships endured by the Koreans. Only in this way can the study of Korean history be properly related to the study of world history and, at the same time, related to people living here and now.

With this in mind I have attempted to write this history of Korea. I will not say that I have fully achieved this objective, but I hope that I will have served to advance the study of Korean history a step further.

In the writing of this book I have been aided by many people: in particular, by the helpful advice and encouragement of Professor Ikeuchi Hiroshi even while he was on his sickbed, and by the work of Mr. Sakurai Yoshiyuki in the matter of references. I extend to these my most heartfelt thanks.

                                                        Hatada Takashi

July, 1951

I

Formative Period

Stone Age

On the Korean peninsula the first man may have appeared in the paleolithic period. It may be assumed that he arrived there from the adjoining part of Asia, where paleolithic remains make it clear that mankind has existed since remote antiquity. Such remains, however, have not been definitely identified in Korea, although chipped stone artifacts have been found in North Hamgyŏng Province and in some other areas.

Man's existence in Korea, in the neolithic period, on the other hand, is clearly evidenced by the shell mounds along the sea coasts and in river basins, and by the remains-bearing strata found in these locations and on the hills and mountains.

The discovered remains include pottery and tools made of stone, antler, bone, and in the late neolithic even metal. The great variation in the artifacts indicates that for these people the stone age extended over a long period, probably several thousand years, during which slow progress was made, and that men of diverse cultures contributed. For we see coarse stone tools shading into finer ones, some of the finest appearing to be imitations of metal tools, and pottery ranging from poorly fired, brittle, and crudely made items to some fired at high temperatures, hard, and skillfully executed.

To seek the source of the diverse cultures, one naturally turns to that part of continental Asia which is contiguous to the Korean peninsula. We know that in later historic periods cultural progress in Korea followed that of the rest of Asia, so it seems fair to assume that the same relationship existed at an earlier time. However, many ethnic and cultural strains are mixed in Asia. It is not easy to determine which among them gave Korea her original inhabitants and her earliest culture.

A significant clue to a solution of this problem is furnished by pottery found in the remains-bearing strata. Thus the predominant comb-marked pottery links the culture to that of Siberia and Manchuria; unmarked pottery to that of Mongolia, Manchuria and northern China; and red-painted, polished pottery to a different northern China culture.

Therefore, the first people who entered Korea probably moved south from Siberia and Manchuria, following the sea coasts and rivers. Some of them seem to have crossed the sea to Japan, and others to have climbed the mountains and hills of the interior of Korea. Not all of them were from the far north. Some apparently came from northern China, Manchuria and Mongolia. Such migrations must have occurred repeatedly during a long period of time. The older cultures first brought in and established were partly submerged by those of later ones. Thus the cultures were gradually mixed, which probably explains the variations throughout the stone age and the characteristic regional differences which later developed.

During this early period existence was at a low level and progress was slow. The people lived by hunting and fishing, eating fruit and nuts, and searching for shellfish. Whether they were close to the seashore and rivers or in the hills and mountains, all were dependent on nature for their precarious hand-to-mouth existence. There was a beginning of primitive agriculture, but it alone was quite inadequate to satisfy man's needs. Since agriculture had to be supplemented by natural products, the search for these was the essential task, thus precluding a long stay in any one place. Roaming over wide areas in pursuit of game then settling in an area for a while, the people led a semi-nomadic life. Meanwhile, tools were gradually improved. Gradually, too, agriculture developed in some places. In these, more permanent residences came to be established. Eventually the fishermen in the streams, the hunters in the hills, and those who farmed on the warm plains developed characteristic ways of life different from each other. These diverse patterns, evolving at different speeds in different regions, became the basis for the tribal differences of the peninsula's inhabitants. These were described later in the "Eastern Barbarian" section *(Tung-i-ch'üan)* of *Wei-chih* (History of the Wei), a third-century Chinese history.

The rate of progress was sluggish. Man devoted all his energies to keeping himself alive. He had not reached the stage where he lived by controlling the labor of other men. The people lived in blood-kinship groups which had developed naturally and in which they apparently had to remain. It was the kinship group, undoubtedly, which decided co-operatively the apportionment of labor and distribution of goods to its members. There seems to have been almost no class distinction. Nor have any remains been discovered in the old sites indicating wealth or authority, in contrast with the marvelous finds in the mounds of later periods — finds which were undoubtedly the possessions of the wealthy.

This slowly developing primitive society was finally changed by an outside force. Two influences penetrated the peninsula from the northwest which fundamentally altered the long-existing pattern: metal culture and the concept of authority. Relations of domination and submission, of mastery and subordination, appeared, as well as differentiations based on tribe, class, and culture. Because these two influences appeared simultaneously the introduced metal tools were confined to those in authority, and their general use was not widespread until centuries later.

Activity of the Hsiung-nu and Chinese
Domination of the East

While Korea was still in the stone age, two great movements arose on the continent which, reaching the peninsula, had a profound effect on its population. These were the activities of the Hsiung-nu (Huns) and the Chinese drive to the east.

The Hsiung-nu were a nomadic people who lived largely in the Mongolian plateau of the northern Asiatic steppe belt and who diffused the so-called Scytho-Siberian culture. Their activity, as recorded in history, extended from the fourth or fifth century B.C., but it was from China's period of the Warring States (403-221 B.C.) to the Ch'in (221-207 B.C.) and Former Han (206 B.C. - 8 A.D.) dynasties that the Hsiung-nu united the people of the steppes into a powerful force, extended their power to threaten the Chinese to the south, and expanded as far as Manchuria to the east. The Great Wall, built by the Ch'in, shows how much the Chinese feared the Hsiung-nu. The high metal culture of the Hsiung-nu was transmitted to the various tribes in the east, including the Puyŏ and Koguryŏ peoples. The use of metal accelerated their development and became a source of strength for them in their later expansion into Korea. At the same time, the eastward movement of the Hsiung-nu stimulated opposition to them by the Han Chinese in their own eastern expansion, such as the occupation of much of Korea by the Emperor Wu of Han in 108 B.C. The activities of the Hsiung-nu caused great changes in the political situation of all of East Asia, including Korea.

The drive east of the Chinese had an even greater and more direct effect on Korea than that of the Hsiung-nu. In China, for several millennia B.C., an agricultural civilization had existed in the basin of the Yellow River. By about 2000 B.C., rice was cultivated in paddy fields, domestic animals were raised, and bronze articles were in use. At length the Yin, more commonly known as Shang, and Chou dynasties were established, forming the earliest advanced civilized society among the peoples of Asia. During the Spring-and-Autumn *(Ch'un-ch'iu)* period in China, from the eighth to the fifth century B.C., iron articles first appeared in this essentially bronze culture, and in the period of the Ch'in and Han dynasties, bronze tools were replaced by iron. This development of Chinese culture brought with it the assimilation, colonization, and absorption of surrounding uncivilized peoples. The drive east of the Chinese, a phase of this process, is first distinguishable in the period of the Warring States from the fifth to the third century B.C. The Yen, one of the powerful contenders among the Warring States from northern China, penetrated southern Manchuria and established commanderies *(chün)*[1] and prefectures *(hsien)* in Liao-tung and Liao-hsi, which were incorporated into the territory of China. Since that time, the

---

[1] The term *chün* stands for a geographical and administrative subdivision originally used in early China in frontier areas under a military commander. It is translated as "commandery" in this book when reference is made to subdivisions of areas administered by the Chinese; but when the Koreans adopted the term for the internal division and administration of Korea, it has been translated as "county." The Korean pronunciation of the term is *kun.*

colonization and development in the east by the Chinese became vigorous; they moved from a spearhead in southern Manchuria to the Yalu River and penetrated Korea. There they subdued the natives, took tribute, and either cultivated the land themselves or traded Chinese goods for locally produced articles. In this way their influence became strong in northwest Korea. About the third century B.C., a state was born governed by these Chinese. It was known as Ch'i-tzu Chao-hsien-kuo (K:Kija Chosŏn-guk)[2] — Ch'i-tzu being the name of the founder.

Since that time colonists continued to arrive from China, especially during the period of upheaval following the change of dynasties from Ch'in to Han, when many Chinese refugees escaped to Korea. These immigrants were absorbed into Chao-hsien-kuo which had its center in the lower basin of the Taedong River and controlled a region roughly comprising the two present-day Korean provinces of Hwanghae and P'yŏngan. Then, in the early part of the second century B.C., a Chinese refugee, Wei-man (K:Wiman), seized power in Ch'i-tzu Chao-hsien-kuo and established a new state, Wei-shih Chao-hsien-kuo (K:Wisi Chosŏn-guk). This state, too, received refugees from China and subdued the natives, becoming much more powerful than the earlier Ch'i-tzu Chao-hsien-kuo.

At that time bureaucratic China, ruled by the Han Dynasty, developed on an unprecedented scale. Outside China the Han rulers embarked on great military campaigns against the Hsiung-nu to the north and against Min-yüeh (present-day Fukien Province) and Nan-yüeh (present-day Vietnam) to the south. This activity naturally extended also to the east. Wei-shih Chao-hsien-kuo, although established by a Chinese, avoided paying tribute to Han China. In fact, there are indications that it was allied to the Hsiung-nu when they spread from Mongolia into Manchuria. This state, therefore, constituted a menace to the Han Dynasty, and its existence could not be tolerated if the Han were to control Korea as an eastern base and were to have a protected flank in their fight against the Hsiung-nu.

A first attempt to gain control was made when a Korean tribal chieftain, Yegun Namnyŏ, surrendered to Han forces. The latter seized this opportunity to create the commandery of Ch'uang-hai as part of the Han empire (128 B.C.), but it lacked sufficient military support, and the Han forces were soon ousted. Then, in 109 B.C., the Han Emperor Wu sent armies by land and sea to attack Wang-hsien-ch'eng (present-day P'yŏngyang), the capital of Wei-shih Chao-hsien-kuo. In the following year Wei-shih Chao-hsien-kuo was destroyed.

Emperor Wu incorporated Korea into territory under the direct jurisdiction of the Han rulers and established four commanderies, Lo-lang, Chen-fan, Hsüan-t'u, and Lin-t'un. These were subdivided into a number of prefectures with Chinese administrators. In this way the commandery-prefecture system, which was the method of governing the Chinese homeland, was introduced on the

---

[2]Traditionally, Ch'i-tzu Chao-hsien-kuo was established by Ch'i'tzu, a minister of the last ruler of the Chinese Shang (also called Yin) Dynasty. Ch'i-tzu is said to have come to Korea in 1122 B.C. with five thousand followers, after the overthrow of the Shang Dynasty. While the author of this book accepts the existence of early Chinese influence in Korea, his wording in the text and his dating of Ch'i-tzu Chao-hsien-kuo indicate that he rejects the legend of Kija's arrival and Sinicizing of Korea as early as 1122 B.C. Ch'i-tzu is pronounced Kija in Korean.

peninsula, and the authority of a Chinese dynasty was extended into Korea.

The general locations of these four commanderies, in present-day geographical terms, were: Lo-lang Commandery from P'yŏngan Province and Hwanghae Province to Kyŏnggi Province, with its center in the Taedong River basin; Chen-fan Commandery in the area of Ch'ungch'ŏng Province and Chŏlla Province; Lin-t'un Commandery in Kangwŏn Province; and Hsüan-t'u Commandery in the area of Hamgyŏng Province.

The larger part of Korea thus came under the direct administration of Han. Soon, however, various Korean tribes rebelled, and the area under Chinese control was reduced in size: twenty-six years after their establishment, the two commanderies of Chen-fan and Lin-t'un were discontinued; a large part of Hsüan-t'u Commandery was abandoned and a part merged with Lo-lang; and the capital of Hsüan-t'u Commandery was moved to the headwaters of the Yalu River. Hence, the only commandery remaining on the peninsula was Lo-lang. From 82 B.C., for about 280 years, the Chinese administered only the northwestern and central parts of Korea. At the beginning of the third century, the southern part of Lo-lang Commandery was separated and made into the commandery of Tai-fang. The two commanderies continued to be administered by the Chinese for another hundred years, until they were destroyed by Koguryŏ early in the fourth century.

From the establishment of the four commanderies to the disappearance of the last two, a period of about 400 years, Chinese officials governed in Korea. During that time, Chinese dynasties rose and fell: after the Former Han, the Hsin (8 – 23 A.D.), then the Later Han (23 – 220), the Wei (220 – 265) and the Chin (265 – 316). Yet during this period, when northwestern and central Korea were under the direct jurisdiction of China, Chinese officials in Korea forced various local tribes into submission, and even crossed the sea to control magnates in Japan.

Introduction of Metal Culture

Scytho-Siberian articles such as bronze weapons and horse trappings, brought by the Hsiung-nu to eastern Manchuria and Korea, have been found throughout eastern Manchuria and in Korea even as far as the Naktong River basin in the south. The tribes in Manchuria to whom the Scytho-Siberian culture was first transmitted led a pastoral-hunting life; when they learned to use metal, they developed rapidly and were able to dominate other tribes. Thus the eastern Manchurian Puyŏ people, and then the Koguryŏ, the earliest tribes to be reached by metal culture, subdued their neighbors and became the first Manchurian and northern Korean peoples to establish tribal states.

The eastern expansion of the Chinese, however, had the greatest effect on the people of Manchuria and Korea, far greater than the influence of the Hsiung-nu. Metal knife-money used in China in the Warring States period (403 – 221 B.C.) has been found in excavations in southern Manchuria and in the basins of the Yalu and the Ch'ŏngch'ŏn rivers, and coins of the Wang Mang period (8 – 22 A.D.) have been recovered from Kŭmhae, in southern Korea, in the Naktong River basin. In addition, bronze swords, spearheads, halberds, mirrors, javelin heads, bells, belt fasteners, and other objects have been found in every part of Korea. Although most of these items were brought from China, some were made locally,

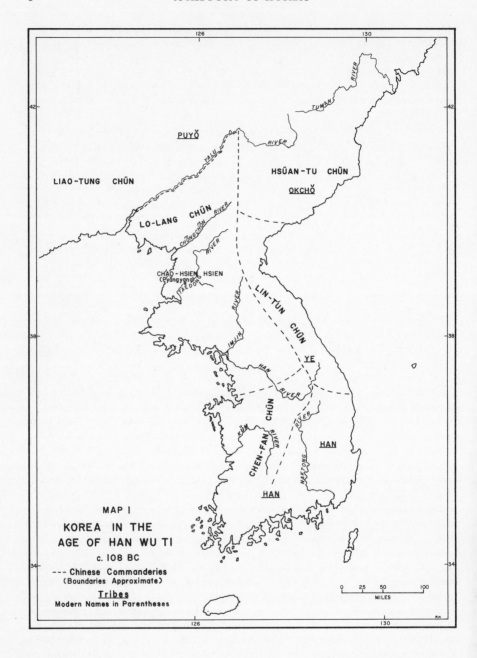

MAP I

KOREA IN THE
AGE OF HAN WU TI

c. 108 BC

--- Chinese Commanderies
(Boundaries Approximate)

Tribes
Modern Names in Parentheses

and we, therefore, know that the method of manufacturing metal objects was introduced, together with their importation. After bronze objects came iron tools. Javelin heads, sword blades, lance heads, axes, spades, sickles, and kitchen knives made of iron have been excavated in North P'yŏngan Province together with knife-money and bronze articles. Also at Kŭmhae, iron axes and knives have been found. These were used as agricultural tools or weapons, or as tools to make bone or horn articles.

Significantly, along with metal articles, rice plants were introduced. It is clear that rice was raised in southern Korea as early as the first century A.D., for, in the Kŭmhae shell mounds, rice grains have been recovered together with Wang Mang coins. The importation of metal and rice undoubtedly was an important factor in the progress of Korean culture. However, the civilization fostered by this advanced culture did not enter Korean society uniformly. In some areas a high degree of development occurred, while in others stone implements continued to be used. These considerable regional differences were partly caused by geographical factors, and to a greater extent by political circumstances. The higher culture from China entered the peninsula from northwestern and central Korea, where the Chinese commanderies and prefectures were first established on the site of the old state of Chao-hsien. This Chinese culture was an integral part of the life of the administering officials there. The concept of a fixed governmental pattern went hand in hand with the transmission of skills in the use of metal. Those reached by one were also affected by the other.

The Lo-lang Commandery can be taken as an example of this pattern. It was large, consisting of twenty-five prefectures, about 60,000 households, and a population of roughly 400,000. At its center, near present-day P'yŏngyang, Chinese officials lived, built Chinese-style government offices and residences, and imported beautiful Chinese art and craft objects. In the vicinity of P'yŏngyang are old mounds in profusion, graves of Lo-lang officials. From these have been excavated many splendid examples of Han culture; and through them the name Lo-lang culture has become known to the world. However, "Lo-lang culture" was the culture of the Chinese officials who lived in Lo-lang, not the culture of the native Koreans. Even in China proper there was a vast difference between the life of an official and the life of a peasant, and one can imagine how much truer this was in a colony where the officials and the natives were of different origin. This may explain why the advanced Lo-lang culture had little relation to the Koreans who composed a large part of the population governed by Lo-lang. They continued to live primitively, and unaffected by this culture.

Nor was it easy for the Koreans to improve their own culture. Under the commandery-prefecture system, the Chinese officials extorted labor and goods from the subject people, keeping them in poverty. Whatever Korean development took place occurred not in the northwestern part of the peninsula administered by Lo-lang, but far away on the upper reaches of the Yalu River among the Koguryŏ people and in the south among the Han tribes. Wherever the Koreans were subject to Chinese official administration, their progress was blocked, and they remained at a relatively low level. Thus, although the introduction of metal culture paved the way for, and ultimately played a part in, the progress of Korean society, its influence was not beneficent as long as it was associated with the political administrative policies of the Chinese.

Although, on the whole, the commandery-prefecture administration converted the various Korean tribes under Chinese domination into a subject people, it brought about certain changes in the internal structure of Korean society. Many persons in the service of the officials came from the local people, and these, through the authority they served, had special rights over others. On orders from the commandery-prefecture, they collected tribute and labor, and received in compensation minor government posts. Thus there appeared within Korean society, where relationships of domination and subjection had been hitherto unknown, petty native officials working under the authority of a powerful dynasty. In places distant from the commandery-prefecture, the traditional tribal chieftains were made petty officials, while in places where the power of the commandery-prefecture was strong, persons other than the chieftains were selected. In the former case, the authority of the tribal chieftains, coupled with the power of the dynasty, was heightened, and the tribal organization, unchanged, became the administrative organization. In the latter case, where authorities different from the tribal chieftains appeared, the tribal organization was destroyed. In both cases a type of power different from the traditional arose. The bronze articles, such as the Korean bronze swords, bronze spearheads, and bronze mirrors, which have been found in various parts of the peninsula, are thought to show the authority of the new chieftains, since in China, during the Ch'in and Han dynasties, iron articles were for practical use and bronze articles were symbols of authority. However, even the chieftains, as long as they were subjected to the domination of the commandery-prefecture, were not able to expand their own power. Their limited authority was derived from the fact that they were working under Chinese officials, who held this power in check and prevented its extension. Until the domination of the Chinese officials could be broken, the Korean people could not develop.

The Development of the Koguryŏ People

The local people resisted the domination of the commandery-prefecture from the start. The four commanderies created by Emperor Wu had to be reorganized and merged after a little more than twenty years, since they could not resist the opposition of the natives. In northwestern and central Korea, where the power of the Chinese administration was strongest (Lo-lang Commandery area), this opposition was suppressed and ineffective, but it was successful in the peripheral regions, where the power of the commandery-prefecture was difficult to extend. Therefore, the Korean people were able to develop only in these regions. This progress was made first by the Koguryŏ people of the north, and, much later, by the Han people of the south.

The Koguryŏ, a branch of the Puyŏ of Manchuria, originally lived in the basin of the Sungari River. About the second century B.C. they moved east and lived a life of hunting in the mountains and valleys between the T'ung-chia and the Yalu river basins. When the eastern expansion of the Hsiung-nu and the Chinese expansion began, about the third century B.C., bringing metal culture to Manchuria, the first people to be affected were the Puyŏ, and later the Koguryŏ. The latter were under the administration of the Hsüan-t'u Commandery, but they were so far away in a mountainous area that complete administrative control was impossible. Their continued resistance to Chinese direction was so successful that, in the latter part of the first century, their chief was called king. At that time, the Koguryŏ invaded the Chinese territory of Liao-tung and even crossed the Liao River to attack the region of Chang-ch'eng, undermining Chinese domination in that area. In retaliation, China sent several expeditions to suppress them. The Koguryŏ home territory was put to the torch, and attacks were pressed against them. The severest of these attacks occurred in the third century A.D. when a great punitive expedition led by General Wu Ch'iu-chien of the Wei laid waste all the Koguryŏ areas in eastern Manchuria and north Korea. However, the Chinese were unable to maintain control over such a mountainous region. The Koguryŏ were a hunting people who easily rebuilt their bases or moved. They were able to recover from each attack, and, after years of bitter conflict, succeeded in creating by the fourth century a great state extending over much of Manchuria and Korea.

Throughout this struggle, the development and solidification of the Koguryŏ people progressed. Indications of their early development can still be seen in the dolmen tombs in the mountainous areas of eastern Manchuria and northern Korea. They were made by arranging stone slabs above the ground to form a square. Over a compartment so formed was placed another huge slab. These dolmen tombs were found in groups from a few to several tens in a row. It is apparent that an enormous amount of labor went into their construction. Their funerary content was meager. A single tomb usually contained only one stone sword and one or more stone javelin heads. Stone swords and stone javelin heads modeled after metal ones have been found, but almost none of metal. There is nothing in these tombs that indicates wealth, only bare strength. It was a surprising strength which developed from such a poor level of life. But these dolmen tombs are not the communal graves of savages; they are apparently the graves of powerful chieftains who erected them as symbols of their domination of a wretched subject people and of the power of the Koguryŏ over the weaker and smaller tribes they had conquered.

The dolmen tombs, after the first and second centuries, were supplanted by stone tumuli and earth mounds. Many large tumuli, made of rocks piled up to form squares, and large earth mounds, constructed in a square shape, remain in the T'ung-kou basin midway up the Yalu River. If the smaller ones are included, their number reaches several thousand. Most of the large mounds, after the first and second century, are the graves of kings and important men of Koguryŏ. These old tombs contain splendid funerary ware and beautiful wall frescoes. Whereas the dolmen are the expressions of strength, these tumuli and earth mounds indicate wealth and a high culture together with power. This difference is undoubtedly the result of the development of the society of the Koguryŏ people during the intervening period.

The situation of the Koguryŏ people during the third century is recorded in the "Eastern Barbarian" section of *Wei-chih*. This Chinese history describes how the old tribal organization was crumbling. Originally, the Koguryŏ people were divided into five tribes, each with its own chieftain of whom one became king, controlling the entire group. By the third century, some tribes were without chieftains. The family lines from which chieftains came were fixed in tribes that still had chieftains. The tribe from which the king was chosen was fixed as well as the tribe which supplied brides to the king.

However, a sense of tribal independence still remained, as the kings, the king's household, and each chieftain controlled their own direct subordinates (tribesmen), and powerful tribes had their own ancestral mausoleums. The royal family and the chieftains of each tribe occupied the highest social positions; below them were their retainers and members of the so-called "great houses" made up of ten thousand or more persons; these ate and sat together with the tribal chieftains. It is thought that the "great houses" were the warriors of the Koguryŏ people, who were divided into tribes. These warriors were the nucleus of the fighting strength of Koguryŏ and the main force which developed the Koguryŏ nation. The lowest strata were the "under the door" class and slaves who worked for the other groups. The "under the door" class and the slaves included degenerates and criminals, and also people from subjugated tribes. These members of the lowest classes labored for the king, princes, nobles, and warriors and were used to transport rice, fish, salt, and other foods over great distances, since Koguryŏ had an inadequate supply of local food. They also served in the army under the direction of the warriors.

During that period, the old clan tribal society was gradually being superseded by an authoritarian regime. The most powerful chieftain, with the largest tribal group of followers, was able to overcome other chieftains and their subordinates, thereby increasing his authority and at the same time causing the dissolution of the other tribes. Nevertheless, some evidence exists that characteristics of the old clan tribal society persisted: there were no prisons, criminals were killed; a "son-in-law hut" was built just outside the wife's home, and the husband met his wife there until the children that his wife bore were grown. Only then could he move into his own home with his wife.

This immature society was dependent on the subjection and services of the neighboring tribes. Since, as mentioned, the Koguryŏ people, living in mountainous areas with poor resources, had to obtain raw materials and food from other regions, and needed people to transport them, they invaded Chinese territory to the west and penetrated to Korea's eastern coast held by the Okchŏ tribes (Hamgyŏng Province) and the Ye tribes (Kangwŏn Province). Although war with China was not conclusive, the Koguryŏ subdued the Okchŏ and the Ye tribes, reducing them to slaves. These tribes were originally of the same stock as the Koguryŏ but had long been separated. In the early period of the four Han commanderies, the Okchŏ and the Ye had been attached respectively to the Hsüan-t'u and Lin-t'un commanderies. Subjugated by the Koguryŏ, they supplied them with food, cloth, women, and other necessities as tribute. They also transported this tribute through the mountains for their masters. This rear base, with subject people to depend on, made it possible for the Koguryŏ to resist successfully when they were attacked by China from the west.

Growth of the Han Tribes

In the central and southern part of the Korean peninsula lived the Han tribes. They were later to control Korea, but in the beginning they were much slower to develop than the Koguryŏ in the north. About the time that the Koguryŏ people were uniting the strength of their various tribes and resisting China, the Han tribes were divided and scarcely able to withstand the imposition of the commandery-prefecture system, though their resistance to the Chinese may have contributed to the abolishment of the Chen-fan Commandery in the first century B.C., soon after its establishment by Emperor Wu of Han. By the beginning of the third century A.D., we know they were oppressed and retarded by the Lo-lang Commandery, as well as the Tai-fang Commandery, which had been created from Lo-lang's southern section.

There was, however, slow progress in cultural development and concentration of power, especially in the eastern and southern coasts and in the interior — places less affected by the commandery-prefecture administration. Indicative of somewhat retarded development are the tombs of the Han tribes similar to the dolmen tombs built by the Koguryŏ. The Han dolmen were constructed very much later, during a period ending in the fourth century A.D.

In contrast to the development of the Koguryŏ as a hunting people, the Han tribes developed as an agricultural people. From the shell mounds at Kŭmhae of about the first century A.D. rice grains have been recovered, along with shells, fish, and animal bones. These finds indicate that rice was already being cultivated in southern Korea at that time, but that the chief occupation was still hunting and fishing; agriculture was secondary. However, the climate and terrain of southern Korea were suitable for agriculture and, with the diffusion of rice cultivation, agriculture grew in importance. According to the "Eastern Barbarian" section of *Wei-chih*, which records the conditions in Korea in the third century, the Han tribes grew the "five cereals" (hemp, millet, rice, wheat, and pulse), planted rice and the mulberry tree, reared cows and pigs, made silk cloth, and became a completely agricultural people. Their life was altogether different from that of the Koguryŏ who depended, for food and raw materials, on the tribute payments of the peoples they had conquered.

The eastern branch of the Han tribes (Chin Han) mined iron. The surrounding Han people, and even the Ye and the Japanese, came to obtain iron from them. Iron was used to make articles for home consumption and as an object of barter. It was also sent to the Chinese commanderies as tribute; therefore, although their productive capacity was high in the third century, since their painfully produced iron articles were taken from them, their life continued to be wretched.

At that time the Han tribes were divided into three branches: the Ma Han, the Chin Han, and the Pyŏn Han. The Ma Han lived in the area of present-day Ch'ungch'ŏng Province and Chŏlla Province with more than one hundred thousand households divided into more than fifty "states" *(kuk);* the Chin Han lived in the area of North Kyŏngsang Province and were divided into twelve states; the Pyŏn Han, living in the area of South Kyŏngsang Province, were also divided into twelve states. The total number of Chin Han and Pyŏn Han households together was forty to fifty thousand. What was termed a "state" was probably a collection of a few villages whose inhabitants were bound together by blood ties. These states had their chiefs. A great chief was called *sinji*, lesser chiefs were known as *ŭpch'a, hŏpch'ik, punye,* or *sarhae.* They all were either appointed by the Chinese officials or tribal chieftains. There was no clear administrative relationship among them, nor was there any fixed relationship between the chiefs and the village people. The Han people made no status distinction between young and old, or male and female, and they did not know the ceremony of kneeling and

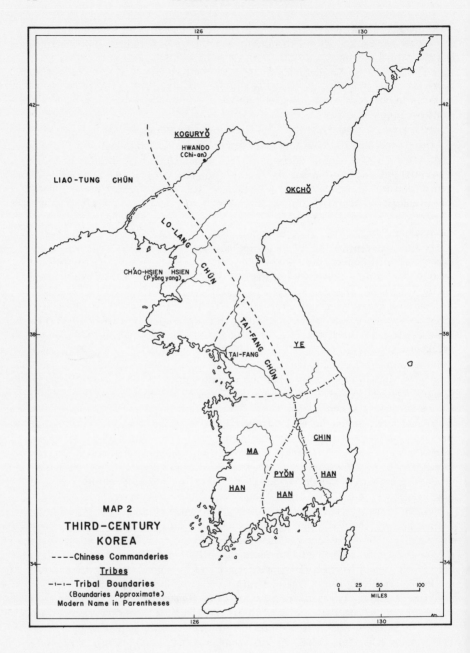

MAP 2

THIRD-CENTURY
KOREA

----Chinese Commanderies

Tribes

—·—·— Tribal Boundaries
(Boundaries Approximate)
Modern Name in Parentheses

worshiping. Their customs were considered contemptible by the Chinese officials who were exacting in their regulation of degrees of domination and submission. They regarded the natives as criminal slaves lacking in propriety.

The Han tribes had not established a strong administrative system and they were less powerful than the Koguryŏ, although their level of production and population was considerably higher. This was because they were wholly under the control of the Chinese commandery-prefecture, much more so than Koguryŏ. This control was exercised by conferring official seals to Han tribal chiefs in addition to titles such as district lord and district chief. Seals were given also to those traveling in and out of the commandery-prefecture on official business. Probably more than a thousand seals were issued in Ma Han alone. Those possessing them gained prestige in their villages. This created new power, but one which could not be consolidated because of the number of seals issued. The system served simply to spread more widely the petty authority of those working in the service of the commandery-prefectures.

China's traditional policy in controlling foreign peoples from ancient until recent times has been to divide and rule through the use of seals. At that time the system was also applied to Japan, but it was most effective in Korea "at the knee" of the commandery-prefectures, especially among the Ma Han tribes. The system accounts for the long retardation of the Han tribes in political development. Real progress had to wait until the commandery-prefecture system was overthrown. This was not an easy task, but gradually, as the power of the Chinese officials weakened, the strength of the people to resist increased.

II

Emergence of the Ancient States;
Three Kingdoms Period

The Fall of Lo-lang and Tai-fang Commanderies

Chinese commanderies and prefectures, from the time they were established in Korea at the end of the second century B.C., were in control of the administration of that country until the fourth century A.D. Their control was unaffected by dynastic changes in China during these five centuries. It could ultimately be broken only through the efforts of the Koreans themselves. Finally an opportunity for this presented itself.

At the beginning of the third century A.D. when the Later Han Dynasty was overthrown, China was split into three states, Wei, Wu, and Shu (Minor Han). By the end of that century, after much fighting, the country was again unified by Chin, but the government was unstable because of the rivalry among noble and wealthy families who were struggling for supremacy. This disunity made it possible for barbarians successfully to invade China, and the result was a period of disorder lasting throughout the fourth century, known as the era of "The Five Barbarian Nations and the Sixteen States." It was during this time of unrest, early in the Chin period, that the Mu-jung clan of the Hsien-pi (a tribe in eastern Mongolia, long an enemy of China) invaded Manchuria and occupied the Liao-hsi Commandery in Chinese territory, establishing a state known as Yen. This state cut communications between China and Korea, and isolated the two commanderies of Lo-lang and Tai-fang from China.

Thus at last an opportunity to get on their feet presented itself to the tribes of the peninsula who had suffered so long under Chinese control. The first action was taken by the Koguryǒ people, who had already spent many years in bitter warfare against the Chinese. They attacked Liao-tung and, continuing into Korea, overcame the Lo-lang Commandery and absorbed its territory in 313. Thus, the Lo-lang Commandery, which had existed for about four-hundred years, was abolished. Shortly thereafter, about the middle of the fourth century, the Tai-fang

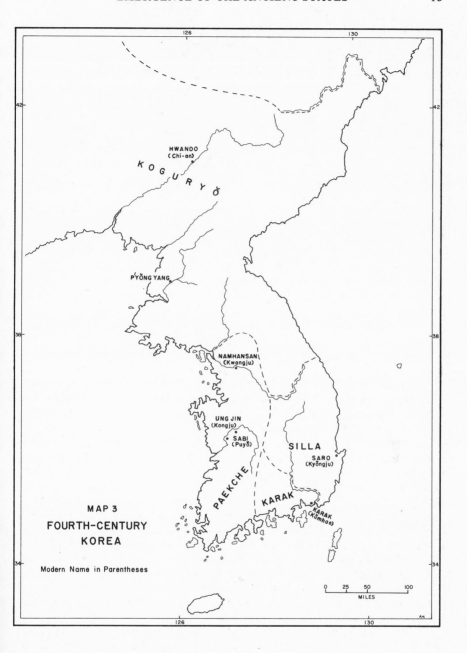

MAP 3

FOURTH-CENTURY
KOREA

Modern Name in Parentheses

Commandery was overthrown by Paekche,[1] one of the fifty-odd Ma Han "states" under the jurisdiction of the commandery. Because of the weakness of the latter, Paekche was able to unify the Ma Han people and successfully attack and defeat it. In this way the Chinese commandery-prefectures were obliterated, and the administration by Chinese officials, which had retarded the development of the Korean peoples, was at last eliminated.

While Paekche was unifying the Ma Han, the Chin Han in the east were being unified by Saro (later called Silla), one of the twelve Chin Han "states" which had recently risen into prominence. Thus, Paekche and Silla constituted the dominant powers among the Han tribes. Only the Pyŏn Han states remained disunified because Japan, then a unified state centered about Yamato, had gained a foothold among the Pyŏn Han and brought the various states under her control.

The destruction of the two commanderies of Lo-lang and Tai-fang was a signal event in the development of Korea. Chinese officials who had directly administered Korea for several hundred years were no more, and the independent development of the various Korean peoples became possible. The suzerain-tributary relationship to the Chinese dynasties persisted, but since it did not involve direct administration as under the commandery-prefecture system, the Korean peoples had more freedom to develop than they had ever had before, and the road was open for their brilliant achievements in the following centuries.

Koguryŏ

While Koguryŏ was expanding her territory by annexing the Lo-lang Commandery, attacking Liao-tung, and extending from Manchuria into the northern half of Korea, to the west of Koguryŏ, the state of Yen, established by the Mu-jung clan of the Hsien-pi, grew in strength. About the middle of the fourth century a large army from Yen attacked in the Yalu River basin, occupied the capital of Koguryŏ, desecrated royal mausolea, and carried off much treasure and more than fifty thousand men and women (345). As a result of this blow, Koguryŏ had to cease its advance to the west and to send tribute to "barbarian" states like Yen and Ch'in, and directed its major effort southward into Korea.

While this was happening in northern Korea, Paekche and Silla grew stronger in the south. Japan, meanwhile, conquered the Pyŏn Han area known as Karak (Mimana in Japanese), and was planning to extend her control over more of Korea. After the latter half of the fourth century, Koguryŏ ventured to challenge these states and attacked southward. King Kwanggaet'o (also known as King Hot'ae, 391-412) several times led large armies south, threatening Paekche, Silla, and territory held by the Japanese, and enlarging Koguryŏ's territory to the south. A record of these successful campaigns was inscribed on the Hot'ae-wang-bi, a stone stele erected at the old Koguryŏ capital of Kungnaesŏng (modern T'ung-kou, in Manchuria). The next ruler, King Changsu (413-491), moved the capital from Kungnaesŏng to P'yŏngyang (417), which he used as a base in continuing attacks south. These two kings, through their southern campaigns, turned a large

---

[1] See glossary for difference between the Chinese characters for the state of Paekche and Ma Han Paekche.

portion of the peninsula into Koguryŏ territory, not including the present-day provinces of Kyŏngsang, Chŏlla, and South Ch'ungch'ŏng. Thus, Koguryŏ became an extensive country, embracing Manchuria east of the Liao River and the northern half of Korea.

With this expansion of territory a greatly increased number of people came under Koguryŏ control. Later, at the time of the fall of Koguryŏ, the population comprised about 690,000 households. The majority of these, however, were conquered people. Thousands, perhaps ten thousands, of these people were prisoners that had been captured in battles; it is recorded that Paekche, when defeated, presented a thousand men and women to Koguryŏ. It would almost seem that the aim of the territorial expansion was to acquire prisoners and increase the slave population.

To control this extensive area and this large number of subject people, it was necessary to have a large powerful organization. To this end numerous large and small forts were built at strategic locations in Manchuria and Korea, such as the capital P'yŏngyang, the old capital Kungnaesŏng in Manchuria, and Hansŏng (present-day Kwangju, Kyŏnggi Province), which had been seized from Paekche. The organization was essentially a military one to enable Koguryŏ to resist any foreign invasion or domestic rebellion and also to make possible the control of such an extensive territory and such a large population by a relatively small number of Koguryŏ people. At P'yŏngyang the class of officials was divided into more than ten ranks headed by the highest, entitled *taedaero*, and responsibility for internal and external affairs of state was allotted among these. Civil administrators were stationed at the various regional forts, and below these officials were military officers. In addition, the forts were garrisoned by military units and stocked with food and weapons.

The administrative positions of this state were occupied by nobles and warriors of the Koguryŏ people. They were essentially officials or military men directly serving the king. Their presence throughout the wide realm served to break down even further the already crumbling tribal organization. However, the nobles still used the names of the five clans to show their lineage and still enjoyed a privileged social position derived from the old tribal relationship. The fact that the highest-ranking official positions were rotated every three years and were passed down among the nobility may also have been a survival of the old system. These nobles and military men owned slaves, fields, and residences and riches, clear evidence that class differentiation had developed. Yet all classes united when Koguryŏ was opposed by its subject population or faced a foreign foe. In order to preserve the unity of Koguryŏ severe punishments were imposed. Rebels were burned to death by common people with torches; and persons who surrendered a fort to the enemy when entrusted with its defense, persons defeated in battle, robbers, and murderers were decapitated.

The people controlled by Koguryŏ included many natives and officials from the former Lo-lang Commandery. Some of these were mixed in with the Koguryŏ people, but most were integrated into the subject population. Cloth and millet were collected as poll and household taxes from them, and they were forced also to supply labor.

During this period of growth of the Koguryŏ state, ideology and religious beliefs developed. Originally the various Koguryŏ tribes worshiped individual divine ancestors, but all worshiped the heavens in a religious observance called *Tongmyŏng*. The worship of nature continued into later centuries. In the weaker tribes, however, the worship of a special ancestor was gradually abandoned, and for it was substituted worship of Chumong, regarded as the highest ancestor of the Koguryŏ people. About 372 A.D. Buddhism reached Koguryŏ from China. The state encouraged the Buddhist concept of obtaining happiness through protecting the nation, and built many Buddhist temples.

About this same time, Confucianism, astronomy, medicine, and other branches of learning were introduced into Koguryŏ, a college was established for the sons of nobles, and laws were codified (373). Presumably, the Chinese in Lo-lang Commandery contributed greatly to this progress, but the basis for the cultural advance was the fact the Koguryŏ had overthrown the Lo-Lang Commandery and so had opened up a free world for themselves.

Paekche

Paekche, as mentioned, was one of the more than fifty Han "states" which made up the unified Ma Han in the fourth century, overthrew Tai-fang Commandery, and gave its name to the new state. About that same time, on the eastern coast of the peninsula, the Kingdom of Silla was established. To the southeast, in the Naktong River basin, Japan subjugated the Pyŏn Han and gained a foothold for expansion on the peninsula in Mimana; from the north, Koguryŏ continued to launch strong attacks southward. Koguryŏ, Silla, Japan, and Paekche were the four powers competing for control of the Korean peninsula. The mightiest enemy of Paekche was Koguryŏ, which had overthrown Lo-lang Commandery and was driving south. To defend itself against Koguryŏ, Paekche tried various diplomatic maneuvers; joining forces with Japan, at times allying herself with Silla, and exploiting the prestige of various Chinese dynasties against Koguryŏ. This was during the period of the Northern and Southern dynasties in China (386-589). Most of all, Paekche depended on secret alliances with Japan. In spite of this, Paekche could not resist the pressure of powerful Koguryŏ and was gradually compressed into the southwestern part of the peninsula. At first the capital was at Hansŏng (Kyŏnggi Province, Kwangju), from about 350 to 474; then at Ungjin (South Ch'ungch'ŏng Province, Kongju), from 474 to 538; and finally at Sabi (South Ch'ungch'ŏng Province, Puyŏ), from 538 to 660. During this period Paekche continually faced grave crises. In 396 a large Koguryŏ army besieged the Paekche capital, and Paekche sent Koguryŏ a thousand men and women and sued for peace. Again, in 404 Paekche's forces were defeated and surrendered to a Koguryŏ fleet. Then, in 475, the Paekche capital was taken, and the Paekche king captured and decapitated. Besides this pressure from the north, Silla, to the east, had gradually gained in strength and was beginning to encroach upon Paekche. In the middle of the sixth century Silla conquered Mimana and menaced the eastern border of Paekche. Faced with these conditions, Paekche allied herself with Japan and, using southwestern Korea as a base, put up a determined resistance, often counterattacking and threatening Koguryŏ and Silla. The strength of Paekche, while it lasted, was due partly to its alliance with Japan and partly to its large population and fertile agricultural lands. The final overthrow of Paekche by the less-developed Silla must be attributed to lack of cohesion in its national structure.

Of all Korean states at that time, Paekche had the land most blessed by nature and the largest population, but it lacked organization and popular support because Ma Han, the predecessor of Paekche, had for so long been exposed to administration by Chinese officials. This had caused her own tribal order to break down, leaving no indigenous order to rely on when Chinese control was removed. Under the strong administration of Tai-fang Commandery, many Ma Han people became agents of the Chinese officials and collected tribute and labor from the Ma Han. Many of these agents, however, were not traditional chieftains or tribal leaders. They depended on the power of the commandery-prefectures in order to govern the Ma Han people, and not on any authority of their own as tribal chieftains. Thus the traditional authority of the chieftain declined, and there was too little left of the tribal organization to serve effectively as a nucleus for a new nation when the Kingdom of Paekche was created. It was necessary therefore for Paekche to unify the Ma Han through an outside tribe, instead of strengthening a native Ma Han tendency for that purpose. A branch of the royal clan of Puyŏ, which was the most famous of the tribes of Manchuria and Korea, was made the royal house of Paekche. This house governed the Ma Han people, but never ceased to boast that it was of Puyŏ and not of Han origin. The fact that the state of Paekche was first formed and supported by the royal family of an outside tribe, probably indicates how difficult it was to bring about the unification of the Ma Han people.

Thus it happened that in Paekche a royal clan of different blood, few in numbers, virtually enslaved the Ma Han people. Up to the beginning of the sixth century the royal clan lived in the capital and in fortified towns in the country, called *yŏmno*, from which its members controlled the native people. These *yŏmno* were bases for military and civil administration and places for gathering tribute and labor. Powerful men among the Ma Han were appointed subordinate officials of the royal house, but the central and regional administrative positions were held by sons of the king or members of the royal family. While this system gave the royal house unique authority in the country, it also made the Ma Han into virtually a subject people with no awareness of national unity.

This state structure developed and reached a high point by the beginning of the sixth century. At that time, Paekche, which was compelled to move its capital from Ungjin to Sabi under pressure from Koguryŏ and Silla, reformed its state structure to meet the critical situation. And thus came into being the system of the "five areas" and the "five parts": the capital was divided into "five parts" (top, center, bottom, front, and back), and the people beneath the local magnates were gathered in the capital and distributed to the five parts, each part headed by a commander (*talsu*) who led five hundred soldiers; at the same time, the country districts were divided into "five areas." At the "area fort," or *pangsŏng*, which was the center of the area, there were from 700 to 1,200 troops under a commander; at strategic points within each area, large and small forts were built in which garrisons were placed, each under a commander. In short, a national structure was established whose core was the military. By these reforms local magnates were elevated to the position of nobles protecting the royal house. By uniting the strength of these nobles, foreign invasions could be resisted, but such a unity, being temporary, was essentially weak as compared with the traditional clan-tribal unity of Koguryŏ and Silla.

Paekche came to have a subject and slave population, not unlike that of Koguryŏ, and it was upon this that its culture depended. Paekche's subject people were chiefly engaged in agriculture, and agriculture progressed further in Paekche than in any of the other three kingdoms. Slaves operated the exclusive handicraft industries maintained by the royal household, and produced cloth, leather articles, metal and wood objects, and weapons.

Since communication with China was geographically easy, and since the southward attacks of Koguryŏ needed to be countered, Paekche had frequent intercourse with a number of southern dynasties during the period of division between north and south China after the collapse of Western Chin in 317. Paekche attempted to absorb Chinese culture. After Buddhism was introduced in 384, it attracted the nobility, and many temples were built and Buddhist statues and Buddhist paintings made. Remains of this culture are rare, but from the little that has come down to us, it is known that Paekche art had made great progress. The Paekche kings and nobles built splendid palaces, raised rare birds and foreign plants, and encouraged Buddhist art. This Paekche art was transmitted to Japan where it became the basis for the art of the Asuka period (about 552-644).

Silla

Silla was the nation formed when Saro, one of the twelve Chin Han "states," unified the Chin Han. It was established about the same time as Paekche, in the middle of the fourth century.

At that time, Koguryŏ was already driving south, and Japan had entered Korea and had established a foothold in the Pyŏn Han region. Paekche, allied with Japan, was pressing upon Silla from the west. Silla's position was extremely difficult and the existence of the state was threatened on several occasions, yet Silla successfully defended her cradle district in the Kyŏngju area, then turned the tables and launched counterattacks against Koguryŏ, Paekche, and Japan. Silla drove the Japanese from the peninsula in the latter half of the sixth century, absorbed Koguryŏ and Paekche in the latter half of the seventh century, and created for the first time a unified state covering all of Korea. These efforts of Silla extended from the fourth to the seventh century, and the resulting unification with the Han people as the nucleus laid the foundation for the later brilliance of Silla.

Silla and Paekche were both populated by the Han people. Paekche had more fertile land and a larger population than Silla. Nevertheless, Silla was the final victor and gained control of the whole peninsula. The reason for this was that the Chin Han, the predecessors of Silla, in contrast to the Ma Han, the predecessors of Paekche, were distant from the Chinese commandery-prefectures and therefore were not directly under the control of the Chinese officials. Consequently, a stronger element of unity remained among the Silla people upon which the organization of the state could be built.

Saro, the nucleus of the Kingdom of Silla, was a tribal union of clans in the area of Kyŏngju in North Kyŏngsang Province. According to legend, the chieftains of six villages there, each of which had its own ancestors, assembled on a river bank for a conference and called upon a great man to assume joint leadership. Such conferences of chiefs, always held on river banks or mountain tops, were called *hwabaek*. At the *hwabaek* important problems were deliberated, and unanimous consent of all present was required for a decision. The chiefs must have been able to look beyond the confines of their primitive society. The custom of the *hwabaek* was continued, long after Silla became powerful, and it was entrusted with the appointment of kings and other vital matters of state.

The founder of Silla, Hyŏkkŏse, had the title of *kŏsŏgan*, and his successor, Namhae, was called *ch'ach'aung*. The third to the eighteenth rulers were called *nisagŭm*; the nineteenth to the twenty-second were called *maripkan*; and after them the Chinese title of *wang* (king) began to be used. Many different explanations have been given for the etymology of the titles *kŏsŏgan, nisagŭm,* and *maripkan*, and how they should be pronounced, but undoubtedly they all meant chief or paramount chief. *Ch'ach'aung* seems to have meant a shaman who served the spirits. The fact that the ruler was for so long called by one of these titles, instead of king, and that his position was not hereditary but depended on the decision of the *hwabaek*, shows the persistence of the ancient customs and of the early state structure.

As Silla grew, it conquered other tribes. These were subservient to the original clans, and their chieftains did not participate in the *hwabaek*. The king was selected from the victors only. They were recognized as the privileged ruling class, and their tribal organization was not changed. The conquered also retained their old tribal group structure, although they became essentially a subject people. Thus the tradition of a clan-tribal society was preserved, but a subject-ruler relationship was introduced. Within both groups significant class divisions developed. These divisions, related to social stratification and tradition rather than to actual power, seem at first to have been quite simple. Later, subdivisions were introduced and the classification became rigid and developed into the *kolp'umje* or "bones" status system.

The *kol* (bone) part of *kolp'umje* represented blood relationship; the *p'um* (status) represented rank and social position. Thus *kolp'umje* was a system of classification based on all three factors: blood, rank, and social position. The clan one was born into determined one's class, and one's whole way of life, as well as governmental and social position, depended upon the class.

The "first bones" category, also known as *sŏnggol* (sage bones) or *chin'gol* (true bones), was the highest noble class of the Kingdom of Silla. It was made up exclusively of men and women from certain clans, such as the Pak, Sŏk, and Kim. No lower-class person could become a "first bone." Only a first bone could marry a first bone. Only a first-bones man or woman could occupy a high official position or become the ruler. Kingship was not hereditary. It moved freely among first-bones clans and depended solely on the selection by the *hwabaek*, which had only first-bones members and assembled at intervals to appoint a king or to discuss matters of state.

Below the first-bones class was the second-bones class; below that the third; and below that several more bones. Each bones class was formed from certain clans. Slaves and subject people were probably outside the bones status order, but chieftains and powerful men from the conquered people were sometimes, by marriage or some other method, absorbed into high bones.

As mentioned, many traditions of the old clan-tribal society were preserved within the bones status system. This applies to the ruling class and was probably even more true of the subject population. The chronicles of the time recorded only matters pertaining to the higher social levels and ignored the lives of the lower classes. However, by projecting backward from conditions of later ages and by analogy to the society of the ruling classes of that time, it can be concluded that among the subject people the old ways were preserved intact and life went on for the majority in accordance with past traditions and customs. Only in the groups who became direct slaves of the king, princes, and nobles was the way of living altered. For the most part, contact with administrative authorities was limited to the furnishing of tribute, labor, and military service. These were exacted and collected at the garrisoned fort towns inhabited by nobles dispatched from the capital city of Kyŏngju.

The people organized along the lines of the bones status system, especially the first bones, were the nucleus of the Kingdom of Silla. The fact that this system permitted the continuance of group relationships made possible the development of loyal warriors, called *hwarang*. These were young noblemen who prided themselves on bravery and honor and offered themselves to fight a common enemy or to advance the common welfare. Since the development of the country took place in the midst of wars with Koguryŏ, Paekche, and Japan, strong fighting forces were essential. Had it not been for the fighting qualities of these warriors, who possessed the traditions of young men's associations of the clan society, Silla could not have escaped disaster on repeated occasions. The *hwarang* headed the army of Silla, fended off its enemies, and increased the national power.

Gradually Silla developed a more autocratic and bureaucratic system of government. After the reign of Naemul Maripkan (356-402), the position of the ruler was no longer determined by the *hwabaek*, but was made hereditary in the Kim clan. From the beginning of the sixth century, the chief came to be called by the Chinese title of *wang* (king). At the same time, a bureaucracy following the Chinese pattern was set up and era names were adopted. Buddhism was made the state religion in 528. The idea of a single omnipotent deity gradually supplanted ancestor worship and shamanism, which up to that time had been the sole religious beliefs of the people. In short, the ideas and institutions in Silla were significantly modified by Chinese culture throughout those years.

This was also the period during which Silla enlarged her territory markedly. In the reigns of King Pŏphŭng (514-539) and King Chinhŭng (540-575), Silla absorbed Mimana, Japan's base in the Naktong River basin (562). To the north Silla occupied what is now Kangwŏn Province and the southern part of Hamgyŏng Province, and in the west the basin of the Han River; besides, Silla gained an outlet on the west coast of Korea, a valuable location for communication with China and the importation of Chinese culture.

From about that time Silla became the strongest nation in Korea in size and state structure and was able to apply pressure on her old enemies Koguryŏ and Paekche. Through successful campaigns against them, Silla greatly increased the population of subject peoples and the power and prestige of her nobles. Supported by the bones status system, the king and the people surrounding him became very powerful. The prime minister now was also important and owned several thousand slaves and a large number of domestic animals.

Changes in the Political Situation of East Asia and the Invasions of Sui and T'ang

The fighting between Koguryŏ, Paekche, and Silla lasted from the fourth century to the seventh century. In China this was the period covering the turbulent era of the "Five Barbarian Nations and the Sixteen States" and the "Northern and Southern Dynasties", to the time of the T'ang unification, or 317 to 618. In Japan it was the period extending from the national unification under the political power of Yamato until after the Taika reform of 645. On the continent the northern tribes attacked China during these centuries and set up states in different parts of northern China. They even drove the Chinese dynasties south of the Yangtse River and occupied the land north of the river. They established the Northern Dynasties consisting of Northern Wei, Eastern Wei, Western Wei, Northern Ch'i, and Northern Chou. The Chinese who escaped south of the Yangtse River established the Sung, Ch'i, Liang, and Ch'en dynasties, known as the Southern Dynasties, which opposed those to the north. Besides this conflict between north and south, these states fought among themselves, and assassinations of emperors were common. Internally political conditions were unsettled and the various Chinese dynasties therefore lacked their former power to control Korea. The Three Kingdoms in Korea presented tribute to various Chinese dynasties, imported Chinese culture — Buddhism, Confucianism, arts and crafts — and borrowed Chinese political institutions to enhance their own power, and were never menaced by China.

Japan and Korea had been in contact in prehistoric times. After Han China had established the four commanderies in Korea, Chinese culture entered Japan by way of Korea, stimulating the civilization of Japan. Since Japan, unlike Korea, did not experience the direct oppression of China, she developed earlier than Korea, and already by about the middle of the fourth century became a unified state centered on Yamato. When Chinese power was withdrawn from Korea and the Three Kingdoms were fighting among themselves, this unified Japanese state advanced into Korea. First the Pyŏn Han states of the Naktong River basin (Karak) were conquered and became the Japanese colony of Mimana. Then the Japanese began to penetrate into the interior of Korea. The first counterattack against their advance was launched by Koguryŏ. From the end of the fourth century to the beginning of the fifth, Koguryŏ armies led by King Hot'ae repeatedly fought the Japanese on land and sea. After that Japan continued to govern part of southern Korea, but as Silla grew in strength, Japan's fortunes changed. Although Mimana was allied with Paekche in opposition to Koguryŏ and Silla, Silla annexed Mimana (about the middle of the sixth century), and Japan lost her base in Korea.

After the withdrawal of the Japanese, the three kingdoms of Korea began to oppose each other without outside interference. However, this did not last long because the political conditions in China changed. China, which had long been divided, was unified by Sui at the end of the sixth century. During the period of division between North and South she had not been in a position to threaten Korea, but now she was again able to do so. Sui, which was menaced by invasion, especially from the Turks in the north, found that, in order to forestall them, it was necessary to secure her flanks. To do this she had to occupy Manchuria and northern Korea and cope with Koguryŏ, which was in contact with the Turks. To this end Emperor Wen of Sui sent a large army of 300,000 to attack Koguryŏ in 598. Later, Emperor Yang personally took to the field three times between 612 and 614; in the first campaign more than a million men were mobilized. Yet these efforts to subdue Koguryŏ failed. These defeats caused insurrections in China, which contributed to the overthrow of the Sui Dynasty (618). The T'ang Dynasty, who replaced the Sui and established a great empire that exceeded that of Sui, continued the Sui policy of planning the conquest of Korea and Manchuria. T'ai-tsung attacked Koguryŏ three times between 644 and 646, and the next ruler, Kao-tsung, also dispatched expeditionary armies (655-659). However, these expeditions also ended in failure. After this, the T'ang rulers gave up frontal attacks and decided to strike first at Paekche in Koguryŏ's rear. They sent a fleet to invade Paekche, attacked the capital Puyŏ, and succeeded in subjugating the country in 660. At that time Japan was struggling to reestablish Paekche as a nation, but abandoned the attempt after her fleet was defeated in a battle at the mouth of the Kŭm River in 663. With the destruction of Paekche, Japan lost her last sphere of influence on the peninsula. Many fled from Paekche to Japan at that time, which stimulated Japanese culture.

After the conquest of Paekche, T'ang China then attacked Koguryŏ and finally occupied P'yŏngyang in 668. From the time of the first Chinese campaign, for about seventy years, Koguryŏ had fought against the huge armies of the Sui and T'ang empires, but finally fell. These seventy years of resistance reveal the stout development of the various Korean tribes and their surprising strength, as compared with their condition earlier when Korea had been conquered by the Chinese. Because of Koguryŏ's resistance Silla was able ultimately to throw off Chinese military control and realize the unification of Korea.

The Sui and T'ang expeditions against Paekche and Koguryŏ had presented a difficult problem for Silla. She saw in them an excellent opportunity to dispose of her mortal enemies in Korea, but she recognized the danger of being subjected to Chinese military control. Silla, at the time of the T'ang expeditions against Paekche and Koguryŏ, participated in the fighting as a wing of the T'ang army and provided the army with rations and other military supplies. Such services won her the right to a voice in the arrangements after the enemy had been defeated. After the T'ang invaders had occupied the former territories of Paekche and Koguryŏ and administered them through a military government, they wished to integrate them into China. Silla, however, wanted to regain them and to establish a unified state embracing all Korea. The opposition of Silla to China came into the open with the fall of Koguryŏ, and war broke out between the two countries, which lasted for six years. As a result of the determined resistance of Silla and of revolts among the defeated people of Koguryŏ and Paekche, the T'ang invaders were finally forced to abandon their occupation of Korea and to withdraw from the country. Silla began her unified rule of Korea in 675.

III

The Kingdom of Silla

Unification of Silla

Before Korea was unified by Silla, the tribes which inhabited it differed greatly in customs, language, and form of government. Although the Koguryŏ people in the north and the Han tribes in the south may have originated from the same ethnic group in prehistoric times, they had grown far apart because of the different environment and political conditions under which they had been living. When Silla, which emerged from the Han tribes, drove out the T'ang army and brought about a political union of the country, it also achieved an amalgamation of all Korean tribes and made dominant the customs and language of the Han tribes. This unification provided a basis for the development of the modern Korean people and thus was an important turning point in the history of the country.

By preventing a division of Korea by the T'ang army, Silla undoubtedly saved the country from what would have been a period of stagnation and retarded development. If the T'ang army had continued the occupation, it probably would have made the Koreans a subject people such as they had been earlier under the Han Dynasty. We need only consider that T'ang forces during their occupation of Koguryŏ and Paekche sent 200,000 Koguryŏ and 13,000 Paekche prisoners of war to China as slaves, to realize that all of Korea would have been enslaved if Korea had become a part of T'ang territory. At that time slaves meant prosperity for a country, and there were slaves even in Korea. Had the Koreans been made a subject people, the slave system there would undoubtedly have been discontinued. When one recalls the retardation of Korean society by the administration of the Lo-lang and Tai-fang commanderies, the Silla unification appears even more as an epoch-making event.

Chinese dynastic authority was not, however, entirely eliminated. T'ang, as a suzerain nation, dominated the Silla kings. This was more than a mere formality. It entailed the presenting of considerable tribute to the suzerain. In comparison, however, with the direct administration by Chinese officials, this was a relatively light burden. The Koreans had a measure of freedom and an autonomous government by their own countrymen, and this made possible the development of self-rule and the brilliant culture of Silla.

Creation of the Unified State

Silla's territory expanded enormously when Koguryŏ and Paekche were added. Hitherto it had extended over the southeastern portion of the peninsula north to about the 37th parallel, but now it reached in the northwest to the Taedong River, and in the northeast to the southern part of Hamgyŏng Province. At the same time, the number of people under Silla administration also increased. The greater part of Paekche's 760,000 households and a large number of Koguryŏ's 690,000 households were incorporated into Silla. The administration of a population and territory that had grown so suddenly posed a serious problem.

A part of the land and people was distributed to Silla nobles. As in the past, land and people were given to the victors and to the chiefs of tribes who had surrendered; or those who surrendered had their own lands and people granted back to them as emolument estates *(sigŭp)*.[1] For example, in 532, the 19th year of King Pŏphŭng (514-539), it appears that Kim Kuhi, a chieftain of Kŭmgwan-guk (a state in the Naktong River basin) who had surrendered, was given Kŭmgwan-guk as an emolument estate. In this estate probably no change was made in the traditional internal relationships. Kim Kuhi's right of rule was confirmed, and the people living there rendered tribute and labor to the ruler of the estate.

In cases where a noble received land from the king, the noble probably did not manage the land himself, but only took crops as tribute, for landowners who managed their own lands appeared much later in Korean history. It would seem that landownership at that time was an immature control relationship in which the person controlling a fixed area of land simply took crops and corvée.from the people who lived on it. There were cases where only the tax revenue from the land was granted to men of merit, but in reality there seems to have been little difference between the presentation of land and the granting of the tax revenue from the land. The granting of these emolument estates, and of land and tax revenues, increased with the expansion of the territory of Silla, especially with the annexation of Koguryŏ and Paekche. To Kim Yusin (595-673), who had helped in the unification, 500 households and 500 *kyŏl*[2] of rice paddies were presented as an emolument estate; to Kim Inmum (629-694) went an emolument estate of 500 households; and Kang Su (died 692) was granted a 200 *sŏk*[3] rice tax revenue from Sinsŏng. Futhermore, civil and military officials were given official paddies in 687.

---

[1] *Sigŭp* is a term for land tenure occurring repeatedly in Korean historical texts. It is difficult to translate because its connotations change in different periods. For example, it sometimes appears to be hereditary, and at other times not. While it has often been translated as "fief," this word would imply certain conditions of European feudal land tenure such as military service, which are not implicit in land tenure in Korea under *sigŭp*. "Emolument estates" has been chosen for translating this term in this book because it suggests the least common denominator for *sigŭp* in various periods.

[2] *Kyŏl* is a unit of land measure, used in Korea especially for measuring the area of cultivated fields. The area of a *kyŏl* has varied vastly at different times in the history of Korea, being sometimes determined by the yield of the fields; in 1069 it was approximately 490 square feet, in the nineteenth century about 10,000 square feet.

[3] *Sŏk* is a unit of dry measure for grain, similar to the Anglo-Saxon bushel. Like the term *kyŏl*, the measure of a *sŏk* has varied during the centuries, making it difficult to determine precise numerical values for use in translation. The present-day *sŏk* in Korea is equivalent to nearly 5 bushels.

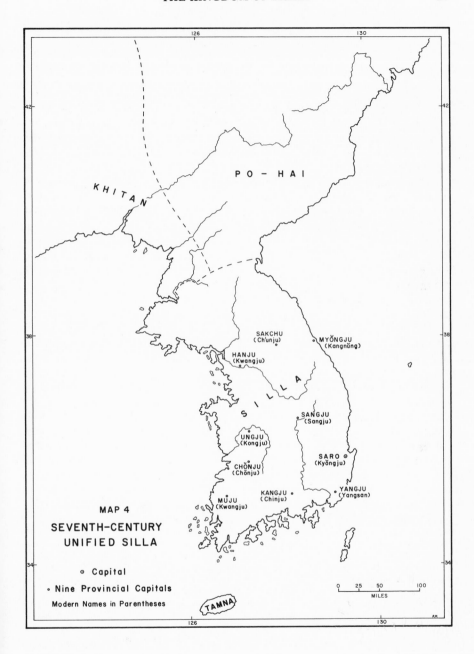

KHITAN

PO - HAI

SAKCHU
(Ch'unju)

MYŎNGJU
(Kangnŭng)

HANJU
(Kwangju)

S I L L A

SANGJU
(Sangju)

UNGJU
(Kongju)

CHŎNJU
(Chŏnju)

SARO
(Kyŏngju)

MŬJU
(Kwangju)

KANGJU
(Chinju)

YANGJU
(Yangsan)

MAP 4

SEVENTH-CENTURY
UNIFIED SILLA

○ Capital

● Nine Provincial Capitals

Modern Names in Parentheses

TAMNA

0   25   50   100
        MILES

In the same year, the granting of stipend estates to all former officials was changed to supplying them with tax income, but the stipend estates were restored again in 757. To both large and small chieftains of Koguryŏ and Paekche who had surrendered, official posts were given together with land, and temples had paddies bestowed upon them.

In addition to the emolument estates, land, and tax revenues, people also were distributed. Most of them had been made subject people, and only their crops had been taken, but some among them were separated from their land and were allocated to nobles as slaves. The general population, too, was without rights, not knowing when they might be removed from the soil. This was especially true of the many war prisoners who could easily be distributed. One of the principal objectives of the wars of that time was the capture of prisoners for slaves, and these were distributed among the nobles of Silla as booty along with domestic animals and other property.

The victorious nobles became wealthy. Chinese chronicles record that the prime minister lived an extravagant life and owned 3,000 slaves, a large number of domestic animals (cattle, horses, and swine), and troops. The Silla leaders as conquerors became a privileged group, and the men who accompanied them shared in the spoils. Some Silla nobles were powerful enough to own several thousand slaves. These nobles endangered the ruling class based, as it was, on the mutually beneficial *kolp'umje* (bones status) system. There was a strong tendency for clans within the bone system and families within the clans to seek personal advantage, regardless of the interests of the bone or clan as a unit, and to center their attention on the realities of their lives. These families, which posed a threat to the bones system, were quite different from those originally composing the bones, in that they were large and widely inclusive, sometimes connected with several clans. This tendency was combated by those who upheld the traditional *kolp'umje* system. At about the time of the unification of the peninsula by Silla, the development of the independent power of families, or conflict between families, was in many cases punished by the execution of nobles. Although powerful men struggled for power, sometimes within the same family, the *kolp'umje* was not undermined. It continued to be the central framework of the administrative and social order, and the rulers depended on the authority derived from it to protect their over-all interests.

The continuing strength of the *kolp'umje* indicates that the power of individual families had not yet developed to a point sufficient for the independent control of land and men. It was still only through the cooperation of all the nobles that the old Kingdom of Silla, as well as the newly acquired territory and its population, could be administered. All the land and people were considered to belong to the state of Silla, or to the king who represented the nobles and not to individual nobles. The ruling positions of the state were monopolized by the fixed bone clans, and since the king was the most powerful person in these clans, that which belonged to the state or king belonged to the bone clans. Although a trend toward breaking down the solidarity of the bone clans had developed, essentially these clans remained unchanged, and most of the land and people were placed under their administration.

However, if the country was to continue to be ruled through a single organization, the state structure had to be enlarged and reorganized. The administrative system of the T'ang empire served as a model. Already, before the unification, T'ang methods had been employed in Silla. Afterward their use greatly increased, and in the reign of King Kyŏngdŏk (742-764), the administrative organization of Silla came to be patterned completely after that of T'ang. At the capital, the central government was organized into a ministry of management *(chipsasŏng)*, boards *(pu)*, bureaus *(pu)*, departments *(chŏn)*, and other subdivisions similar to those used in China.[4]

For regional administration the country was divided into nine districts *(chu)*; at five important points lesser capitals were established, and the districts were subdivided into counties *(kun)*[5] and prefectures *(hyŏn)*; below them the land was further subdivided into country districts *(hyang)* and wards *(pugok)*. At the capital, Kyŏngju, and throughout the country at strategic points, military garrisons called *chŏng* were set up. To each *chŏng*, military units of every branch were attached, and competent men from throughout the country (including survivors from Koguryŏ and Paekche) were assigned to these units. All military and civil officials received official paddies and stipend revenues (originally stipend estates, then changed to tax revenues, and later changed back again to stipend estates); and farmers were furnished tenant paddies (722). Grain taxes, labor service, and cloth were taken from the farmers. It is clear,therefore, that Silla closely imitated the T'ang bureaucracy in organizing her administration.

However, there were great differences between Silla and China, and these were reflected in their state structures. First, in T'ang China candidates for office were selected on the basis of examinations, while in Silla official positions were filled according to a man's standing in the *kolp'umje*. It is true that in China, in spite of the examinations, those who became officials were likely to be sons of powerful and wealthy persons. Nevertheless, the examinations opened the door to many individuals by removing the limitations of social and family position for prospective officials. The effect of the examination was to absorb into the official hierarchy many influential persons instead of confining it exclusively to a few nobles of the best families. In Silla, on the other hand, official positions were restricted to people of fixed "bones." Family and official position were inseparately tied together. Central and regional posts for high civil and military officials were the monopoly of the first bone, the one from which the king came. Beneath the first bone was the noble stratum of the second bone, whose members occupied the next lower level of positions. Below them were several lower strata, and each determined the limits to the posts that one could assume. A man's official position was determined by birth, not by ability or talent. The subject peoples who were not attached to any bone were excluded from all official positions. This system of social stratification severely circumscribed not only official position, but affected dress, residence, and even who should have mounts and vehicles. Such a system of stratification into castes differed greatly from the T'ang system.

Secondly, there was a difference between China and Silla in the position of the agricultural population vis-à-vis the dominant official hierarchy. The agricultural population of China, living on "equally divided fields," preserved some

---

[4]The author includes here a long list of government offices, but this has been omitted in the translation because it was felt to add little to the reader's comprehension of the administrative system.

[5]See note 1 in Chapter I for an explanation of "county" as a translation of *kun*.

characteristics of servitude from the past, but, in addition to these, had characteristics of the freer and more independent agricultural population in China, which
developed after the Sung Dynasty (960-1279). We know little of the material life
of the agricultural population of Silla, since the records say only briefly that
farmers were provided with fields. But from the fact that the peasants were said to
live in country districts and "wards," we can guess something of their slavelike
position, because the country district and ward, as administrative subdivisions
under the county and prefecture, continued from the Silla period into the Koryŏ
period, and the people of the country districts and wards were different from the
ordinary free citizenry. They occupied special inferior positions as slaves and
unfree people. Originally "ward" was a Chinese term, and in China the word was
used to designate various types of slaves. In Korea it was the name of the lowest
regional administrative unit from the Silla period to the end of the Koryŏ period.
This suggests that the farming population had the status of slaves, and the
"wards" of the Koryŏ period, as is clear from the use of the word, indicated
people discriminated against because of their low social position. This point will
be discussed again in the section on the Koryŏ period. Undoubtedly this was the
case in Silla too. One can safely conclude that all of Silla's agricultural population
were slaves. The system of government based on the *kolp'umje* probably made the
existence of a subject agricultural population inevitable.

Thirdly, the court occupied a relatively more important position in the
organization of Silla society than in that of China. In addition to the great number
of government bureaus associated with the Silla court, a department of handi-
crafts was directly attached to it. At such factories, under formal planning and
management, all sorts of manufactured items were made, such as cloth, embroi-
dery, dye stuffs, shoes, leather goods, wooden articles, ceramics, lacquer ware,
tiles, metal articles, weapons, and also boats. Undoubtedly these industries were
carried on by slaves. In T'ang China, too, handicraft industries were attached to
the court, but, in addition to these, handicraft industries of the people rose to a
high level. In Silla this was not the case. There, most handicraft industries were
directly attached to the court or concentrated there to such an extent that, for all
intents and purposes, no others could be said to exist. This was because the court
was the center of the administration from which the bone clans controlled the
subject people.

The Silla administration was the first to create a unified state in Korea and to
administer a vast territory and a large population. But the early bone-clan administrative system was not eliminated. The capital of Silla from beginning to end
remained at Kyŏngju, which indicates the strength of this traditional system. Silla
was a nation in which a small bone-clan class, based in Kyŏngju, ruled a large
number of subject people. In order to control this vast area and population, it was
necessary strictly to maintain the solidarity and cohesion of the bone clans and to
keep the governed at a low social status. With the expansion of the state, the
kolp'umje became all the stronger. Neither the rulers nor the ruled could escape
from the constrictions of their clan, and their ranks were determined by the clan
into which they were born. The *kolp'umje* was the foundation of the national
order and of society. Within this tribal order there existed persons in authority
with great powers and slaves.

Silla Culture

The period in which Silla flourished on the peninsula corresponds roughly to the period during which T'ang rule spread throughout the mainland of Asia. Silla looked to T'ang China as her suzerain. Besides year after year sending envoys to T'ang, she dispatched students and priests to study T'ang culture. The brilliant T'ang civilization which dominated the Oriental world of that day had a profound effect on the culture of Silla, and Silla's civilization may be considered to be the civilization of T'ang on a reduced scale. However, since the development of the two countries was basically different, there were limits to what Silla could adopt. Silla was more inclined to the culture of Buddhism, and studied it rather than Confucianism. Confucianism, which was the basis of the power of the Chinese dynasties, had been introduced into Korea quite early, and at the Silla capital of Kyŏngju a Confucian state academy was established, but it did not appeal greatly to the Silla nobility. In a society where "bone status" and not examinations set the standard for the selection of officials, Confucianism, which theoretically relied on examinations for determining qualification for office, could hardly become the principle for the direction of the state or be admired by the people. On the other hand, Buddhism was much esteemed. It had entered the country during Silla's period of development and flourished increasingly as Silla prospered. During the reign of King Pŏphŭng, it became a national faith. Beginning with the area around Kyŏngju and spreading from there throughout the country, many temples were built on famous mountains. Renowned monks such as Ŭisang, Wŏnhyo, Sŭngjŏn, and Hyech'o appeared, and Hyech'o studying in China, even traveled on a pilgrimage to India. Because Buddhism was revered as the doctrine that protected the state, the state was lavish in its support. Vast amounts of state funds were expended on the building of temples, Buddhist images, bells, and stupas; and temples were given paddies as sources of income. Special government offices, known as *sŏngjŏn*, were created for the repair of the great temples associated with this religion, and the highest nobles of the first "bones" were placed at the head of these offices. Among the more famous Silla temples for which *sŏngjŏn* were created were those of Sach'ŏnwang, Pongsŏng, Hamŭn, Pongdŏk, Pong'ŭn, Yŏngmyo, and Yŏnghŭng. Priest-officials were appointed, called *kukt'ong* (state abbots), *chut'ong* (district abbots), and *kunt'ong* (county abbots). The celebrated King Munmu (661-681), who unified the peninsula, was an ardent believer in Buddhism; legend has it that, according to his death-bed injunction, his remains were cremated in conformity with Buddhist practice and the ashes scattered upon a big rock in the "Eastern Sea." For generations, first the kings and then the nobility vied with each other in donating property and land to temples, and some built their own temples. People were fascinated with Buddhism to such an extent that the state had to curb such overenthusiasm. Buddhism was served because it was believed that it protected the state and brought the nobles good fortune. This belief was the essence of Buddhism at this time; there was in the religion little consideration of ways to relieve human suffering.

As Buddhism flourished it colored the culture of Silla and affected her arts and crafts. Famous examples of Buddhist art are the Pulguk Temple and Sŏkkuram, a stone grotto, both of which survive today on the outskirts of Kyŏngju. They were begun in 751, the tenth year of King Kyŏngdŏk, and took several decades to be completed. The stone altar at Pulguk Temple (together with the bell tower), the Tabo stone stupa, the Shaka stone stupa, the Locana Buddha and Amitâbha Buddha statues, as well as the stone Buddhas of Sŏkkuram, have rarely been equalled in beauty. The bronze bell of Pongdŏk Temple and the stone lanterns of Sach'ŏnwang Temple are superb. Other outstanding creations of Buddhist art of that time include the bell of the nine-storied stupa of Hwangnyong Temple (weighing about 132,000 pounds completed in 754) and the bronze image of Yaksa (the Buddhist king of medicine) of Punhwang Temple, weighing 396,000 pounds, which was completed in 755. These last two have not survived, but they suggest the grandiose manner of the Buddhist art of the time. The existing great bell of Pongdŏk Temple (diameter: seven feet, six inches; height: eleven feet; thickness: seven inches) is of great beauty, indicating the artistic heights achieved in the period.

Other examples of Silla culture which survive in the region of Kyŏngju are the remains of palaces and royal tombs. These date from practically every period in Silla history. Royal crowns of nearly pure gold and silver, and other ornaments were buried in the old mounds from before unification. These clearly show the wealth and power of the nobles of that time, but they still suggest a certain lack of polish. Compared with these the guardian stones, stone men, tortoise bases, stone lions, and similar figures found at tombs of the united Silla period, also displaying the power of the kings and nobles, are more beautiful, superior even to their T'ang Chinese models. Silla could produce this superb art because of the wealth and power enjoyed by the nobles.

Silla's brilliant culture was built, however, on the rule of the nobles over subject peoples. It was the culture of a nobility dwelling in a world separate from that of the common man, who continued to live in wretched poverty. In the capital, Kyŏngju, neatly divided into rectangles, were built magnificent palaces, government offices, and temples. There were palace gardens containing rare flowers, animals, plants and trees, but just a step outside of this area were the squalid houses of the poor. Kyŏngju flourished upon the wealth brought there by the poor subject population.

Revolts of the Nobles and Uprising of the Subject Population

The Silla nobility who beat off the T'ang army and established a unified state were effective warriors, fighting at the head of the army in order to gain Korean independence. Sons of nobles, heedless of personal safety, they fought unto death for the country. They formed *hwarang* groups, the elite warriors of whom Kim Yusin is representative. To them was due not only Silla's unification, but also its cultural progress. Although their power derived from their control over subject peoples, a condition usual, perhaps inevitable, at the stage of development society had reached at that time, they were not idle parasites but true leaders.

Later, with the struggles for unification past, the nobles became simply a privileged class. Art grew weak and narrow, lacking grandeur and beauty, and production of artistic objects decreased. State construction of temples, stupas, and statues ceased. The *hwarang*, formerly warriors, became a group of effeminate young men. This metamorphosis occurred throughout the body of Silla's nobility.

Its power, position, and property still depended on the *kolp'umje,* but with these changes the *kolp'umje* became unstable. No longer was it supported by concerted action of the nobles. The disruptive tendencies observed earlier among the "bone" clans became stronger. Clans within the same bone, and families within the same clan, took independent action. Among the nobility, conflict and discord came to the surface. With the solidarity of the bone group lost, hostilities could no longer be checked. During the reign of King Hyegong (765-779), several revolts broke out, ending in the assassination of Hyegong, with his assassin ascending the throne as King Sŏndŏk (780-784). The 150 years from Sŏndŏk to the last king of the dynasty, Kyŏngsun (927-935), called the period of Silla's decline, was marked by succession quarrels. Twenty kings ruled during this period, most of whom came to untimely ends, victims of the struggles between the bone clans. The position of the king, formerly established through the cooperation of the bone clans, now became the object of a fight for power among them. Those who won the throne massacred and banished the opposing factions, and the defeated group countered by plotting to regain power. Since their struggle was a fight for the throne, the conflict was usually staged at the capital. However, in the fourteenth year of King Hŏndŏk (822), the governor of Ungch'ŏn district, Kim Hŏnch'ang, resentful that his father Kim Chuwŏn had not become king, started a rebellion in the hinterlands of Ungch'ŏn (present-day Kongju) in South Ch'ungch'ŏng Province. There he established a new state, which he named Changan; for a short time, it included Chŏlla and Kyŏngsang provinces.

In the seventeenth year of the rule of King Hŏndŏk (825), an incident occurred in which Kim Pŏmmun, son of Hŏnch'ang, tried to set up a capital at Yangju (present-day Seoul) in Kyŏnggi Province. Rebellions in the hinterland such as these were, however, rare and easily suppressed. Their object was the capture of the throne, but leading regional officials or even district governors like Kim Hŏnch'ang had no strong support from the rural subject population. It was in the capital that the nobles with no roots in the countryside struggled against each other for power. It was there on that narrow stage that the fighting took place, that control passed from one to another with bewildering speed, and that changes in government repeatedly occurred, followed each time by bloody massacres.

During these conflicts the *kolp'umje* changed in character. It still retained its traditional authority, and still without the prestige of the bone status no one could become really powerful; but it was no longer possible to gain power through the *kolp'umje* alone. Material strength was also required. The importance of the individual had greatly increased, and powerful figures and families appeared on whom clan factions became centered. Such families which combined the authority of the noble "bone" with real power, engaged in bitter rivalry for the throne. It was between these clan factions that the conflicts occurred, and as one or another clan gained control, the appointed king came to represent not the "bone" as a whole, but a clan faction.

While at the capital the nobles created clan factions and quarreled among themselves, conditions were changing in the country. In years of bad crops, vagrants and bandits appeared in many places. Those who lived near the sea set out in boats and ravaged the coastline, some going as far as Japan and China, and some seizing farmers along the coast whom they sold as slaves in China. The famous Kungbok (Chang Pogo) emerged from this bandit group, went to

Hsü-chou in China and became a soldier. He now regretted the fate of the Koreans who had been carried away as T'ang slaves. He returned to Korea, was put in charge of coastal operations and was appointed deputy at Ch'ŏnghae-jin (present-day Wan Island) in South Chŏlla Province (828). He controlled seafarers from his base at Wan Island and traded with Japan and China, becoming increasingly powerful. Then he participated in the struggle of the nobles at the capital for the seizure of the throne and aided Kim Ujing, who had sought his assistance, to become king (839). Kim Ujing was called King Sinmu.

Away from the capital, Kungbok was also able to develop considerable strength, sufficient in fact to enable him to become very powerful politically for a short time. However, Kungbok was not a magnate in control of a farming population, and he never attempted to expand his authority in that area. Rather he controlled the sea as a pirate chieftain, and was placed in high positions by King Sinmu and by Sinmu's son King Munsŏng. He planned to enter the nobility by marrying the daughter of King Munsŏng. When this was refused, he revolted and was quickly killed (846). Powerful as he was, he could not oppose the court.

Besides Kungbok, no other persons who exercised power outside the capital became involved in the struggles of the nobility for political control. Local power had not yet developed to that point. Its influence at the capital was still very weak, but it was slowly growing. By the end of the Silla period, Buddhist temples were being built by the local faithful everywhere in Korea, in contrast to the diminishing construction of huge temples by the government. In an effort to curb this trend, an edict was issued in the seventh year of King Aejang (806) forbidding the building of new local temples. Further evidence of growing local power may be inferred from the adoption of the examination system for officials in the fourth year of the rule of King Wŏnsŏng (788). The objective was probably to strengthen the kolp'umje, but it may also have signified a recognition of the increasing local strength and an attempt to absorb it into the official class.

While the nobles of Kyŏngju struggled for the throne, the life of the subject people became more difficult. Great demands were made upon the population — demands no longer held in check by the deteriorating state system. While King Hŏn'gang (875-885), accompanied by courtiers paid visits to the Wŏlsang pavilion, offered prayers for the prosperity of the capital, and, on the other hand, reveled in drinking, poetry, and music parties, outside the capital the land was in turmoil. Long smouldering rebellion now suddenly spread and began to endanger the foundation of the government. In the third year of the reign of Queen Chinsŏng (889), signs of the decline of the dynasty clearly appeared. Taxes in the countryside had not been collected, and when the queen dispatched officials to press for collection, bandits attacked them. Wŏnjong, Aeno, and others of unknown antecedents took advantage of these uprisings to revolt at Sangju in Kyŏngsang Province. Uprisings and revolts instantly spread throughout the country, and conditions were such that it was said, "Outside the capital, districts and prefectures take part in rebellion and, near and far, bands of thieves arise and swarm like ants." In the tenth year of the queen's reign (896), bandits wearing red trousers, chŏkko, arose in the southwest part of the country and advanced almost to the capital. Queen Chinsŏng could not cope with the situation and, since the rise of banditry and the misery of the peasants were attributed to her "lack of virtue," she abdicated.

This wave of uprisings greatly increased the power of the local subject people.

To them, long oppressed as they had been, came an opportunity at last to take advantage of the confusion in the government's administrative machinery. Throughout the country, men with local authority became influential. First, following the uprising of Wŏnjong and Aeno, bandit chieftains appeared in many parts of the land. Among them the strongest were Yanggil of Pugwŏn (present-day Wŏnju) in Kangwŏn Province, and Chinhwŏn of Mujinju (present-day Kwangju) in South Chŏlla Province. Yanggil attacked Kangwŏn Province, and Chinhwŏn took control of Chŏlla Province, moved to Wansan (present-day Chŏnju) in North Chŏlla Province, and called himself king of Later Paekche (892). Later, a priest of the Silla royal family, Kungye, overthrew Yanggil and, establishing his base at Chŏrwŏn in Kangwŏn Province, called his new state T'aebong (901). Now Silla was weak controlling only the Kyŏngju region, while all other areas were split up among rivals.

Growth of Regional Political Power

The regional revolts, sparked by the violence of the peasantry, continued for about half a century, until Korea was unified by Koryŏ in 936. During that time the power of the Silla court rapidly declined, and opposition to it by the subject population supplied the motive force for the uprisings. These were large-scale revolts that spread throughout the entire country and were powerful enough to bring about the downfall of the court. However, they were not well organized. The common people, under the miserable conditions in which they had been living, were incapable of organizing and of assuming leadership. To oppose the power of the Silla court effectively, they had to rely on local magnates. Among these were sons of Silla nobles who had not achieved their ambitions at court, persons of unknown origin, seafarers, and probably even men who had emerged from the subject population. They profited from the wave of uprisings, or, simply carried along by it, expanded their power. Some of these men, in the process of extending their influence, became absolute rulers, and the areas under their control resembled despotic states. Kungye, an illegitimate son of King Hŏnan, is an example. When he was about to be executed by his father, he was rescued by his slave wet nurse. He later became a priest, but nurtured rebellious feelings against the Silla nobles. Seizing the opportunity offered by the rising of bandit groups, he gathered together a band, threw in his lot with Kihwŏn, a bandit chief of Chukchu and became active as a general of the bandit chieftain Yanggil of Pugwŏn. Because he shared success and adversity with his troops and took nothing for himself, he was popular with his subordinates. However, as Kungye increased his strength, he set up a state, called himself prince, and established central and regional government posts in imitation of the dynasty. Then he bestowed Silla titles and, following the Silla system, created a government official hierarchy. Now he became a tyrant, hated by his subordinates. In 918 he was overthrown by one of his generals, Wang Kŏn (later to become Koryŏ's first ruler, T'aejo).

Kungye represents the type of rebel who, riding the wave of peasant discontent and taking advantage of the uprisings of the period, gained control and became a tyrant. Kungye, from childhood, loathed Silla. He slashed a picture of the Silla king with his sword, called Silla the "Capital of Extermination," and so hated Silla that he slew all emissaries from Silla. Nevertheless, when he became powerful, he adopted the Silla administrative system, even the titles, and planned to reestablish a Silla-type court, for there was no other way to create power enough to oppose Silla. Accordingly, the new regional authority that derived its power from the uprisings, was materially not different from what had preceded it. There was still no other force great enough to produce a new political authority sufficient to negate that of the Silla court.

The uprisings developed and expanded, carried forward men like Kungye, or were used by them to their advantage. Although they were successful in overthrowing Silla, they produced rulers similar to those of Silla. The peasants who were the backbone of the revolts had strength enough to shake the old kingdom, but not enough to bring forth a new type of authority. They were still helpless under overlords who had the same characteristics as those formerly in control. The subject population had not developed to the point of liberating itself.

IV

Kingdom of Koryŏ

The Reestablishment of a Unified State

Wang Kŏn, the founder of Koryŏ, generally known in history as T'aejo, was a general in the army of Kungye and later succeeded in replacing him on the throne (918). Unlike Kungye, who adopted the Silla system while despising it, Wang Kŏn openly joined hands with Silla, welcomed the Silla king and nobles to his court, and included them in the formation of the new state. When the last Silla ruler, King Kyŏngsun (927-935), known as Kim Po after his abdication, surrendered in 935 with all Silla officials, T'aejo greeted him with an obeisance and gave him his eldest daughter in marriage. Had it not been for the petitions of many courtiers, he would not even have permitted Kim Po to render him the usual royal courtesies. He granted him the highest office, *chŏngsŭng* (Minister of State), and a stipend of a thousand *sŏk* of rice; he built a palace for him, bestowed the former capital city of Kyŏngju on him as an emolument estate, and appointed him supervisor of Kyŏngju. This position entitled Kim Po to live in the capital and control from there the appointment and supervision of local chiefs and subchiefs in the country districts. Thus, T'aejo granted Kim Po the highest office at the capital, and also confirmed his administrative rights over his native city. To the Silla nobles who accompanied Kim Po, T'aejo gave paddy stipends and welcomed them to the capital. He treated the Silla king and nobles so generously because by this time they represented no real threat in terms of political power. Koryŏ, by absorbing in these ways the strength of the traditional authority of Silla, increased its own prestige. The structure of the Koryŏ state did not differ basically from that of Silla. In both states the nobility was the nucleus around which the government and the court were built. This undoubtedly hastened the consolidation of Koryŏ.

The new state continued the T'ang administrative system upon which Silla was based and reestablished the old court pattern. But this was not simply a revival of the former exclusive bone status system, for it created a new official class which included a wide range of constituents. However, the two systems were alike in that they were both based on the government of a subject population by officials. The basic policy of the Koryŏ state was to bring together under the court a broad administrative class which embraced the old nobility and the regional village magnates; and to reduce the farming population to a position of servitude through the power of the organized bureaucracy. The years of the reign of King T'aejo (918-943) to those of King Sŏngjong (982-997), particularly the latter, were years of development of the state. Changes continued to be made during the reign of King Munjong (1047-1082), by which time the basic organization of Koryŏ's autocratic administration was completed.

T'aejo's generals, local magnates who had submitted, and their descendants, became civil and military officials and received government posts and paddy stipends from the state. But men who had gained power in local areas during the disturbances toward the end of the Silla period now too became officials, with fixed positions in the state machinery; in this way their strength was added to that of the state. All land was under the control of the government, and those connected with state service from the highest minister down to the minor officers and common soldiers were provided with fixed amounts of rice land and firewood land according to their position. At their death, this land returned to the state. Land under this system of distribution was called *chŏnsigwa* or "paddies and woods by class." Besides, there was land called *kongŭmjŏnsi*, "merit paddies and woods," which at first was given only to those who had rendered distinguished service in the establishment of the dynasty, and to local magnates who had submitted. Later, high officials were granted fixed amounts of such land according to their rank, and, in addition, this land was recognized as inheritable. Still other lands, known as *sajŏn*, "paddies bestowed by the king," were presented in varying amount as marks of special favor, and these were also inheritable. Of the named lands, the *chŏnsigwa* were the most numerous since they were for officials and troops. However, neither in the case of the *chŏnsigwa*, nor the *kongŭmjŏnsi*, nor the *sajŏn*, was the land itself given, but only a fixed income derived from it. The officials received this revenue from the state, but did not live on, or manage, the land themselves. This arrangement permitted direct control of the land by the state. The fact that the state administered the land and divided the income from it among the officials constituted the economic basis of Koryŏ.

In addition to the land revenue, regular officials were provided with a fixed allowance, according to their position, in rice, barley, or millet from the national granaries. Minor officials who acted as agents of regular officials were treated in like manner. If they served and supported the state, their living was guaranteed. Except for the few low-ranking officials appointed to provincial offices, all officials who were provided with land revenue and stipends lived at the capital, Kaesŏng.[1] This concentration of the ruling group produced a centralization of authority, the extent of which is suggested by the scale of construction at the capital.

Construction in the capital continued intermittently for approximately a century, from the establishment of the capital at Kaesŏng in the second year of

---

[1] Kaesŏng, the present-day name of the capital of Koryŏ, has also been known as Songak, Songdo, Kaegyŏng, and by other names in the past. The author uses both Kaesŏng and Kaegyŏng in his book, but for the sake of uniformity, only the name Kaesŏng has been used in this translation.

T'aejo's reign (919) to the twentieth year of Hyŏnjong's reign (1029). It is said that when Hyŏnjong built the outer wall, a corvée of 344,400 laborers was used. We know on what a grand scale the capital, the symbol of this bureaucratic state, was constructed, from its well-designed boulevards which divided it into districts, from its beautiful palaces, pavilions, and temples which stood there side by side, from its higher-government offices known as the Six Boards and Nine Courts, and from its lower-government offices. In the first year of Injong (1123), Hsü Ching, an envoy from Sung China, came to Kaesŏng. He admired the splendor of this capital and praised it as being indeed the old fief of Ch'i-tzu. However, Hsü Ching pointed out that, compared with the magnificence of the capital, the dwellings of the common people were miserable. The Koryŏ officials were embarrassed by them and endeavored to keep the Sung envoy from seeing them. But the foreigner noticed the contrast between the squalid homes of the common people and the grandiose royal palaces.

In this capital lived the king and his family, civil and military officials and their families, Buddhist priests and the suites that attended them, artisans who labored in the shops of government bureaus, the royal guard that protected the palace, and public and private slaves. Although there had been many slaves from the time of Silla, their number since then had greatly increased as a result of the taking of prisoners of war and of the destitution brought about by the upheavals at the end of the Silla regime. They were classified into public slaves, official slaves, and private slaves. The public slaves belonged to the state and served as petty clerks or servants. They performed minor tasks in the palace and government offices. Official slaves were allotted in small or large numbers to civil and military officials. When officials traveled abroad, they went on horseback accompanied before and behind by official slaves called *chŏngni* (attendants to the mount) and *kusa* (drivers of the mount). Their number was fixed in accordance with the rank of the official; for important ministers, the scores of official slaves made quite a procession. Private slaves were owned by the king, princes, officials, and temples, and entered into the registers of their masters. They were used to cut firewood, draw water, and do similar work. Some were entrusted with important tasks such as supervision of land and household affairs. These were called *kano* (male household slaves), *kabi* (female household slaves), and *kadong* (young male house slaves). They were bought and sold or held as pledges, and their children and grandchildren inherited the social status of slaves.

The royal guard *(pubyŏng)* was selected from the peasantry. Able-bodied peasants could not avoid military duty, which was one type of service that the peasants rendered to the state. In time of war several hundred thousand farmers were mobilized; in time of peace about 30,000 peasants in the royal guard protected the capital.

The wealth of the nation was gathered in the Koryŏ capital. Agricultural products, such as rice, wheat, and millet, as well as cloth, gold, silver, copper, iron, oil, silk, paper, ink, tiles, charcoal, salt, fish, ceramics, and other items were all brought there to satisfy the needs of the king, princes, and officials. These goods were produced as tribute and taxes by the free *(yangmin)* and unfree people *(ch'ŏnmin)*[2] of the country, and, through manual labor commandeered by the state, were transported over great distances. Without using merchants, the wealth of the nation was concentrated in the capital by the state, and from there distributed to the king, princes, officials, their retinues, and the government offices.

Although many people lived at the capital, and wealth was accumulated there on a grand scale, yet there were no stores. Merchants carried their stock on their backs, but none built shops. The only fixed locales for trading were a few drinking halls frequented by the officials. Markets were established where daily necessities and vegetables were bartered, but no metal currency was used. Cloth and rice took the place of money. When envoys from other lands arrived, active trade was carried on with them, but this was the only time that government bureaus traded with foreign merchants. Aside from this, there were almost no business transactions.

Within the city walls stood many magnificent palaces, stately government offices, and majestic temples, yet there were no shops or places of amusement. Temple bells and the sound of chanted sutras could be heard, but no noise of entertainment or mercantile activity. This was completely different from the ancient cities of Greece and Rome. It was different also from T'ang Chinese cities, however similar the shape and names of palaces and pavilions may have been, since there were no bustling city crowds. The Koryŏ capital was completely an administrative city, a city of officials, the symbol of Koryŏ.

The rural districts were organized to serve the capital. The entire country, with the capital and capital province as the centers, was divided into provinces *(to)*, districts *(chu)*, counties *(kun)*, prefectures *(hyŏn)*, villages *(ch'ŏn)*, country districts *(hyang)*, wards *(pugok)*, and places *(so)*. At important points of communication there were ferries, courier stations, and official residences; at strategic points were fortresses. Special resident officers *(yusugwan)* were placed at the ancient centers of the Western Capital *(P'yŏngyang)*, the Eastern Capital *(Kyŏngju)*, and the Southern Capital *(Seoul)*.[3] Officials sent out by the central government were stationed at these various administrative subdivisions down to the level of prefectures and fortresses. The position of local officials was lower than that of officials who lived in the capital, and prefectural officials had the lowest rank. There were relatively few local officials, for authority was concentrated at the capital.

Those who had direct contact with the people below the level of prefecture were not officials, but the country-district clerks *(hyangni)* who were selected from

---

[2] *Yangmin* means "good people" and *ch'ŏnmin* "despised people." *Yangmin* will be translated as "free" or "free men" and *ch'ŏnmin* as "unfree" or "unfree men." *Ch'ŏnmin* include slaves, serfs, outcastes who engaged in unclean, menial or socially or legally undesirable occupations, as well as the holders of some low offices. In the Yi period monks and nuns were added to the class. As a group the *ch'ŏnmin* suffered from legal disabilities, but within the group there was wide variety in personal freedom and social acceptance.

[3] Seoul is a Korean word meaning "capital" and is used at the present time when referring to the capital of Korea. Present-day Seoul has also been known in the past as Hansŏng, Hanyang, Kyŏngsŏng, Namgyŏng, and by other names. Under the Japanese it was called Keijō. In this translation, whenever the present-day capital is referred to by one of its old names, the word "Seoul" is added in parenthesis or used directly.

the local populace. To them was assigned the service of collecting taxes, applying corvée, and tending to minor legal matters. Because they represented the state, they had great power over the local peasantry, but their own social position was very low. The state considered them to be unfree persons, almost slaves of the officials, and imposed many restrictions on them to prevent their attaining independence.

High officials at the capital were appointed inspecting officers *(sasimgwan)* of their home areas. They supervised the country-district clerks who administered these areas and controlled the local people. Any connection between the inspecting officer and the country-district clerk was forbidden. They could not be of the same family or related by marriage. Special restrictions were placed on the examinations to prevent country-district clerks from becoming officials. Their sons were held at the capital as hostages, called *kiin* (literally "their men"). Their position in the country district was similar to that of the petty clerk at the capital who was an official slave.

The people administered by them lived in villages, country districts, wards, places, ferries, official residences, and courier stations. They included both free and unfree persons. Among the latter, besides slaves, there were large numbers who approximated the status of slaves. For example, at places *(so)* there were special organizations established to provide the gold, silver, copper, iron, silk, paper, ceramics, and charcoal needed by the state; the craftsmen who worked in these organizations were unfree persons or criminals. Again, wards *(pugok)* were administrative units which sometimes had larger populations than prefectures, and the people who lived in them were not free. The ward was established in the Silla era. During the Koryŏ period there was a trend toward its dissolution, but it still existed throughout the country up to the end of the period. Whenever there occurred a serious offense that threatened the state, the prefecture or county where it occurred was reduced to a ward as punishment. The country district *(hyang)* was an administrative division similar to the ward; the majority of its inhabitants, as well as those of ferries, courier stations, and official residences, had the social status of unfree people. The unfree people who were neither slaves nor free, lived in hamlets *(purak)* widely scattered throughout the country. Furthermore, their hamlets had official standing as regional administrative units. Thus, besides public slaves, a vast group of base people existed in the Koryŏ administrative structure whom the state made into an important lower-class organization.

The free people included probably most of the peasantry. The way was open for them to take the examinations to become officials, and they could also become Buddhist priests. As a practical matter, however, such an idea probably never entered their heads. It could hardly be expected that these people who paid the taxes, carried out labor service, and were called upon unceasingly for emergency requisitions, would have much time for studying. They had the social status of the free but, in everyday life, there was little difference between them and the unfree people. They were always on the verge of sinking into slavery, and there were many instances when they sold themselves as slaves. As an indication of how different the world of the official must have been from that of the free and unfree people in country villages, is the report that, when officials committed serious crimes, they would be sent away to the villages as punishment.

The people who lived in the villages formed large family groups, quite different from present-day families. They were so widely inclusive as to be close to being clans. There were families numbering as many as ninety-five adults. Probably it was only because they could rely on these extensive family connections for protection that the poor and those of low station were able to survive. Since punishments for crimes against group heads, and especially against a person's grandfather or father, were very severe, we can assume that the authority of the family or clan head was absolute in the family and clan.

The poor farming villages provided the wealth for the officials in the magnificent capital. Although there were status differences among the free and unfree, as well as among the officials, by far the widest division lay between the two classes of officials and nonofficials; the complete collective power of the former was the special characteristic of this absolute bureaucratic state.

Aristocratic Government and Buddhist Temples

King T'aejo rewarded handsomely the men who had fought with him and helped him to victory. He gave them important posts and provided them with land, income, and public slaves. They lived at the palace in wealth and splendor with private slaves and petty clerks to serve them and perform minor duties. Soon they became nobles and lived as parasites on the state. Their descendants inherited their power so that, as the state developed and became stabilized, a man's position depended not on his own ability, but on the meritorious service of his forefathers and the standing of his family and relatives.

At the beginning of the Silla period, a man's position was primarily dependent on the "bone" to which he belonged. Later, individual families became powerful and influential, until eventually, at the end of the period, they became all-important and the "bones" became meaningless. The word "family" must be understood to cover a wide range of relationships. Not only direct lines, but collateral lines and members of the mothers' and wives' families were included. Even slaves were entered in the family register. Although so large a family, almost resembling a clan, did not act as a unit in daily life, it was important in any political activity or connection with outsiders and became the chief determining factor of a person's position in society.

Since the possession of land, income, and slaves depended on one's position, and one's position depended less on individual ability than on one's family connections, it became important to seek ties with the best clans and the highest nobility. The royal house represented this group. At the beginning of the Koryŏ period, in order to elevate the power of the royal family, marriage between its members and outsiders was forbidden. But eventually marriages took place with important unrelated persons, to the great advantage of the latter. Daughters and sisters would enter the palace, and in-laws gained supreme authority among the king's ministers. As they were now members of the royal family, they became powerful. The Kim family of Ansan, after three daughters of Kim Ŭnbu became consorts of King Hyŏnjong (1009-1031), took over political control and, during approximately fifty years covering the four reigns of Hyŏngjong, Tŏkchong, Chŏngjong, and Munjong, became wealthy nobles. The Yi family of Kyŏngwŏn, after three daughters of Yi Chayŏn became consorts of King Munjong

(1046-1083), held the reins of power for nearly eighty years during the reigns of seven kings from Munjong to Injong. During this period, the Yi family sent women to the palace, one after the other, set up the heir to the throne, and used their position as in-laws to extend their power. If a man became an important official, his family and clan rose; when he fell from power, his family and clan were banished.

The struggles of the nobles for position, honor, and property quite naturally developed into quarrels between clans. In these disputes, relations with the royal family were of prime importance. Consequently, there were many bloody incidents involving the enthronement and dethronement of kings and queens. The second king of Koryŏ, Hyejong, the third king, Chŏngjong, and the fourth king, Kwangjong, all died violently; the seventh king, Mokchong, was assassinated by a minister. The queens were beset by even more woes than the kings.

Tragedies and plots ceaselessly darkened the gaudy but isolated life of the nobility at the capital. Within the high walls of the palace, secret feuds and conspiracies unfolded in which the people outside the city had no part. The countryside was entirely separate. Sometimes those who fell from power went to the country, and powerful figures there were not entirely lacking, but the strength of the countryside had not yet made itself felt at the capital.

The nobles, wishing to increase the splendor of their way of living, became dissatisfied with the income from their *chŏnsigwa* and *kongŭmjŏnsi* lands. They petitioned the king for other land and took away the fields of others. These newly acquired agricultural holdings were known as *chŏnjang, nongjang,* or *changwŏn,* and collectively will be called here private agricultural estates. They were not directly administered by the nobles, but entrusted to cultivators; and the nobles only collected the income. In this way they did not differ from *chŏnsigwa* and *kongŭmjŏnsi.* The nobles who lived at the capital used the authority of the dynasty to extract taxes from the peasants, and otherwise had no relations with the land or peasantry. The development of these conditions brought about a decrease in land that provided taxes to the state and thus threatened to destroy the economic base of the nation. Nevertheless, since the nobility were not opposed to the state but simply parasites on it, the trend was uncontested. The expansion of private agricultural estates caused an increase in land-grabbing among the nobility, and this in turn created internal disturbances in the administration.

With the development of government by the nobles, Buddhist temples flourished. Buddhism had entered Korea quite early, the traditional dates being 372 in Koguryŏ, 384 in Paekche, and 528 in Silla. In the Silla period, Buddhism was venerated as the state religion, and many temples and Buddhist statues were created, but the golden age of Korean Buddhism came in the Koryŏ period. King T'aejo is said to have admonished his descendants to protect and revere Buddhism. The succeeding kings and nobles faithfully adhered to T'aejo's counsel and became zealous Buddhists. Since Buddhism was considered to be most efficacious in protecting the state, it was made into a royally sponsored religion.

Confucianism also had come to Korea early, and was encouraged in the Koryŏ period. The Confucian examination system was adopted in 958, but to the kings, princes, and nobles at that time, the more magnificent and sumptuous Buddhism had greater attraction than the severe Confucianism. Much later, during the Yi dynasty, Confucianism was to become the guiding principle for Korean bureaucracy.

Meanwhile splendid temples were built, some even within the palace walls. Temples were erected also outside the capital and on famous mountains throughout the country. Most of these were built at state expense and received from the state vast paddy fields and many slaves. Buddhism thus received not only spiritual but material support from the state.

Among the many priests in the temples were persons who had left the royal household or noble families because of their adherence to Buddhism. Also among the priests were the poor, because priests were exempt from taxes and the corvée. This practice became so common that the state had to restrict it. Observances were held in the temples on the king's birthday and on religious feast days, and at these times the state feasted the priests. The number of *hansŭng* or "rice priests" at that period amounted to tens of thousands. This large number of priests was organized hierarchically, the lowest ranks performing minor duties while the highest were able to live in a manner similar to that of the nobility. When a priest reached the rank of *kuksa* ("instructor of the nation") in the hierarchy, even the king had to make obeisance before him.

The temples, which were sanctuaries for the protection of the state, also served as pleasure sites. Situated in areas of natural beauty, besides being places to listen to the prayers and sutras of the priests, they were ideal spots for amusement. Kings, princes, and nobles enjoyed themselves there composing poems and feasting; even in this way Buddhism was suited to the requirements and desires of the nobility.

Thus, through the veneration and protection given to the temples by the state, the priests held a dominant spiritual and material position. They sometimes used the income from their vast paddy holdings to engage in money-lending. To protect their power, they had their own weapons and trained organizations of warrior-priests. Their military strength made itself felt in the struggles of the nobles and was influential in changes of government. The temples reached the height of their development in the Koryŏ period, but this efflorescence of Buddhism was subjected to curtailment and pressure in the Yi Dynasty which followed.

Revolts of the Military

As the struggles of the nobles became more intense, they increasingly resorted to violence. Some nobles had designs on the throne. The Yi family who were the in-laws of the royal family throughout the seven reigns from King Munjong to Injong, held absolute power in the palace by the time of the reign of Injong. The family head, Yi Chagyŏm, planning to make himself king, attacked the palace and burned it in 1126. However, a quarrel arose between him and an associate, T'ak Chun'gyŏng, in which Chagyŏm was killed and the Yi family banished. The fall of the Yi family foreshadowed the fall of the government of the nobles. During the fight between Yi Chagyŏm and T'ak Chun'gyŏng, many palaces were burned, and the beautiful capital was all but destroyed.

It was during this period of unrest that a doctrine became current based on *yin-yang* and dealing with the magical influences of geography. It was said to have been first introduced into Korea by the priest To Sŏn (827-898) at the end of the

Silla period. A priest who practiced this geomancy, Myo Ch'ŏng, from the Western Capital (P'yŏngyang), impressed the uneasy populace and King Injong with the doctrine. He persuaded the king to move the capital from Kaesŏng to P'yŏngyang in the belief that such a move would restore the vitality of the royal house. The attempt to do this was checked by the opposition party led by Kim Pusik who feared that moving the capital would bring about a change of political power. The faction supporting Myo Ch'ŏng rose in revolt at the Western Capital in 1135. It was finally defeated, but only after a year of conflict. Uprisings like those of Myo Ch'ŏng and the previous Yi family rebellion indicate the atmosphere of unrest and instability in the government of the nobility. As soon as the disturbances were brought under control, the nobles resumed their lives of pleasure behind the high walls of the capital. King Ŭijong (1146-1170), who succeeded Injong, a devotee of hedonistic pursuits, was called "Lord of Tranquility and Literature Appreciation." He built villas in many places and almost every day set out on a round of pleasures accompanied by literary men, feasting and composing poems.

In 1170 an incident occurred that became known as the uprising of *Kyŏngin* (the Korean cyclical name for the year). When, one night, the royal pleasure party was about to pass through the gate of Pohyŏn Palace, the accomplices of Chŏng Chungbu, a military official of the guard accompanying the party, drew their swords and began cutting down the civil officials escorting the king. Then this group sped to the capital and hunted down the civil officials within the city, killing a large number. The troops within the city also rose and killed every civil official in sight.

This was not the end of the massacre of civil officials by military officials. When the commander of the northeastern provincial forces, Kim Podang, tried to raise an army to attack Chŏng Chungbu, the military officials carried out a thorough massacre of civil officials. This was called the uprising of *Kyesa* (for the Korean cyclical name for the year) and occurred in the third year of the reign of King Myŏngjong (1173).

The military officials had long been downtrodden and despised by the civil officials and the nobility. The achievements of the military, highly prized while the dynasty was establishing itself, were quickly forgotten after order and bureaucratic control had been introduced. The civil officials had seized the right to direct military matters, so that the military officers became their subordinates, which caused dissatisfaction among the military officers. Almost sixty years earlier, in the fifth year of the reign of King Hyŏnjong (1014), they revolted and temporarily seized power. This and similar attempts at rebellion were of short duration and were easily crushed by the civil officers. The uprisings of *Kyŏngin* and *Kyesa* differed from these earlier revolts in that they were on a vast scale destroying nearly all civil officials.

These uprisings were different from previous ones also because they affected the lower ranks of the army and not only the military officials. The soldiers were conscripted for military service from the peasantry as one form of the corvée, so the peasants were much aware of the hardships of the troops. The following passage from the *Koryŏ-sa* (History of Koryŏ), shows clearly how difficult the life of the people was at that time. "Previously, when building a pavilion, conscripted troops had to bring their own rations; one of the soldiers was so poor he could not bring any food with him, so the other soldiers divided their own portions of rice for him to eat. One day his wife prepared rice and brought it. She said, 'Call your close friends and eat this with them.' The soldier said, 'How did you prepare this when we are so poor? Did you get it by selling your body or did you steal it from somebody?' His wife said, 'What a cruel thing to say. I am ugly. To whom could I offer myself? Don't worry. I didn't steal it. All I did was to cut off my hair and sell it.' She showed him her head and the soldier sobbed and could not eat. All who heard this were moved to tears."

These were the conditions existing when King Ŭijong, "Lord of Tranquility and Literature Appreciation," built pavilions for his pleasure. It was on the sacrifices of such pathetic fellows as described above that the culture of the nobles flourished. These conditions produced dissatisfaction among the military officials and their conscripted troops. The uprisings of *Kyŏngin* and *Kyesa* were strengthened by the wide-spread popular opposition to the administration of the nobles.

With the uprisings of *Kyŏngin* and *Kyesa*, the period of rule by civil officials and nobles, which had lasted almost two centuries, came to an end. For a time after that, counterattacks by powerful civil officials continued against the administrative control of the military officials, but each time the military suppressed the civil bureaucracy and finally all the principal government offices, both in the capital and in the country, were occupied by the military. Surviving civil officials surrendered to the military and were permitted to exist under the administration of the military. It took considerable time for the military to stabilize their control of the government, but control by the civil officials was over.

As indicated above, the unrest and opposition to civil control by the peasantry and conscripted troops helped the military officials to gain control of the government, but it was the military officials themselves who overthrew the old nobility. These officials had no direct ties with the peasants, and the troops never became a primary source of power for them.

The armed strength of the military officials rested mainly on their division into units of martial *mun'gaek* (retainers) and *kadong* (young male house slaves). The commanders of these units had close ties with other commanders. The units themselves were tightly knit and, like clans, were centered on their chieftains. The civil officials had no such clan relation with their troops. Their clan groups were made up solely from the nobility and upper classes. At the time of the uprisings of *Kyŏngin* and *Kyesa*, though the regular conscripted troops (royal guard) were under the direct orders of the military officials, the civil officials held the highest positions of command. When the military officials rebelled, the troops followed their example, and their defection from the civil command resulted in its easy defeat. However, this was still principally a revolt of the military officials supported by the armed strength of their clans and, though it occurred amid simultaneous uprisings of discontented peasants and troops, the power of the latter had still not developed to any great extent.

The military officials who overthrew the civil officials replaced them in high government positions and, like them, expanded their private agricultural estates, increased their holdings of slaves, and squeezed the peasantry. They differed from the civil officers by maintaining clan-like private military organizations and not depending on a royal guard. The military officials were each supported by their private armies, and they fought among themselves.

Uprisings of Peasants and Slaves

In the Koryŏ bureaucratic state, the officialdom, which lived on a plane entirely different from that of the peasantry, used the country-district clerks to collect the taxes and forced labor service from the peasants. These exactions were made through strong outside forces by persons with whom the peasants otherwise had no relations. The peasantry were dissatisfied with this arrangement but unable to resist. But when the exploitation became too severe, they could not remain passive if they were to survive. From the time of King Munjong, vagrancy became common. Free peasants tended to become slaves; some peasants drifted into the capital to become retainers of influential persons. The greater number of peasants, however, could not even leave their home villages. During the reigns of Injong (1123-1146) and Ŭijong (1147-1170), uprisings occurred all over the country, and it was in this turbulent atmosphere that the military officials overthrew the government of the civil officials in a successful *coup d'état*. But this change in the personnel of government resulted in no improvement in the life of the people.

While the military were contending with each other for control at the capital, resistance to their authority by civil officials increased in the provinces, and government machinery for controlling it became disorganized. In particular, the chief official of the Western Capital (P'yŏngyang), Cho Wich'ong, who controlled more than forty forts in Pukkye (Northern March, P'yŏngan Province) and Tonggye (Eastern March, Hamgyŏng Province), rebelled against the government of the military officials, and it took three years to subdue him (1174-1176).

These confused conditions provided the best opportunities for new peasant uprisings. The first of these centered on Kongju in southern Korea. Its leaders were Mangi and Mangsoi of Myŏnghak Place, Kongju. Here products needed by the state were made by unfree people. They provided the backbone of the revolt. The fighting spread throughout Ch'ungch'ŏng Province and continued for nearly a year and a half (1176-1177). About the same time, uprisings broke out in Chŏlla Province, Hwanghae Province, and P'yŏngan Province; then the government slaves of Chŏnju in North Chŏlla Province revolted and seized Chŏnju (1182). An uprising took place even at the Eastern Capital, Kyŏngju, in North Kyŏngsang Province (1190). During this period outbreaks of banditry occurred throughout south Korea. Those of Kim Sami at Unmun and of Hyo Sim at Ch'ojŏn, both in North Kyŏngsang Province, were especially large. They spread, attracting vagrants and the poor who ravaged districts and prefectures to the south. When this group fought the government army at Miryang, it was so large that the government forces were reported to have been able to take more than seven thousand heads (1193-1194). After that, uprisings followed in waves. At the capital, public and private slaves plotted together with the objective of "abolishing the status of unfree people in the 'Three Han' (Korea)," and they planned to burn the registers of public and private slaves and to kill civil and military officials (1198). This was followed by uprisings at Myŏngju, Samch'ŏk and Ulchin in Kangwŏn Province and another uprising at Kyŏngju (1199). Other uprisings were instigated by the slaves of Chinju in South Kyŏngsang Province in 1200; in that year, more than fifty government slaves at Miryang in South Kyŏngsang Province seized government property and fled to join the bandits of Unmun. The peasants of Kŭmhae in South Kyŏngsang Province also banded together in 1200 and tried to kill the

powerful local families; and at about the same time, the people of Nool Ward at
Sŏmch'ŏn in South Kyŏngsang Province revolted. An insurrection occurred on
Cheju Island in 1202, and, following this, between 1202 and 1203, the people of
Kyŏngju allied themselves with the people of Unmun, Ch'ojŏn, and Ulchin and
rebelled. Buddhist monks at the temples of Pusŏk, Puin, and Ssangam in North
Kyŏngsang Province also rose in revolt in 1203. Besides these, uprisings occurred
elsewhere about which little is known.

The above uprisings extended over a period of about thirty years after the
coup d'état of the military officials. They occurred in rapid succession in the
capital and in the provinces, especially throughout southern Korea. The main
participants were public and private slaves, the unfree people of the wards and
places, monks, country-district clerks, and similar persons of low status. These
people, long squeezed and oppressed, rose up simultaneously against the officials,
taking advantage of the confusion in government at the capital and of the disorder
in the administrative system.

These revolts deserve special attention in Korean history because they lasted
so long, covered such a wide area, involved so many people, and were led by
persons from the lowest strata. The revolts of these people threatened autocratic
rule, and the government armies had great difficulty in suppressing them. When
they could not be suppressed, the king himself granted official rank to the unfree
people who had plotted the uprisings, and adopted conciliatory policies, such as
liberating unfree persons of wards and places. Finally, however, all revolts were
put down. The wave of uprisings shook the throne, but failed to overthrow it. The
military officials who first had destroyed the power of the civil officials, exerted
all their strength in an effort to suppress further uprisings and gradually succeeded
in breaking them up.

Control of the Government by the Ch'oe Family

The success of the military in repressing the revolts consolidated their authority
and wiped out all traces of civilian rule, yet there was unrest because the officials
quarreled among themselves for control. In 1174 Yi Ŭibang, an ambitious military
leader and associate of Chŏng Chungbu, was killed by the son of the latter, and
then, in 1179, both Chŏng Chungbu and his son were killed by another military
man, Kyŏng Taesŭng. Kyŏng Taesŭng became a rival of General Yi Ŭimin. These
two gathered warriors to protect themselves in a military organization known as
tobang (general chamber). In the struggle between these two, General Ch'oe
Ch'unghŏn prevailed, executed Yi Ŭimin, and seized the government in 1196.

Ch'oe Ch'unghŏn killed or banished all members of Yi Ŭimin's family and his
supporters and slaves. He conducted a thorough search for all who had opposed
him, and eliminated them. He also took firm measures to suppress the peasant and
slave revolts which had been recurring for thirty years. To do this he built up a
strong military force. He was instrumental in deposing King Myŏngjong and
putting Sinjong on the throne in 1197. Members of the royal family, ministers or
military officials who objected to Ch'oe's acts, he put to death. He did not spare
even members of his own family who opposed him. In this way Ch'oe gathered all
authority into his own hands. Later, during the period that his son Ch'oe U

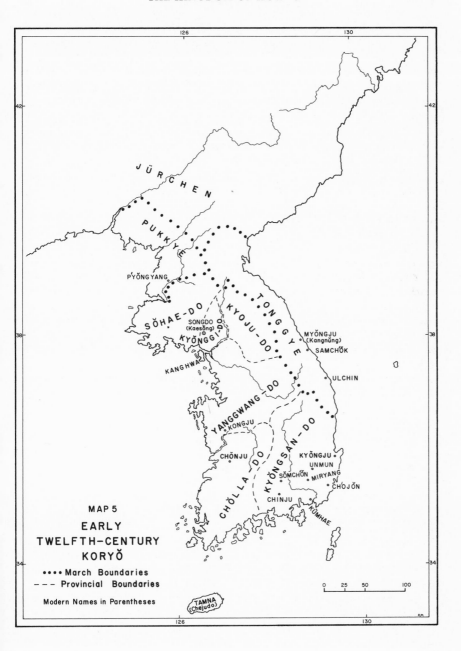

MAP 5

EARLY
TWELFTH-CENTURY
KORYŎ

•••• March Boundaries
– – – Provincial Boundaries

Modern Names in Parentheses

controlled affairs, a private administrative office known as the *chŏngbang* (administrative chamber) was established where all regular officials stood in attendance on the Ch'oe family. The *chŏngbang* may be considered the counterpart on the administrative side of the private military organization *(tobang)* of this time. It was through these private organizations that the king was bypassed; real power moved into the hands of the Ch'oe family.

Ch'oe family control continued for four generations, under Ch'unghŏn, U, Hang, and Ŭi. During nearly sixty years, from the last years of King Myŏngjong, through the reigns of three other kings, up to the forty-fifth year of King Kojong (1258), members of the Ch'oe family were the real rulers of Koryŏ. Control by military officials, which began with the uprisings of *Kyŏngin* and *Kyesa*, came to fruition in the autocratic rule of the Ch'oe family.

The Ch'oe family maintained a position of power with somewhat different methods than the civil officials who had dominated the court earlier. For example, when Ch'oe Ch'unghŏn's younger brother, Ch'ungsu, wished to marry his daughter to the heir of King Sinjong, Ch'unghŏn was absolutely opposed because he did not want power based on a female royal in-law relationship, and he had his younger brother put to death for disregarding his wishes. Moreover, Ch'unghŏn did not rely on a royal guard *(pubyŏng),* but depended on his own retainers *(mun'gaek)* for his military support. Also when Ch'oe U established the *chŏngbang* at his private residence, there was no precedent for it. Yet, despite these differences, the Ch'oe family were still intrinsically bureaucrats. Although they might enthrone and dethrone kings, they did not try to overthrow the dynasty, but directed the government in the king's name. In this the Ch'oe family resembled the earlier civil ministers.

The strength of the Ch'oe family depended primarily on their large force of private troops. Other powerful military officials before them had maintained private troops, but never on such an extensive scale. The military strength of the Ch'oe family far exceeded that of the national army. The core of the private troops was the *mun'gaek*. These were units of warriors bound by a clan-like bond to the family and said to number as many as three thousand. Among them were men who had been raised from *kadong* (young male slave) status. Ch'oe allied himself with other military officials who also had *mun'gaek*, and thus increased his strength. Actually, the prinicipal members in this alliance were persons related to him — brothers, relatives, and in-laws. Therefore the subordinate organizations were clan-like groups, and the combination of these formed a clan-like alliance, an arrangement making for great power for Ch'oe Ch'unghŏn. Although these vertical and lateral unions had a broader compass than the earlier organizations of the civil ministers, they were quite similar to them in that the basis for the clans of both were real or fictive blood ties. Also, the Ch'oe family clans, like the previous ones, were centered in the capital and isolated from the farming villages. Although there were people who left the villages to join the Ch'oe clans, no village-based clans were established.

The second basis of the Ch'oe family strength lay in its extensive emolument estates and private agricultural estates. The former comprised whole counties or prefectures that the king had bestowed on the family. The taxes and tribute from them, which normally should have gone into the state warehouses, went into the hands of the Ch'oe family, and the conscripted labor to transport this wealth was furnished by the state. These estates could not be inherited, and from time to time their location was changed. They were called Ch'oe family emolument estates, but the family did not administer them directly; it simply received the produce from them. In essence, then, the system merely meant the control of royal land receipts by parasites. The Ch'oe family living in the capital had no contact with the slaves and farmers cultivating the emolument estates. The same was true of the private agricultural estates except that the produce from the latter was collected by house slaves of the Ch'oe family. In this way these estates were like the earlier private agricultural estates of the civil officials and aristocrats. It was by the income from both types of estates that the *mun'gaek* were supported, but no land was given them by the family. If, on the recommendation of the Ch'oe family, an official rank was granted to one of their members, land and income were provided by the state, without alienating any of the Ch'oe family-held land.

The third source of strength of the Ch'oe family was its numerous slaves. Its private troops were in effect slaves, and even among the *mun'gaek*, who constituted the core of the private troops, some had been house slaves. In public and private life at the capital and on private agricultural estates, many slaves were employed, and hence life under the Ch'oe regime was very much as it had been earlier under the regime of the civil officials and nobles. However, during the period of Ch'oe family control, slaves, hitherto excluded from the official class, could come to occupy official positions. Although few achieved this, it marks an important new trend, albeit an incipient one.

Thus we see that the Ch'oe family, martial though they were, were bureaucrats of the old court, not medieval warriors. In some ways they had made advances over the earlier civil officials and nobility, but the life at court was not very different from that of their predecessors. Imitating the ways of the aristocrats and officials, they gathered together scholars, spread feasts, amused themselves composing poems in Chinese, and even invited civil officials into the *mun'gaek*. Some former civil officials fled from the capital and refused to have anything to do with the military men, but there were many men of letters and civil officials who became affiliated with the Ch'oe family, received government support, and were in attendance at the Ch'oe family *chŏngbang*. Two notable representatives of this kind were Yi Illo and Yi Kyubo.

The Mongol Invasions and the *Wakō*

From ancient times, Korea has been directly affected by changes occurring in the adjoining part of Asia, and her fate has been intertwined with continental Asiatic affairs. For example, it was during the chaotic period on the continent coinciding with the end of T'ang and the Five Dynasties (907-960) in China that Wang Kŏn, the founder of Koryŏ, overthrew Silla and established a new dynasty. Since this was a time when Chinese authority had diminished in Korea, Wang Kŏn was able to found the new dynasty without interference from the continent. But once the unification of Korea was completed, tribute was immediately sent to the various states of the Five Dynasties, and when Sung unified China in 960, Koryŏ rendered tribute to Sung. In each case this was necessary to enhance the authority of the ruler of Korea by the support of the ruler of China.

Koryŏ's relations with Sung were peaceful, and for a time she was not threatened. That situation, however, did not continue for long, because the Khitan, the Jurchen, and the Mongols arose in the north to threaten Koryŏ. In the thirteenth year of the reign of King Sŏngjong (994), Koryŏ submitted to the Khitan and adopted their calendar, yet in the reign of King Hyŏnjong (1010-1031) there were numerous Khitan invasions, and even the capital Kaesŏng was occupied. The first carving of wood blocks for the Koryŏ Tripitika (the Buddhist Canon) was planned as a means of warding off such invasions, and this carving project continued for almost sixty years, during the reigns of four kings, from Hyŏnjong to Munjong.

After the Khitan, the Jurchen rose to power in Manchuria. In the first year of King Yejong's reign (1106), General Yun Kwan of Koryŏ, in an effort to secure the northern frontier, attacked the Jurchen with a force of more than a hundred thousand men and constructed nine forts in north Korea in 1108. These were surrounded and seized by the Jurchen; thereafter Koryŏ suffered from many Jurchen attacks. Finally the Jurchen established the Chin Dynasty (1115-1234) and joined the Sung to destroy the Khitan in 1125. Soon after that they drove the Sung south of the Yangtse River (1127). Faced with this situation, Koryŏ submitted to both Sung and Chin and strove to avoid foreign difficulties. These invasions, however, appear insignificant in comparison with the invasions of the Mongols.

The Mongols, who came from north of the Gobi desert, destroyed the Chin, and occupied Manchuria and north China in 1234. Then they proceded to conquer the Southern Sung area and, at the same time, carried out a major invasion of Korea. In the eighteenth year of the reign of King Kojong (1231), when the Ch'oe family was still exercising autocratic power in Koryŏ, a large Mongol army crossed the Yalu River and attacked Korea. Soon Kaesŏng was surrounded, and the Koryŏ army was forced to surrender. When the Mongol army withdrew, Koryŏ, fearing other attacks, moved the capital from Kaesŏng to Kanghwa Island. Under the leadership of the Ch'oe family, the Koryŏ king, princes, and major officials, intent on their own personal safety, loaded their property onto boats and fled to the island. The Mongols, though excellent horsemen, were inexperienced sailors and unable to cross to Kanghwa and capture the Koryŏ's rulers.

The people who remained suffered great hardships. The Mongols regarded the removal of the capital by the Koryŏ rulers as a rebellious act. For more than twenty years, until the royal family surrendered and left the island, the Mongols repeatedly invaded Korea and trampled the entire country down to its southern boundary. In the forty-first year of the reign of Kojong (1254), the wretched conditions resulting from the invasion of the Mongol troops are recorded in the *Koryŏ-sa* as follows: "This year men and women seized by the Mongol troops reached the enormous number of 206,800, and innumerable people were massacred. All of the districts through which the Mongol troops passed were reduced to ashes." This is not an exaggeration, and similar events happened repeatedly.

While the mainland was suffering so severely the Koryŏ king, princes, and officials who had escaped to Kanghwa Island were living a life as though in another world. Taking advantage of the fact that the Mongol troops were blocked by the sea from coming over to the island, the court built splendid palaces and pavilions, and enjoyed Yŏndŭnghoe and P'algwanhoe (indigenous spring and autumn festivals with Buddhist trappings), and reveled in feasts. Tax rice and goods were brought in by sea from southern Korea, and the court nobles and officials led a carefree life. Refusing to take any notice of the misery of the peninsula, they tried to ward off the invasions of the enemy by invoking the power of Buddha. They did, however, recarve the wood blocks for the Tripitika. The ones carved earlier on the occasion of the Khitan invasions had been burned in 1232 by the Mongols. These second blocks carved on the island in the midst of turmoil and war are preserved today at Haein Temple on Kaya Mountain in South Kyŏngsang Province and constitute an important source for Buddhist culture.

The Mongol invasions seemed endless and so did the constricted life at the island capital. The divine protection of the power of Buddha did not manifest itself by driving out the Mongols. Uneasiness increased on the island, and so did dissatisfaction with the real rulers, the Ch'oe family. In the forty-fifth year of Kojong's reign (1258), Ch'oe Ŭi was assassinated and the Ch'oe family overthrown. This resulted in a complete change in government policy. The king, nobles, and officials now left the island and surrendered to the Mongols. The crown prince went personally to the Mongol court and apologized to the emperor.

After the crown prince returned from China he ascended the throne as King Wŏnjong (1260-1274). From this time on, Koryŏ became in name as well as in fact a vassal state of the Mongols. Koryŏ-Mongol relations were strengthened when the next king, Ch'ungnyŏl Wang, who had married a daughter of the Yüan[4] Emperor Shih-tsu (Khublai Khan)[5] ascended the throne in 1274. In this way the Yüan imperial house and Koryŏ royal house became united as a single family, and the descendants from this line became the kings of Koryŏ for generations. They represented not only Koryŏ but also the person of the Yüan emperor. They could now live in tranquility, no longer menaced by powerful and ambitious ministers as in the past, supported by the might of the great Yüan Empire. On the other hand, the price of this peace was the loss of independence. The traditional title of *chong* for the Koryŏ king was changed to the less-exalted *wang*, indicating a position of princely subservience. The king now used *ko*, the princely "we," in place of *chim*, the royal or imperial "we." Yüan supervisors were stationed at key points throughout the country, a great network of roads was built, and a courier system set up.

Yüan pressure on Korea was felt throughout the country. Even the northern part of Koryŏ was separated and taken by the Yüan, without any opposition being possible. But the greatest burden that the Yüan placed on Koryŏ was the demand that she assist in the subjugation of Japan. The reasons for and objectives of the expedition against Japan are not clear, but, bearing in mind that at that time communications and trade between Japan and Southern Sung, and Japan and Koryŏ, were flourishing, it is thought the attempt to subjugate Japan may have been connected with the Mongol conquest of Southern Sung. In the first invasion of 1274, Koryŏ mobilized some 30,000 laborers, built nine hundred warships, and was responsible for providing five thousand troops and a vast quantity of military rations. The Koryŏ peasant had already been impoverished by the long and devastating Mongol invasions and by the stationing of Mongol troops in Korea after Koryŏ's surrender, and for him this new burden was difficult to bear. Conditions

---

[4] The Chinese branch of the Mongol Empire took the name of Yüan in 1271.
[5] Khublai is the Mongol name of Emperor Shih-tsu.

were so serious that it was said, "The farmers are all eating grass and the leaves of trees." About that time, Koryŏ military units called the *sambyŏlch'o* revolted and occupied various islands off the coast of South Chŏlla and South Kyŏngsang provinces. When the Mongol and Koryŏ government army fought the mutinous units, the peasants of the southern districts, unable to bear the extreme demands of the Yüan any longer, cooperated with the rebels. But this revolt was crushed and a Mongol army of 20,000 (including Sung Chinese) and a Koryŏ army of five thousand sailed from Happ'o (present-day Masan in South Kyŏngsang Province), attacked the islands of Tsushima and Iki, and then anchored off Hakata Bay in Kyūshū. However, a hurricane and the strong resistance of the Japanese warriors thwarted this overseas expedition. A second expedition was undertaken in 1281, on an even greater scale than the first; the Yüan army had a total strength of 140,000 men — 100,000 from armies south of the Yangtse River and 40,000 from the "eastern-route army" in Korea. Koryŏ was required to provide 900 warships, 15,000 sailors and crew members, an army of 10,000, and 110,000 *sŏk* of military rations. The Koryŏ king, Ch'ungnyŏl Wang, son-in-law of the Yüan emperor, cooperated energetically in this undertaking, for the fate of the Koryŏ royal house was bound up with that of the Yüan imperial house. However, the second expedition, as the first, ended in failure.

The Yüan attempt to subjugate Japan failed, but the unification of Yüan and Koryŏ proceeded, and the Korean peasants were subject not only to rule by Koryŏ but brought into close contact with the rule of the vast Yüan empire. For Yüan officials not only used the Koryŏ government, to make demands on the people, but even entered the farm villages themselves to exact tribute. Furthermore, the Yüan princesses who became Koryŏ queens, well aware of their prestige as Mongols, took what they pleased of the people's slaves and treasure or made entire counties into personal appanages. The Koryŏ royal house and officials were completely subservient to the Yüan; they changed over to the Yüan administrative system and adopted Yüan customs and manners. At frequent intervals, the Koryŏ king would leave Kaesŏng and live at the Yüan capital, directing the officials of Koryŏ from there. Thus even the most superficial pretense of independent rule of Koryŏ disappeared. The administration of Koryŏ, dependent entirely on the support of the Yüan regime, lasted about a hundred years. Under kings so powerless, it is easy to imagine how wretched the life of the Korean people must have been.

Then the country was subjected to another calamity with the advent of the *Wakō*, Japanese marauders. These had appeared fairly early on the Korean coast, but their depredations increased after the reign of Ch'ungjŏng Wang (1348-1351). The *Wakō* continued their activities from about that time to the early period of the Yi Dynasty in Korea. This corresponded in Japan with the disturbed era from the wars of the Northern and Southern Courts (1336-1392) to the early part of the Muromachi period (1392-1573). During these years, the *Wakō* raided Korea and also the coasts of China. In Korea almost the entire coastline was ravaged, and at times even the capital Kaesŏng was threatened. Coastal rice and wheat were carried off, people were seized, and government food cargo ships were attacked. Because of these raids, the residents of the coastal districts fled into the interior and, we are told, the coasts became uninhabited wasteland. Some poor and vagrant Koreans joined the *Wakō* and participated in the looting, others imitated the *Wakō* and became marauders themselves. Farming villages, devastated by Yüan oppression, were still more shaken by the *Wakō* raids. The nation was unable to defend itself.

Expansion of Private Agricultural Estates and the Resulting Confusion Between the Free and the Unfree

The basis of the Koryŏ bureaucratic state was its unified control of the people and land of the entire country. This was accomplished through the concentration of power in the bureaucracy at the capital. The people constituted a slave-like population but the bureaucracy had no more freedom, and depended on the dynasty. Only the dynasty's preservation assured the livelihood of the officials. Although restricted under this system, the official, because of his relation to the state, gradually increased his power and acquired more private agricultural estates.

According to the paddy system, introduced when the dynasty was established, officials were generally allotted a fixed amount of land corresponding to their rank; this land could not be inherited. However, the land known as *kongŭmjŏnsi* and *sajŏn*, held by high officials, was inheritable. Also, particularly powerful persons were granted emolument estates. At first, the amount of such privately held land was comparatively insignificant, but with the development of a hereditary nobility among the officials, individual holdings soon greatly increased through such methods as the extortion of *sajŏn* from the king, annexation of the land of other persons, and the growth of land commendation. During the period of military control in Koryŏ, this tendency became more marked. The increase in private land holdings caused conflicts among the officials. Because these conflicts threatened to undermine the bureaucratic system, the problem of curtailing the permanent alienation of land was frequently aired but no solution was reached. One of the major reasons for the inability to prevent such alienation of land was that the officials themselves had become too involved in the process. Not only lawless individuals, but also powerful persons, such as the king, the royal family, temple and secular officials, used their authority to enlarge their land holdings, until there were no influential groups without private agricultural estates. In the period of Yüan rule, this trend grew, and with the passage of time, the relative importance of owning private agricultural estates increased. Now a person in authority no longer relied on the land and stipends that had been bestowed on him in accordance with his rank, but depended mainly for his livelihood on his own holdings. The form of organization of the officials did not change, but its basis did.

The growth of private agricultural estates brought about a decrease in the amount of land directly under the control of the state, with a resultant instability in state finances. However, this did not cause the immediate fall of the dynasty, for the increase in private estates was not connected with opposition to the state, but rather was carried out by those dependent on the state. This is obvious since most holders of private agricultural estates were persons like the king, princes, and nobles who lived at the court. Basically, private land holding did not conflict with the control of state land.

There were various types of private agricultural estates. The first was the type from which the king, princes, and nobles of the capital collected crops through the power of the state. Lands known as *ch'ŏ* and *chang*, held by the royal family, were included in this category. These were tilled by free men whose taxes were collected by state officials. They differed from the general state paddy fields in that their crops did not enter the state granaries, but went directly to the households of the king or princes. Their administration was similar to that of emolument estates and depended on the authority of the state. It was in this type of private agricultural estate that the king, queen, and royal family chiefly enlarged their land holdings during the latter part of the Koryŏ period.

The second was the type which the king, princes, and important members of the bureaucracy had tilled by personal slaves or tenant farmers, and from which their own house slaves or retainers collected the crops. Compared with the first type the administration of these was relatively autonomous. Nevertheless, those who held these private estates lived in the capital and held title to the estates only by reason of their high office there. If this office were lost, the private estate would be lost too. Therefore the primary concern of the owners of such estates was to be in constant attendance at the palace to make sure of retaining their position. Little attention was given to the administration of the estate itself.

These two types of private agricultural estates were established by, and were totally dependent on, the authority of the dynasty, so that it was impossible for opposition to the state to develop on this land. But since these private estates changed hands according to the changes in the government position of their owners, any instability in the government caused the land administrative system to fall into disorder. When this occurred, many persons appeared claiming to hold rights to the same piece of land, often causing the cultivators to be reduced to extreme poverty by excessive assessments.

Differing from these two types of private agricultural estates was a third type, managed by its owners in the country, such as country-district clerks, locally influential men, retired officials, and Buddhist monks. The local proprietors built their own country villas, gathered slaves and *chŏn'gaek* (tenant farmers), and managed the land themselves. Some officials at the capital apparently established this sort of independent private estate for themselves, delegating the administration to their own subordinates who were sent out to live in the country. This type of private agricultural estate, since it was not dependent on the power of the state, represented a new kind of land administration in which land and people were managed solely by local individuals. In this type, the possibility existed for the development of a power which could be hostile to the state. Indeed, later, during the Yi Dynasty, this type of holding came to predominate, but at that time the trend toward private estates was scarcely perceptible. In these independently administered estates, the slaves and farmers who labored on the land still had the same characteristics of servitude as before. Their relationship to the land was not changed by this new development which was, nevertheless, of great significance for the progress of society.

The increase in private agricultural estates did not immediately put an end to the Koryŏ Dynasty, but it created all kinds of problems. Officials living on their own private estates gained power, replacing officials dependent on land bestowed upon them by the state in accordance with their rank. There was, in other words, a change from a system in which officials depended on public land to one where they depended on private estates. The growth of importance of these private estates created several difficulties.

First, bitter quarrels developed within the ranks of the officials. In addition to the conflicts related to the struggle for private estates, dissatisfaction mounted among lower-ranking officials not powerful enough to hold private estates. The income of the state had already declined, and thus when the granting of stipend allowances became irregular, the living conditions of the officials without private agricultural estates became precarious. The possibility of giving income paddies instead of stipends had been the subject of discussion by the court ministers a number of times during the period of Yüan rule, and, in part, this scheme was carried out. Nevertheless, since it would have been necessary to confiscate and redistribute private estates in order fully to accomplish this, a completely satisfactory solution to the problem was impossible. The dissatisfaction over declining allowances was directed toward powerful persons holding private agricultural estates and even toward the royal house of Koryŏ. While Yüan oppression was strong, this dissatisfaction was crushed by the might of the Yüan Empire and did not manifest itself openly, but when Yüan power began to crumble, discontent at not receiving land and stipends was publicly voiced. Many openly asserted that the vast private agricultural estates monopolized by the king, princes, and nobles should be divided among all officials. How to meet this demand became a grave political problem involving the fate of the dynasty, and Koryŏ finally fell because it was unable to solve it.

The second difficulty brought about by the proliferation of private agricultural estates was the social disorganization that accompanied the disintegration of the peasant class. With the increase of private estates, the peasants, both free and unfree, who had been governed directly by the state, were absorbed into these private estates. This development, however, was not just a direct transfer, but followed a complicated course of social disorganization. This is shown in the confusion of the social status of free and unfree men. Free men tilled land that had been handed down for generations in their own villages, but this land was controlled by the state and was not owned by them personally. The larger portion of the land tilled by free men came under the direct administration of the state, and these free men rendered taxes and corvée to the state. The remaining portion of the land tilled by free men was granted by the state to officials, and the peasantry on this land became tenant farmers of the officials and paid taxes to them.

In both cases the peasantry were cruelly exploited, and even at the time the dynasty was at its peak, their living conditions were extremely difficult. Wandering, uprooted peasants appeared in every period, and when political authority was shaken at the time of the slaughter of civil officials by the military, peasants rebelled throughout the country. After this, in the period of military dictatorship, the squeeze on the peasantry continued unabated; and during the Mongol invasions and control of Korea, the peasants continued to live in extreme misery. In the wake of all this came *Wakō* attacks, and many peasants no longer had a place to live. Faced with these internal and foreign disturbances, it was impossible for many to continue the cultivation of land; they became vagrants and bandits. Some peasants became the *mun'gaek* of powerful men, but the poor were too numerous to be absorbed in this manner. Private agricultural estates were the most promising places to which the poor peasant could go. Some free men even commended their own lands to private estates and stayed on the land, although, in entering a private

estate, they often declined to a position of servitude. Some chose to become unfree in order to no longer be liable for taxes or service to the state. Also, administrators of private agricultural estates compelled free men on the estates to adopt
the status of slaves in order to exempt persons under their direction from military
service.

However, many people were not absorbed into the private estates. Some of
these, reduced to poverty, eked out a bare existence; others sold themselves or
their children or grandchildren into servitude. This conversion of free men into
slaves was disadvantageous to the state because, since slaves were the private property of their owners, the state had no direct control over them. As the number of
slaves increased, the population under the control of the state diminished. Faced
with this situation, the state unsuccessfully tried to block a further increase in the
number of slaves.

At the same time that the distinction between free and unfree was being
confused, as free men became slaves, further confusion was brought about as
unfree men became free. Those of unfree status included public and private slaves,
musicians, artisans, petty officials, people of the wards, and others; the majority
were public or private slaves, and their emancipation was forbidden by order of
the state; they were clearly differentiated from free men. However, during the
period of military dictatorship in Koryŏ, slaves became the *mun'gaek* and private
troops of military men. Some slaves with ability even rose along with their masters
to attain distinction but this did not occur often, for social discrimination was
particularly severe at this time, and for a slave to attain an official position was a
rare event. During this period, slaves and unfree people frequently revolted, and
actively sought to gain their liberation. With the increase in private agricultural
estates, slaves and unfree men entered these estates and misrepresented their social
position. They were able to do this because during the chaotic period at the end
of Koryŏ, brought about by the numerous foreign and internal crises, careful
census registers could no longer be kept. Therefore if slaves or unfree men fled
and joined the ranks of the shifting population, it was often possible for them to
conceal their status. There were at that time many legal cases regarding social
position which the courts had difficulty in deciding.

Despite the increased incidence of interchange of status between the free and
unfree, the distinction between the two classes remained unchanged. Complete
emancipation of slaves and unfree men was never even considered. The distinction
in social status continued long afterward throughout the Yi Dynasty. Still, the
confusion between the free and unfree, resulting from the increase in private
estates and reorganization of the bureaucratic system, was indicative of the progress of the times. Paradoxically, this progress was attributable to the great
increase of slaves on the private agricultural estates. Since these were held principally by officials at the capital, there was only distant contact and association
between the owners and the slaves. The work of the latter was not confined to
simple household tasks, but included tilling the soil and even some administrative
duties. This greater independence from direct control made possible a substantial
improvement in their position.

Decline of Yüan and Fall of Koryŏ

The vast empire of the Mongols, spanning Europe and Asia, had a short life. It was weakened from within by a struggle for the throne among those in power, and from the outside by the revolts of the various khans on its borders which were seeking their independence. Furthermore, the Chinese over whom the Mongols ruled were restive, and a wave of bandit uprisings developed. The strongest band was that of the Red Turbans whose members believed in the rebirth of the Maitreya Buddha. To aid in putting down their revolt which had spread throughout the country, the Yüan rulers requested that Koryŏ send troops to China. This was done, but the Red Turban band not only defeated the Koryŏ army, but moved through Manchuria and attacked Korea in 1359 and 1361. Before long, Chu Yüan-chang, who had emerged from a faction of the Red Turban band, made himself king in south China at Nanking, forming a new state which he called Ta Ming (1368). The Ming army then continued northward, attacking the Mongol capital Yenching (today Peking), and overthrowing the Yüan regime, which, with some of their forces, withdrew to the north. This political change affected Korea. In the government of Koryŏ, till then under the absolute control of the Yüan regime, a strong anti-Yüan movement developed. The Koryŏ ruler Kongmin Wang (1352-1374), killed the Ki family which had dominated the Koryŏ court, through its marital ties with the Yüan imperial house. The Koryŏ army was able to recover the northern part of the peninsula which had been taken from it earlier by Yüan forces. The Yüan regime, unable to prevent this, was forced to recognize the reoccupation, demanding only an apology from Koryŏ.

When an envoy from Ming arrived to announce the establishment of the new state, the Koryŏ ruler, Kongmin Wang, glad to be independent of Yüan, adopted the Ming-era name of Hung-wu (1370) to show his intention of making Koryŏ a tributary to the Ming emperor.

In spite of this, the status of the anti-Yüan movement was extremely precarious. The Koryŏ Dynasty had been oppressed by Yüan, but it had maintained itself internally through the great prestige of the Yüan Dynasty. If relations with the latter were severed, and Koryŏ could not gain the immediate support of the Ming ruler, the dynasty's internal strength would be endangered. Even though it was true that the Yüan regime was weakened, it had established its court north of the Great Wall and was fighting the Ming regime. It was still too early to separate from Yüan. Especially serious was the danger that discontented officials might rise at the opportunity presented by a separation from Yüan. At this point the great problem in Koryŏ became whether the court should attach itself to the Yüan or the Ming regime, and foreign policy was much debated. Kongmin Wang's death was reported to both the Yüan and the Ming regimes because Koryŏ policy had not yet been decided. Conditions, however, did not permit a continuance of such indecisiveness. At the end of the dispute over state policy, Yi Inim, Ch'oe Yŏng, and others of the pro-Yüan faction won out over Chŏng Mongju, Chŏng Tojŏn, and the other members of the pro-Ming faction, and Koryŏ's policy was fixed as pro-Yüan and anti-Ming. The victory of the pro-Yüan faction was at the same time a victory of the royal house and of the aristocracy, possessing private agricultural estates, over a group of discontented officials. The adherents of the pro-Yüan policy tried to suppress elements of discontent within the country caused by former Yüan oppression and to protect the vast agricultural estates of the royal house and the aristocracy.

In accord with this policy, Koryŏ decided to attack the Ming state in order to assist the Northern Yüan regime. The leader of the pro-Yüan faction, Ch'oe Yŏng, became commander-in-chief; Cho Minsu and Yi Sŏnggye were appointed commanders of the right and left and were ordered to advance into the Ming territory of Liao-tung. Yi Sŏnggye was a general who had won a high military reputation for his victories over the Wakō and the Jürchen. He argued that an attack on Liao-tung was impossible, but he was overruled by Ch'oe Yŏng, and was obliged to set out at the head of an army of fifty thousand men. However, there was little promise of victory over the powerful Ming forces, and, besides, the troops were not interested in the war and deserted in large numbers. When the army had proceeded as far as Wihwa Island in the middle of the Yalu River, Yi Sŏnggye resolved to stop the war, gathered the army, and led it back to the Koryŏ capital. There, welcomed by the populace, he entered Kaesŏng, banished Ch'oe Yŏng and his pro-Yüan supporters, deposed King U, and set up the king's son, Ch'ang, as ruler. At one stroke, Yi Sŏnggye had seized the power at the capital. This was in 1388.

The army which returned from Wihwa Island settled the fate of the Koryŏ Dynasty. In 1392, Yi Sŏnggye, encouraged by his supporters, mounted the throne, and this ended the Koryŏ Dynasty.

V

Yi Dynasty

The Land Reform of Yi Sŏnggye

Yi Sŏnggye, the founder of the Yi Dynasty, had come into prominence through his military achievements. He had repelled the invasions of the Jürchen in the northeastern areas (Hamgyŏng Province) and routed the Japanese marauders *(Wakō)* who had been ravaging the entire coastline of Korea. In the critical period at the end of Koryŏ, he had become the chief general of national defense.

Yi was also a statesman. He foresaw the decline of the Yüan empire and with it the loss of power of the old court parties which had long been parasites on Koryŏ. Therefore, after turning back the army from Wihwa Island and taking over the leadership of the nation, he adopted a clearly anti-Yüan and pro-Ming policy and, at the same time, embarked on a determined internal program to overthrow the old court parties. The main part of this program was his plan to confiscate private agricultural estates and to redistribute land. Since the princes and nobles of the Koryŏ court financially depended on these estates, their confiscation threatened to destroy the power of the aristocracy. Heavy opposition from the old court parties to Yi's land reform was foreseeable; but the success of the program was crucial to Yi's political future.

The most ardent supporters of Yi's program were the lower officials who owned no private agricultural estates and who, with the growth of the holdings of the princes and high officials, had been receiving less of the land and stipends to which they had originally been entitled. Their financial situation had become precarious. In their demand for land reform, they were joined by impoverished peasants and soldiers from the peasant class.

Land reform was imperative also from another point of view. Land-control relationships had become confused; often one piece of land had two or three reputed owners; those dispossessed of their land roamed the countryside; the distinction between the free and unfree had become vague. Unless property rights could be clearly reestablished, the position of the ruling class was threatened. Thus, for the four years following 1388 (just after the Wihwa Island incident) to 1391 (the year before the downfall of Koryŏ), the problem of land reform was under discussion.

Yi's proposed system, supported by the groups of disgruntled officials, had persons like Cho Chun (1346-1405) as spokesmen. They argued that the old land system established at the beginning of the Koryŏ period should be restored. It had been modeled after the "well-field" law *(ching-t'ien-fa)* of the Chou Dynasty in China (1122-257 B.C.) and the "equal field" law *(chŭn-t'ien-fa)* of the T'ang Dynasty (618-907 A.D.). They wished to amplify the system to include everyone from princes and high officials to country-district clerks *(hyangni)*, soldiers, peasants, workers in country districts *(hyang)* and wards *(pugok)*, and even immigrants and slaves. The plan, in other words, was to give fixed amounts of land to all holding government positions, from those in the highest ranks to those carrying out menial tasks, graduated according to their station. This plan represented a Confucian return to the past and a stabilization of the life of the people by reestablishing control through officials — a program which met with great enthusiasm. However, the plan remained an unrealized ideal. Gradually the plans of the reformers became modified until finally the needs of peasants, slaves, and unfree persons were forgotten. In 1390, the reform party, supported by the military strength of Yi Sŏnggye, publically burned the old public and private land registers, to the distress of King Kong'yang and the nobles and high officials who owned private agricultural estates.

The next year a new *kwajŏn* (classified field) land system was proclaimed. It gave to officials and to the royal family *kwajŏn* in Kyŏnggi Province according to their rank, to the military *kunjŏn* (military fields) outside of Kyŏnggi Province, and to the various local government offices suitable grants of land. The purpose of limiting to Kyŏnggi Province lands allowed to officials and to the royal family was to concentrate power centrally and prevent officials from growing powerful by holding land in provinces to which they were assigned. In order to distribute *kwajŏn* and *kunjŏn*, the old private agricultural estates were confiscated; it appears that, despite their size, this was accomplished almost completely and with little difficulty. Most landowners were dependent on Koryŏ royal authority and, when this was removed, through the political changes at the capital, they had no strength in the countryside to fall back upon.

Although the *kwajŏn-pŏp* (classified-field law) wiped out the private agricultural estates, it was significantly different from the *chŏnsigwa* of the first part of the Koryŏ period. In both systems the state held a strong controlling power over the land, established a bureaucracy through distribution of land, and aimed at concentrating the power of the officials at the capital. The difference lay in the fact that in *chŏnsigwa,* land holding was limited to the period during which the official held office, while in the *kwajŏn-pŏp*, hereditary tenure was permitted. Even if a landholder committed a crime, his land could not be confiscated. Those who received land through *chŏnsigwa* paid no taxes, while the land received through the *kwajŏn-pŏp* was subject to tax. Thus the officials in this latter period could more truly be considered land owners than those in the early Koryŏ era.

This system marked an advance in the institution of private property and, in addition, signaled a measure of growth for the farming element of the population. The *kwajŏn-pŏp* established the following relationships between tenant and owner: an official tax rate was fixed; seizure of a tenant's land by the owner was prohibited; a tenant was not permitted to abandon the property. These provisions guaranteed the tenant a certain status in society. Within this framework his life was unrestricted, and he was not oppressed to the extent he had been before. He was also bound more closely to the land. His position was greatly improved over that held in earlier times when the state had absolute control over the peasantry.

The *kwajŏn-pŏp* was evidence of progress toward a new type of society. In the latter Koryŏ period, the expansion of private agricultural estates foreshadowed the growth of private land ownership. Although the estates were confiscated through the reforms of Yi Sŏnggye, a tendency toward private land ownership persisted — a tendency which was acknowledged and even provided for in the new classified-field law. Later, during the period of the Yi Dynasty, private agricultural estates gradually reappeared, but local control in these was far greater than in earlier periods. The rights of the officials to the land upon which their power depended had greatly increased, although in most other aspects the relationships of the past continued unchanged. It was under these conditions that the Yi Dynasty of Korea came into existence.

The Development of a Bureaucratic State

The land reform of Yi Sŏnggye destroyed the material power base of the old nobility. They made some futile attempts to oppose the tide, but its course was irrevocably set. Some of the old nobility and officials of Koryŏ refused to serve under the new regime and went into retirement, others opposed it and were banished or put to death, but the majority were absorbed into the new administration. Disgruntled officials of the old dynasty eagerly supported Yi Sŏnggye and were active in the establishment of the new state. The capital was moved from Kaesŏng to Kyŏngsŏng (Seoul). The basis of foreign policy was *sadae* (literally "serving the great" or obeisance) toward the Ming emperor, and the new dynasty received endorsement of its authority from him. At the same time, Confucianism was adopted as the guiding philosophy. King T'aejo (the temple name of Yi Sŏnggye) made the promotion of Confucianism a major program of the new government. In the capital he set up the Sŏnggyun'gwan, a Confucian academy, and the Five Halls of Scholarship (one for each direction of the compass, north, south, east, west, and center) as the highest Confucian centers of learning and ritual; in the provinces he established *hyanggyo* (country-district schools) in the various local administrative subdivisions (municipalities, *pu*; departments, *mok*; counties, *kun*; and prefectures, *hyŏn*) for the teaching of Confucianism. In order to spread the philosophy, King T'aejong (1401-1418) had movable copper type cast and numerous books printed. This encouragement of Confucianism was continued by many subsequent kings so that it gradually replaced Buddhism that had previously held it in check. Confucianism was tantamount to a national religion; all Yi Dynasty officials, unlike their predecessors, were Confucian scholars.

Confucianism had been brought to Korea several hundreds of years earlier and had gradually spread, but during the Koryŏ period Buddhism was the national religion. The change to Confucianism during the Yi Dynasty can be attributed to the altered character of the bureaucracy. The earlier society was undeveloped, and parasite officials were drawn largely from the royal family, in-law relatives, and family followers. In the Yi Dynasty, on the other hand, officials had local political affiliations. With the development of this new official class came a change in both the theory and the actual form of the bureaucratic system. This change will be discussed later in connection with the explanation of the relationship between private agricultural estates and the *sŏwŏn* (literary academies). Korean officials had earlier been unable to grasp the basic tenets of the Chinese system, even though the form of control used by Chinese officials had been introduced. Now Korean bureaucracy had developed to a point where it fitted into the Chinese pattern and even absorbed the basic Confucian intellectual principles. Still, Korean Confucianism was less mature than the Chinese variety, and hence the bureaucratic system of the country was comparatively backward. Confucian officials saw the elimination of the authority and influence of Buddhism and Buddhist temples as one of the primary tasks facing them. The temples which had been centers for the defense and well-being of the state were now to be abandoned, but this could not be brought about overnight. Even after the confiscation of the private estates of the former nobles, temples continued to have extensive land holdings, many slaves, and a large number of priests. The number of Buddhists decreased, but many remained after the Yi Dynasty was established, even within the court. However, as the bureaucratic system developed, the pressure against the temples became stronger. At the time of King T'aejo, the tax exemption enjoyed by the temples was taken away, and the temple lands were taxed. During the reign of King T'aejong, however, an anti-Buddhist policy was adopted. The number of temples, temple lands, slaves, and priests which any Buddhist sect could possess was limited. If the limit was exceeded, confiscation resulted. During the reign of the next king, Sejong (1419-1450), the limitations were made even more stringent, and the number of temples, temple lands, and slaves was further reduced. This policy of suppression continued and grew stronger as the Yi Dynasty developed, until the Buddhist sects became completely powerless.

Through the efforts of the new officials the mechanism of government was reorganized. At first it had been patterned by King T'aejo after the old Koryŏ system. He originally established the *Top'yŏngŭisasa* (Office of Joint Supervisory Councillors) as the highest council of state in which officials of second rank[1] or above, both military and civilian, participated. Its decisions, after receiving the approval of the king, were transmitted to an office known as the *Munhabu* (Chancellery). The *Munhabu* handed them down for compliance and action to the Six Boards of State (Board of Civil Administration, Board of Revenue, Board of Rites, Board of Justice, Board of War, Board of Public Works). In 1400 the name of this highest council of state was changed from *Top'yŏngŭisasa* to *Ŭijŏngbu* (Office of State Councillors) and was made into a council for civilian officials only. In 1401, the *Munhabu* was united with the *Ŭijŏngbu* to simplify the management of the government. After 1414, only the most important affairs were put before the *Ŭijŏngbu*, and ordinary matters were referred directly to the Six Boards of State. These changes indicate the increasing stability of the state and the direction in which administrative control was developing.

In the reign of King T'aejo, the country was divided into the Capital Domain (Kyŏnggi), the Five Provinces (Yanggwang, Kyoju, Sŏhae, Kyŏngsang, Chŏlla), and the Two Frontiers (Northeastern and Northwestern), following the old organi-

---

[1] There were nine ranks in all, each of which was divided into an upper and lower category. The highest rank was the first; the next the second; and so on.

zation of the Koryŏ; but in 1413 this division was changed into the Eight Prov-inces of Kyŏnggi, P'unghae (later called Hwanghae), P'yŏngan, Ch'ungch'ŏng, Kangwŏn, Yŏnggil (later called Hamgyŏng), Kyŏngsang and Chŏlla. Each province was subdivided into *pu, mok, kun,* and *hyŏn.* Country districts (*hyang*) and wards (*pugok*), which had existed as provincial administrative subdivisions throughout both the Silla and Koryŏ dynasties, now disappeared. There were still many public and private slaves, but no separate administrative subdivisions were set up for their control. This is a further illustration of the advance made by the Yi Dynasty over earlier dynasties both in its government and its social pattern.

In spite of these advances, however, many similarities to the dynasties of the past continued within the new state structure. Regular officials managed affairs directly down to the prefectural level, but below that, common clerks, called *sŏri*, (also known as *ajŏn*), chosen from among the local population, were in charge. They had direct control over the peasants living in subdivisions such as *myŏn* (townships), *i* (villages), and *tong* (hamlets). The *sŏri* were similar to the country district clerks (*hyangni*) of earlier periods, and worked under the direction of local government offices. They were employed on a hereditary basis, clothed them-selves with the authority of regular officials, and acted in cooperation with the local families of importance. But although they held positions of influence among the peasants, they were a type of unfree person in state service whose social status was that of the group of unfree peoples called, "the seven classes of the public unfree and the eight classes of the private unfree." Thus, for the peasants, the direct tangible expression of government power was, as in previous dynasties, in the hands of unfree persons. Besides, in central and local government offices many official slaves were detailed to various branches to carry out the miscellaneous affairs of government. These duties could be the tilling of land attached to a government office, taking care of river fords and beacons, making handicraft articles needed by the state, even providing *kisaeng* (singing girls) as companions for the officials of the local and central government. In addition to the numerous public slaves required for these duties for the bureaucratic state, officials owned many private slaves as in earlier times. Thus the traditional slave relationships persisted, however much the Yi Dynasty had advanced in other ways.

With the development and stabilization of the bureaucratic system, the power of Korea became greater than it had been before. The boundaries of the state were expanded northward during the reigns of kings T'aejo, T'aejong, and Sejong until all territory south of the Yalu and Tuman rivers became part of Korea. At the same time, the opening up of the northern area by immigrants from the south proceeded apace, and the northern section of the Korean peninsula became fully amalgamated internally with the rest of the country. Land reclamation and devel-opment were also carried out throughout the entire country. At the end of the Koryŏ period, the total area under cultivation was about 800,000 *kyŏl*,[2] whereas under King T'aejong (1401-1418), it exceeded 1,000,000 *kyŏl*, and under King Sejong (1419-1450), 1,600,000 *kyŏl*. The population also increased rapidly. From 180,000 households under King T'aejong it grew to 220,000 under King Sejong. In Kyŏngsang Province, for example, the population almost doubled (100,000 to 190,000 persons) from T'aejong to Sejong. To obtain these statistics, a thorough census was required, whose efficiency indicates the power of the state. During the

---

[2] See note 2, Chapter III, for area of the *kyŏl.*

reign of King Sejong too, two outstanding geographical works, *Sejong sillock chiriji* (Sejong Veritable Records Gazeteer) and *Tongguk yŏji sŭngnam* (Survey of the Geography of the Eastern Country) were compiled by the government. Agriculture made important advances. In addition to numerous official decrees encouraging farming, a Korean book on farming methods, *Nongsa chiksŏl*, (A Straight Explanation of Agricultural Matters) was put out by the government in 1429, patterned after the famous Chinese work on agriculture, *Ch'i-min yao-shu* (Essential Skills for the People). There is no doubt that agricultural techniques were improved through the efforts of the state.

This movement of expansion and activity is also evident in the cultural sphere. During the reigns of kings Sejong (1419-1450), Sejo (1456-1468), and Sŏngjong (1470-1494), the reigns known as the period of flowering of the Yi Dynasty, such celebrated books as *Ch'ip'yŏng yoram* (Basic Survey for Governing Peacefully), *Yongbi ŏch'ŏn'ga* (Songs of the Dragons Flying to Heaven), *Koryŏ-sa* (History of Koryŏ), *Oryeŭi* (Five Ceremonies), *Kukcho pogam* (Dynastic Mirror), *Tongguk t'onggam* (Complete Mirror of the Eastern Country), *Tongmunsŏn* (Anthology of Korean Literature), *Hunmin chŏngŭm* (Proper Phonetics for Instruction of the People), and *Kyŏngguk taejŏn* (Fundamental Statutes for Governing the Country) were written.[3] Among these, *Hunmin chŏngŭm*, published in 1446, is particularly noteworthy because it was written in Korean script, called *ŏnmun* (also known as *hangŭl*). Up to that time, only Chinese characters (*hanja*) had been used for writing in Korea, and the development of a phonetic script easy to learn attests to the advance of Korean culture. The development of this Korean script is comparable to that of *kana* (Japanese syllabic script) and is an accomplishment of special significance in the history of Korean culture. Also in this period falls the completion of the compilation of *Kyŏngguk taejŏn*, the basic legal-administrative code of the Yi Dynasty. This work was acknowledged even in later generations as a monumental achievement, and indicates the high level of organization which the Yi bureaucratic state had attained at that time.

The Expansion of Private Agricultural Estates

The bureaucratic class which developed the Yi Dynasty was the product of certain social advances. In order to maintain the stability of the system of control, bureaucratic power had to be concentrated in the person of the king. It was a corollary to this that the rise of powerful local officials should be prevented. To this end, ownership of land by officials, allotted according to the *kwajŏn* law, was limited to land in Kyŏnggi Province, and the relationship between landowner and tenant was strictly systematized by the state. To prevent any possibility of an official becoming powerful in his home area, the *hoep'i* (avoid returning) system was followed in which officials were never appointed to their native places. The *sŏri* (common clerks) also could not be allowed to become too influential locally; to ensure this, the dynasty established a place in the capital where the children of the *sŏri* were gathered as hostages (a measure similar to the Koryŏ Dynasty's *kiin* system). Thus, although in regard to property ownership advances had been made, the framework of a central bureaucratic state continued to be

---

[3] A brief description of most of these books may be found in B.H. Hazard Jr. et al. *Korean Studies Guide* (Berkeley and Los Angeles: University of California Press, 1954).

maintained, and every effort was made to prevent the development of local power among officials.

This framework, nevertheless, included the seed from which local power could grow. Agricultural estates gradually expanded at that time, which shows that officials were able to take advantage of their positions in the dynasty to increase their holdings. When the Yi Dynasty was founded, deserving retainers were given, besides the regular *kwajŏn* (classified fields), special land grants known as *kongsinjŏn* (meritorious ministers' paddies) and *pyŏl-sajŏn* (especially conferred paddies). Royal relatives in particular received large tracts of such land. Further, crown land, so-called if controlled directly by the royal house, was acquired when the Koryŏ agricultural estates were confiscated, and originally was in great supply. As long as this was true, there was no land problem, but gradually the amount of land available for grants decreased to the point that made it difficult to furnish officials with *kwajŏn* and impossible to give *sajŏn* to deserving persons. This was so because influential people who already had *sajŏn* grants, in order to enlarge their private estates, had been acquiring additional land by purchase, threats, coercion, and reclamation. These lands, although spread over the whole country, were for the most part concentrated in the rich farming areas from Kyŏnggi Province southward. During the flowering of the Yi Dynasty during the reigns of Sejong, Sejo, and Sŏngjong, the problem of the expansion of private agricultural estates was frequently discussed and plans were made to cope with it. These, however, were ineffective, because the royal house, royal relatives, and high officials had the larger holdings of such estates and, although concerned with the general ill effects of land accumulation, never thought of its specific causes or considered giving up their own claims and holdings.

A comparison of the agricultural estates of that time with those of earlier dynasties shows several marked similarities and, at the same time, two significant differences. The most striking resemblance lies in the concentration in the capital of the owners of the estates (the royal house, royal relatives, important ministers, and high officials), and the wide distribution throughout Korea of the properties held. In lands so scattered no focus of manpower and resources could appear strong enough to oppose the dynasty.

A second similarity was that the managers of these lands were slaves – either official slaves (*sŏri*) in land which was directly controlled by the royal house or private slaves in the lands of royal relatives and great ministers. The actual owners had no part in the running of the agricultural estates, but lived on the taxes collected by the slave-managers.

A third similarity was the prevalence of unfree persons among the tillers of the estates. In the main, land was worked by slaves. They lived on the estates and were always presented with it in the *sajŏn* grant, since they were indispensable for the cultivation of the land. But some of the land was worked by tenants, called *chŏnho* (tillers). Their relationship to the owners was called *pyŏngjak* (joint work) and *pyŏnggyŏng* (joint ploughing), meaning that the harvest was divided equally. As a general rule, tenants were free but some were not. Some gave up their free status to become unfree and thus to escape the heavy taxes, levies, and other exactions to which free men were subjected. There were also many instances, especially in the tenant class, where free men had been forced by influential persons to become unfree. As we use the word "unfree" it should be kept in mind that there were many types of "unfree" men. There were also many gradations among those with a definite slave status. Some slaves even owned other slaves and administered their own lands. However, the fact that unfree men existed who were not slaves would seem to indicate a distinction between the two conditions. However, the unfree could not become free and the free could become unfree. Thus these restrictions of social mobility and the persistence of old relationships are reminiscent of previous periods.

In the situations described above, the private agricultural estates of the Yi Dynasty were similar to earlier ones. However, even in these points of similarity new tendencies were evident. First, although the slaves who worked on the estates were unfree persons, they were more independent than most slaves, some even personally managing their own property. There were many tenants who had the status of free men; their position, first established in the *kwajŏn* system, was recognized in the agricultural estates, and many peasants advanced to the point of being *pyŏngjak* cultivators.

Secondly, not all owners of private agricultural estates lived at the capital. Some lived in villas and residences which they built on their own lands, and many important officials residing at the capital had relatives living on their estates. On these private estates, *sŏwŏn* (literary academies) were established at which the owner's relatives and local inhabitants received instruction. Also, retired officials and those out of favor frequently moved to the country and lived on their properties. In these ways the connection between landowners and their agricultural estates was closer than before.

In these ways, the Yi Dynasty agricultural estates became more independent than in earlier periods, and this, though it represented progress in one sense, became the genesis of the party factionalism to be discussed later.

The control of the private agricultural estates of the Yi Dynasty had both progressive and regressive characteristics. The fact that unfree persons who had the status of slaves were often placed in positions of farm management was offset by the continued separation of the worlds of the unfree and the landowners. The latter were either officials or potential officials whose principal aim in life was to rise in prominence and increase their land holdings. This could be done better if they lived at the capital than if they lived in the country and managed their own estates. They were far from being feudal lords.

Party Factions and Persecutions of the Literati

The cruel recurrent party struggles in the Yi Dynasty bureaucracy are well known. However, such political struggles had taken place in every period and were especially frequent during the Koryŏ era. It is not, therefore, the fact of political conflicts during the Yi Dynasty which is noteworthy, but the character of the conflicts. The political struggles of Koryŏ officials revolving primarily around problems of marriage or succession were, for the most part, confined to the capital. In those days, if a person was able to seize power within the walls of the capital, he could control the whole nation. Any opposition which might occur in the countryside was too weak to stand against the strength of the officials at the capital. Therefore, although the party struggles often produced political change in

Koryŏ times, they did not last long.

But when we come to the Yi Dynasty, political struggles had no connection with either the royal house or the queen's relatives. The plots were no longer revolving about the royal palace and no longer were the conflicts restricted to the capital. They had deep roots in the countryside, even causing the mobilization of party men from country districts. Nevertheless, as in the past, the object was to gain central political control. Essentially the conflicts were between men with similar interests, for all were alike dependent on the dynasty. These officials formed parties, set up definite goals, and fought publicly. Thus in form and scope these disputes were different from those of earlier dynasties, and it is in these aspects that we can observe a significant development.

The main protagonists in the Yi Dynasty political struggles were officials, many of whom were Confucian literati. Their fights first broke out immediately after the reign of King Sŏngjong (1470-1494) in the period of the flowering of the dynasty. In 1498, the fourth year of the reign of Yŏnsan-gun (1495-1505),[4] scores of literati of the school of Kim Chongjik (1431-1492) were sentenced to death on orders from Yu Chagwang, a government minister. After this, in 1504, many more literati of the Kim Chongjik school were executed. Kim Chongjik was a Confucian scholar who, following the tradition of Kil Chae (1353-1419), a Confucianist at the end of the Koryŏ period, rose to the position of chief official on the Board of Justice in the service of King Sŏngjong. There were many famous scholars among his students, and in the reign of King Sŏngjong his school boasted of great influence. The school studied the theories of the Chinese Neo-Confucian philosopher Chu Hsi (1130-1200) and particularly revered the principle of purity. Since those who were not in agreement with this school were branded as rabble, there was strong resentment against it among important government officials. This feeling grew in intensity until the anti-Kim Chongjik party which supported the tyrant Yŏnsan-gun brought about the persecutions of literati in 1498 and 1504.

The strength of the Kim Chongjik school declined, but struggles of the bureaucrats did not cease. In 1519, the fourteenth year of the reign of King Chungjong (1506-1544), a score of court officials headed by Cho Kwangjo (1482-1519) were condemned to death. At the news of the imprisonment of Kwangjo and his group, it is said that more than a thousand Confucianists gathered outside the Kwanghwa Gate in Seoul, sent a memorial to the king averring Kwangjo's innocence, and finally entered the palace where they wailed and wept. When the king ordered them seized, each demanded that he be arrested before the others. They were taken prisoner, and the jails became so full there was no place to put them.

Disputes among court officials continued after this, and numerous small incidents occurred. But in 1545, the first year of the reign of King Myŏngjong (1545-1567), a serious event took place in which many officials of the party of Yun Im (1437-1545; known as the "Great Yun"), were put to death at the instigation of the party of Yun Wŏnhyŏng (died 1565; known as the "Small Yun").

The persecutions of literati described above had different immediate causes.

---

[4]Yŏnsan-gun and Kwanghae-gun were not given the dignity of kingly temple names, but were styled *kun* (prince), indicating moral disapproval of the conduct of their reigns.

The persecutions of 1498 were ostensibly brought about by a sentence written by Kim Chongjik censuring King Sejo. The persecutions of 1504 were caused by the posthumous ennobling of Yŏnsan-gun's mother, and the right or wrong of placing her as a queen in King Sŏngjong's mausoleum. The persecutions of 1519 were said to be due to the tyranny and treasonous plotting of Cho Kwangjo, and the 1545 persecutions arose over the problem of succession. Although the pretexts for these tragic persecutions were different, each was connected with problems concerning the king or the queen. In this type of dispute, the losers were forced into the position of rebels or outlaws without being given the opportunity to refute the charges against them. These were not disputes over government policy, but struggles in which one either took power or lost his life. The fights were so vicious that even the corpses of the losers were disinterred and cut to pieces.

Such struggles over questions of loyalty to the ruler were age-old. But though the subject of the conflicts was still the same, the protagonists had changed: Whereas the conflicts before had been between a handful of court ministers, they were now between many men of various parties and Confucianists.

As these struggles were associated with the Throne, the queen's relatives took part in them, often figuring as leading characters, as, for example, in the persecutions of 1545. Still the object at stake was the power of officials and Confucianists, and the methods used were not mainly plots and assassination, but rather public discussions in which protests were openly made against the present authority, plainly an advance over the methods of political struggle in the past.

The usual pattern of political struggles was now as follows. After opposition parties were disposed of by means of large-scale executions, the political climate would be peaceful for a short time. Then, before long, more opposition parties would appear, and the political scene would again become disturbed. It was in this atmosphere of instability that strong party combinations developed known as "party factions." These groups, organized under a strong leader, were resolved to extirpate other parties and increase their own power. As they developed, they absorbed into their membership entire families. Party factions continued unshaken from generation to generation and became controlling factors in the life and destinies of their members.

The struggles between party factions first began to take shape clearly in the early part of the reign of King Sŏnjo (1568-1608). The leader of one group was Sim Ŭigyŏm (1535-1587), younger brother of the queen of King Myŏngjong (1546-1567) and holder of the chief post (taesahŏn) in the Office of Supervision. The leader of the opposing group was Kim Hyowŏn (died 1590), a relative of the victor in the 1545 persecution of the literati, Yun Wŏnhyŏng, a man of talent who was a Confucianist of the Kim Chongjik school. He held the post of chŏllang (selection officer) in the Board of Civil Administration which controlled the appointment and dismissal of officials. Two factions were formed, spearheaded by these two men and composed of officials and Confucianists, both of whom were dedicated to the advance of their own party and extirpation of all opposition. Kim Hyowŏn's home was situated in the eastern section of the capital, Sim Ŭigyŏm's house was in the western section. Therefore Kim's party was called that of the "Easterners" and Sim's that of the "Westerners." There was hardly a man who was not affiliated with one or the other of these parties. From that time to the end of the Yi Dynasty, the clash between the two factions continued, the subjects at issue being foreign affairs as well as matters of internal government. Their disputes continued through the time of the disastrous Hideyoshi invasions of Korea in 1592 and 1597, and the Manchu attacks of 1627 and 1637.

At first the contest was between Easterners and Westerners; the Easterners divided into "Northerners" and "Southerners," and before long these two groups separated into still smaller ones. The Westerners similarly split into various parties. The major divisions are indicated in Table 1.

These parties each had their rise and decline. First the Easterners attained power and oppressed the Westerners, but in 1591, the twenty-fourth year of the reign of King Sŏnjo, a dispute arose among the Easterners concerning methods of oppressing the Westerners, which resulted in the mentioned split between Northerners and Southerners. During the period of the Hideyoshi invasions of Korea, the leader of the Southerners, Yu Sŏngnyong (1542-1607), was in control of the government. In these years, party struggles died down; but they became intensified again after the Japanese armies withdrew, and Northerners replaced Southerners as wielders of power. Before long the Northerners divided into the "Small Northerners" and "Large Northerners" and fought over matters of royal succession. The Large Northerners who backed Kwanghae-gun (1609-1622) were victorious. Their party held political power during the reign of this king. Toward the end of his reign, however, the Manchu state of the Later Chin arose in Manchuria, and the relation between Korea and her suzerain, the Ming, whom she was bound to assist, became precarious. Taking advantage of these circumstances, the Westerners who for a long time had been subservient, arose, deposed Kwanghae-gun, set up Injo as king in 1623, and, killing and exiling the members of the Large Northerners party, took control of the state. During the reign of King Injo (1623-1649), the Nak party — one of the splinter parties of the Westerners — was dominant, but during the reigns of kings Hyojong (1650-1659) and Hyŏnjong (1660-1674), the Mountain party — another splinter party — led by the great Confucianist Song Siryŏl (1607-1689), held power. It lost its position in a controversy over the length of time the king had to wear mourning and was replaced by the Southerners. These Southerners also were soon overthrown, and Song Siryŏl again appeared in court at the head of the Westerners reasserting their hegemony. Then in a dispute over the manner of exiling the Southerners, the Westerners divided into two contending groups, the Old Doctrine and Young Doctrine. In 1689, the fifteenth year of the reign of King Sukchong (1675-1720), the Southerners again rose to power over the problem of determining the heir-apparent, condemned Song Siryŏl to death, and punished many Westerners. It was not long however before the Southerners were again replaced by the party of the Westerners, though within that party a bitter struggle continued between the Old Doctrine and Young Doctrine groups.

Reflecting these struggles between party factions, political changes at the capital occurred frequently. When one party gained power, it carried out cruel measures against the opposition parties, condemning to death scores of people and meting out lesser punishment to hundreds. The core of the opposition, however, could never be eliminated; after a short time the members of parties who had been in hiding would rise seeking revenge, and the whole process would be repeated. Furthermore, parties which had seized power would suddenly split. No party stayed united and in power for long. This deep-rooted struggling and splintering

TABLE 1
PRINCIPAL PARTY FACTIONS

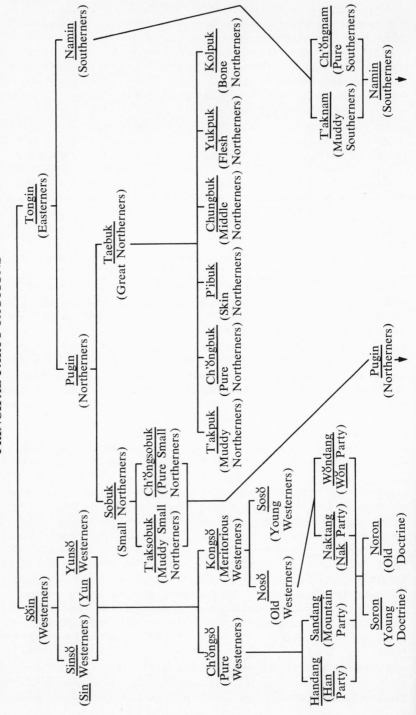

into party factions were characteristics of Yi Dynasty political history, entirely different from anything that had occurred before. They are indicative of the changes that had taken place in the society of that time.

Chiefly involved in these persecutions of the literati and the struggles of the party factions were Confucianists from the class of officials. The study of Confucianism was not new — it had been going on from ancient times — but now, for the first time, due to fundamental changes in Yi Dynasty society, officials were spoken of as Confucianists.

The scholars and literati were either men who, having become officials, practiced Confucianism, or men who studied Confucianism in order to enter the bureaucracy. The philosophy was taught in government schools in the capital and in every country district, and also in the mentioned private institutions *sŏwŏn* (literary academies) and *sŏdang* (literary halls) which existed throughout the land. The number of graduates and persons attending these schools was large. As a whole these persons constituted the so-called "official class" whether they had gone through the examination system (*kwagŏ*) or not, and it was on them that the persecutions of the literati and the party factionalism centered.

Confucianists were everywhere, but of special importance were the Confucianists who taught and studied at the local private educational institutions — the *sŏwŏn* and *sŏdang*. These institutions were usually built by influential men in the local community who were large landowners and had been officials. These men set up villas and mansions on their agricultural estates, and at the same time constructed *sŏwŏn* there for the instruction of the children of the area. The *sŏwŏn* were the cultural pivots of the estates and became the centers of local cultural life. As private agricultural estates became larger and more numerous, there were more *sŏwŏn*, and the number of people studying at them increased correspondingly. Thus three trends became apparent which mark the contrast between this period and preceding ones: the encouragement of the development of local power and settlement in the country on the agricultural estates; the consequent growth of *sŏwŏn*; and the establishment of a literati class.

The highest ideal of those who controlled the agricultural estates was to become regular government officials. If they succeeded in this, they moved to the capital, but still depended on their estates for the material basis of their power. Nor were they entirely disassociated from their estates as in the past, for members of their families continued to live there and, in fact, the estates became centers where family partisans gathered. Even today the remaining endogamous villages in Korea have their origin in the former agricultural estates where members of the same families came to live together. Persons who did not own such estates often attached themselves to powerful landowning families and came to be included in the family party. This explains the existence of members in the larger groups who had different family names. The partisans of such local family parties were dependent on the agricultural estate for their livelihood and derived their culture from the *sŏwŏn* situated on them.

Those who gathered at the *sŏwŏn*, however, were not the peasants and laborers who lived on the agricultural estates. The actual workers on these estates were tenants (*chŏnho*) and slaves, principally the latter. Their social status was clearly that of unfree men, and they could not enter the family parties made up of those who controlled the property. This ruling group scorned labor, and entrusted the task of managing their estates to slaves, while they themselves lived as consumers. Only these men who resided on the land and were free from all labor made up the family parties. It was this non-working consumer class also that studied at the sŏwŏn. Its members were called *yangban*, and they constituted a privileged group who lived in a world entirely different from that of the peasants.

As the agricultural estates developed, the special privileges of those living in the country who comprised the family parties increased. Great value was put on family origins and social rank, and, consequently, powerful families constructed genealogies in order to enhance their reputation and influence. The reason for the many genealogies drawn up during the Yi Dynasty was two-fold. If a person could prove that he was attached to a powerful family, his privileged position was assured; and if a family could show its connection with many outstanding officials, the power of the family was increased. With the latter aim in view, families often united and supported promising men in an effort to produce influential officials from their group, and when one of their own men managed to rise to prominence, they depended on him to increase their own wealth and reputation. It was considered a valuable part of a *yangban's* training to learn to read genealogical tables, to determine a family's lineage, and to memorize names of important officials in these tables.

The power of the literati had its roots in the environment described above. Party unity was guaranteed by family solidarity in local country areas. This provided a strength that could not easily be crushed. Yet at the same time, party rivalry and competition between literati to obtain official posts was decided by political struggles within the capital. Powerful as the literati had become as masters of an unfree population, they were still dependent on the dynasty.

This situation is shown in the problems which engaged the attention of the literati and scholars. These dealt principally with matters concerning the king or the queen. For example, the great Confucianist Song Siryŏl (1607-1689) conducted heated debates in court to determine the proper number of years for royal mourning, and the decision in this matter sealed the fate of numerous Confucianists who had advocated mourning periods of longer or shorter lengths. In a society where family prestige was so important, this was a critical issue. The scholarship of these men, although Neo-Confucianist, was not concerned with study of the philosophical system, but simply with rites and ethics. Even with the rise of the Ch'ing Dynasty school of textual criticism (School of Han Learning) in China in the eighteenth century, Korean Confucianists were not interested in larger philosophical problems, but studied only matters useful to family and party. The change from the Buddhism of the Koryŏ Dynasty to the Confucianism of the Yi Dynasty represented a step forward in that a theory of leadership by officials was espoused, but Korean Confucianism remained immature because it adapted itself to the undeveloped character of the Korean bureaucratic system. Although Korea observed the rite of *sadae* (serving the great) in relation to China during the Yi Dynasty and admired Chinese culture, she was still not prepared to absorb this culture with all its social and political implications.

The Japanese (Hideyoshi) Invasions

From the last years of the Koryŏ period through the first years of the Yi Dynasty, the Japanese marauders, the *Wakō*, had been plundering the coasts of Korea. It was not until the Ashikaga Military Government in Japan had been established and its political control recognized, that these activities were checked. Then peaceful trade began between Korea and the Ashikaga, as well as between Korea and various *daimyos* (feudal lords) in Japan. Envoys traveled back and forth between the two countries. Korea opened up the three ports of Naeip'o (present-day Chep'o), Pusanp'o (present-day Pusan), and Yŏmp'o (present-day Ulsan) and permitted the Japanese to trade in them and to fish in Korean waters. Consequently a fair number of Japanese resided at these three Korean ports. In 1510, these Japanese residents caused an uprising, and there were other incidents which at times threatened the relations between Japan and Korea, but on the whole, the contacts between the two countries were peaceful. Later the Ashikaga Military Government weakened, Japan was reverting to internal strife, and Japanese pirates again became active on the Korean coast. In 1544 they attacked the town of Saryang in South Kyŏngsang Province, in 1555 a fleet of ships from Japan laid waste the coast of Chŏlla Province, and, in 1589, the town of Hŭngyang in South Chŏlla Province was attacked. These Japanese pirates were known as the "latter-day *Wakō*." They differed from the earlier *Wakō* in that their plundering extended far beyond Korea. They ravaged not only the coasts of Korea, but also those of many other countries in East Asia. Because of them, official relations were suspended between Japan and Korea.

At last the period of internal wars in Japan came to an end when Oda Nobunaga (1534-1582) and Toyotomi Hideyoshi (1536-1598) appeared and established order in the country. A stop was put to *Wakō* marauding, but the activity of the Japanese overseas was continued by merchants and traders. Trade was now regulated, and its expansion encouraged. Hideyoshi was especially assiduous in this effort. He was, however, not satisfied with peaceful trade alone and was planning the conquest of the Asiatic continent as far as India. To this end, he wished to cultivate relations with Korea so that she would be in the vanguard in an invasion of Ming China. His plan was first transmitted to Korea in 1587 through the good offices of the Sō clan of Tsushima, and soon afterward was directly disclosed to the Korean envoy who came to Japan. This placed Korea in an awkward position because of her vassal relationship to China. Foreign policy became the subject of violent dispute between the Korean party factions. As this produced a welter of contradictory opinions, the problem was greatly aggravated, and no clear decision could be reached on which to base a definite reply to Japan. When Hideyoshi realized that negotiations were not proceeding as he had hoped, he decided that the first step in the conquest of Ming China would have to be the conquest of Korea. In the fourth month of 1592, with the army of Konishi Yukinaga in the lead, followed by the armies of Katō Kiyomasa, Kuroda Nagamasa, Mōri Yoshinari, Ukida Hideie, and others, totaling 158,000 men, Hideyoshi's forces landed in Korea. They immediately overwhelmed the southern part of the country and occupied the capital in the beginning of the fifth month. There the armies were split into divisions which spread out and soon conquered all of Korea's eight provinces. A military government was set up in the occupied areas and military supplies were collected. While this was being accomplished, the army of Katō Kiyomasa completed the conquest of Hamgyŏng Province, and pushed on into the area of Wu-liang-ha (present-day Chien-tao in Manchuria). The reasons for the success of the Japanese armies were the unexpectedness of their attack, the lack of a united front in Korea due to party factionalism, and the divided and inadequate state of the country's defenses. However, though successful in land warfare, the Japanese were defeated in sea battles by fleets under the command of the famous Korean admiral Yi Sunsin (1545-1598). In losing control of the sea, the Japanese were unable to keep their victorious armies supplied, and their position in Korea became precarious.

In response to a request from Korea, Ming China, to whom Korea paid tribute, first sent southward a force from Manchuria under Tsu Ch'eng-hsün to assist Korea against the invading Japanese armies. In the seventh month of 1592, this force attacked Konishi's army which was defending P'yŏngyang, but the attack was unsuccessful. More Chinese troops were mobilized, and in the first month of 1593 a force of 40,000 men under Li Ju-sung again attacked P'yŏngyang and, defeating Konishi, continued onward to take Kaesŏng. This army even threatened Seoul, but it was defeated in the battle of Pyŏkchegwan and withdrew to P'yŏngyang. The Japanese then gathered their forces around Seoul and prepared to withstand any further southward push by the Ming troops.

This brought the Chinese and Japanese armies face to face with each other. The Japanese, having lost control of the sea, suffered from lack of supplies and were also troubled by cold and epidemics. Furthermore, they were harassed by Korean ŭigun (righteous armies), guerrilla bands which arose throughout Korea to hinder control of enemy-occupied areas. Suppressing them was an exhausting task for the Japanese army. It became obvious to them that a further continuation of the war would be unprofitable. At the same time, the Chinese armies, having been defeated by the Japanese armies, could not hope for a decisive victory. Therefore the chances of concluding a truce were good. In the fourth month of 1593, the Japanese armies started to withdraw; after this, peace negotiations began between China, Japan, and Korea. Japan proposed a peace as if she had been victorious; China, considering Japan one of her "barbarian" neighbors, proposed to enfeoff Hideyoshi as "king" of Japan and to settle matters on the basis of allowing Japan to pay tribute to China. The positions of the two protagonists were thus completely incompatible. The situation was made worse by the failure of those entrusted with the peace negotiations to report these divergent views to the highest authorities in their respective nations. They tried simply to make peace in a hurry. Finally negotiations for concluding a treaty were stalled, and the peace conference broke up. In 1596 Hideyoshi gave orders for the resumption of hostilities, and in the first month of 1597, a Japanese army of 140,000 men took to the field again in Korea. This invasion, however, was not as successful as the previous one because as the Japanese expedition set out, the Chinese sent land and sea forces to help the Koreans who had themselves also been preparing for war and establishing defenses. By the time the Japanese armies had conquered southern Korea up to the Han River line, fall had passed and the cold had become so severe that the forward movement of the troops was paralyzed. The Japanese were forced to gather their forces and retire to the coastal areas of Chŏlla and Kyŏngsang provinces to await there the passing of winter. In the following year, 1598,

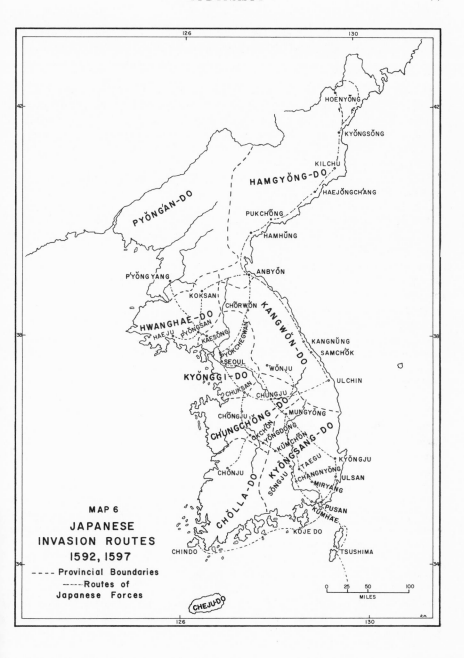

126 130

HOENYŎNG

KYŎNGSŎNG

KILCHU

HAMGYŎNG-DO

HAEJŎNGCH'ANG

PYŎNGAN-DO

PUKCHŎNG

HAMHŬNG

ANBYŎN

P'YŎNG YANG

KOKSAN

CHŎRWŎN

HWANGHAE-DO

KANGWŎN-DO

HAEJU YŎNGSAN

KAESŎNG

KANGNŬNG

SAMCH'ŎK

YŎKCHEGWAN

SEOUL

WŎNJU

KYŎNGGI-DO

ULCHIN

CHUKSAN

CHUNGJU

CHŎNGJU

CHUNGCHŎNG-DO

MUNGYŎNG

OKCH'ŎN

YŎNGDONG

KŬMCH'ŎN

KYŎNGSANG-DO

KYŎNGJU

TAEGU

CHŎNJU

CHANGNYŎNG

ULSAN

SŎNGJU

MIRYANG

CHŎLLA-DO

KŬMHAE

PUSAN

MAP 6

JAPANESE
INVASION ROUTES
1592, 1597

KŎJE DO

CHINDO

TSUSHIMA

- - - - Provincial Boundaries
- - - - - Routes of
Japanese Forces

0   25   50   100

MILES

CHEJU-DO

126 130

the Chinese advanced southward with a great army of 150,000 men and attacked the areas occupied by the Japanese.

While the Japanese army continued fighting under these conditions, Toyotomi Hideyoshi made a death-bed injunction that the Korean invasion should cease. In accordance with this, the Japanese armies began to withdraw. At the same time the Chinese armies, defeated in the battle of Sach'ŏn in South Kyŏngsang Province, lost their will to fight. Peace negotiations were arranged between the armies and, by the end of the same year, both nations withdrew their troops from Korea.

With the death of Hideyoshi, this great war which lasted seven years, including the interim periods of peace negotiations, came to an unsatisfactory end. Japan, who had started it, did not attain her war aims. She simply withdrew from Korea without having suffered heavy losses. In contrast, the loss and damage to Korea from the war reached tragic proportions. The whole country had been a battlefield. Besides suffering from fires set by the soldiers of the Japanese armies, from the killing of her people, from the destruction of her rice fields, and from harsh requisitioning under Japanese military rule, Korea had to bear the wanton vandalism of the Ming Chinese armies which, although they had come to help Korea, brought devastation equal to that inflicted by the Japanese. Her land ravaged by two mighty armies, Korea reaped only disaster from the war and had no way of seeking redress. Both cities and agricultural villages were laid waste. The whole country presented a picture of fearful confusion. Starving people and refugees were preyed upon by thieves, while corrupt officials and local government office clerks (sŏri) took advantage of the disorder in government to further their own interests. Under these conditions, land registers and population figures were lost, manual labor service was not exacted and taxes not assessed. The organization of the government, of the economy, and of the whole society disintegrated. Reestablishment of order was almost impossible. This period marked the beginning of the rapid decline of the Yi Dynasty.

This war also dealt a heavy blow to Ming China. The government was already facing a period of internal difficulties at the end of the sixteenth century. Mobilization of her armies had placed a heavy burden on China financially, and this, combined with the discontent of the people, undermined the strength of the dynasty. Added to this, the sending of the Manchurian forces to Korea had weakened China's defenses in Manchuria, a situation of which the Jürchen took advantage in their drive for independence. This development was to lead to the establishment of the Ch'ing (Manchu) Dynasty, a wholly unforeseen result of Hideyoshi's campaigns, but the one of greatest significance to East Asia.

In Japan, the Toyotomi family was shortly overthrown and the Tokugawa hegemony established. The Tokugawa family wished to reestablish peaceful relations with Korea and, through the good offices of the Sō clan of Tsushima, sought to renew friendly contact. Korea did not readily listen to these overtures, but in 1607 sent an envoy to Japan for the first time since the war. With this, relations between the two countries were restored to their former state, and from then on to the end of the Tokugawa period (1867), peace prevailed between Korea and Japan.

The Invasions of the Manchu Armies

Factional strife subsided temporarily in Korea with the invasion of the Japanese but when the war was over it once again became violent. During the reign of Kwanghae-gun (1609-1622) who followed Sŏnjo (1568-1608), numerous *coups d'état* were carried out. Kwanghae-gun himself became a victim of factional strife and was deposed. The persons of the Western faction who set up Injo (1623-1649) in place of Kwanghae-gun, fought and split over the distribution of rewards for having backed him. At that time Yi Kwal, a northern Korean military commander, who had not been properly recompensed for his service, led an uprising which threatened Seoul. Injo fled from Seoul to escape capture, and Yi Kwal set himself up as king, thus establishing a different royal Korean family. This uprising of Yi Kwal was finally put down and Injo returned to Seoul, but it gave the Manchu armies an opportunity to invade Korea.

While Korean bureaucracy was engrossed in these factional struggles, the political situation in Northeast Asia had changed. This was due to the rise of the Jürchen of Manchuria. The Jürchen in the past had established the Chin Dynasty (1115-1234) and threatened Koryŏ, but on account of the pressure of the Mongols, the Chin rulers lost their power. After the downfall of the Mongols, the Jürchen were subject to the control of the Ming Dynasty of China. In the latter part of that dynasty, however, as Ming control declined, the Jürchen arose and began to threaten the Chinese border areas. They were especially active at the time of the Hideyoshi expedition when the Manchurian defense forces of the Ming were sent into Korea. This weakening of the Ming forces permitted the Jürchen to break loose. The Manchu chieftain, Nurhachi, arose, united the Jürchen, and founded the Manchu Dynasty of Later Chin (1616). Following this, he occupied Fu-shun and defeated a large combined Ming-Korean army at the battle of Sa-erh-hu Mountain (1619). Then he took Shen-yang (Mukden), Liao-yang, T'ieh-ling, and K'ai-yüan (1621), and established his capital at Shen-yang in 1625, one year after the rebellion of Yi Kwal in Korea.

At first Korea had sent troops into Manchuria as ordered by the Ming[5] emperor and had helped him in an attack on Nurhachi, but after the defeat of the combined Ming-Korean forces at Sa-erh-hu, Korea did not attach herself to either the Ming or the Manchus, but adopted a policy of "wait and see." This policy was hotly disputed by the party factions at the capital. The Northerners who had held power during the reign of Kwanghae-gun had been in favor of the "wait and see" policy, but they were ousted in a *coup d'état* by the Westerners who deposed Kwanghae-gun and placed Injo on the throne. This party adopted a pro-Ming and anti-Manchu policy, which aroused the feelings of the Manchus against Korea, and threatened their position in relation to that country. The situation was made worse for the Manchus by a development which was occurring in their rear: Mao Wen-lung, a Ming general who had originally been in Liao-tung, moved to Ka Island off Korea's northwest coast. The major objective of the Manchus was to attack the Ming forces, but before this could be done, they would have·to

---

[5] In the suzerain-vassal relationships of the Chinese system of international relations, one of the duties of a tributary state was to assist its suzerain in military campaigns when requested. Korea was a tributary of the Ming at that time.

eliminate the threat to their rear by defeating Mao Wen-lung and neutralizing Korea. It was just at this time that the rebellion of Yi Kwal was taking place in Korea. Some of the partisans of this unsuccessful rebellion fled to Manchu territory, complained of the injustice of Kwanghae-gun's deposition and Injo's enthronement, and proposed that they take the lead in a Manchu attack on Korea.

This was a perfect opportunity for the Manchu forces. On the pretext of taking revenge for Kwanghae-gun, they invaded Korea in 1627. One group attacked Ka Island, Mao Wen-lung's headquarters, but the principal force overwhelmed P'yŏngan and Hwanghae provinces and moved southward. The Korean government left Seoul and retreated to Kanghwa Island, but soon yielded to the pressure of the Manchu army. Korea made peace on the basis of withdrawal of the Manchu troops and the establishment of elder-younger-brother relations between the two countries. Yet even though at peace with the Manchus, Korea did not turn against the Ming emperor.

With this, the first Manchu invasion of Korea came to an end, but in time, as the power of the Manchu rulers increased, they made many further difficult demands on Korea. They requisitioned food supplies, drafted soldiers for campaigns against China, and demanded a change from elder-younger-brother relation between the two nations to a suzerain-vassal relation. Consequently, Korea again reverted to an anti-Manchu policy, and this brought on another attack by Manchu forces. During this period, Manchu power had greatly expanded, and the name Later Chin was changed to Ch'ing in 1636. The Ch'ing emperor, angered by Korea's attitude, sent out a punitive expedition against her for the second time. In the winter of 1637 a great army of 100,000 men, led personally by the Ch'ing Emperor T'ai-tsung, crossed the Yalu River and made a whirlwind southern invasion. The Korean king and his ministers did not have time to flee to Kanghwa Island before the force was upon Seoul. Korea yielded and, in the first month of 1638, capitulated, agreed to break relations with China, to turn over certain princes and high ministers as hostages, to observe suzerain-vassal relations toward the Manchu Ch'ing, and even to send reinforcements to the Ch'ing forces for their attacks on the Ming emperor. However, even after this, Korea's regard for China was strong; she secretly continued her relations with the Ming emperor, used Ming reign titles even after the fall of Ming[6] and, at one time, even had plans for a northern expedition against the Ch'ing borders. But faced with Manchu pressure, Korea could not make her opposition overt. She continued to send envoys and tribute to the Ch'ing ruler every year, in compliance with the ceremony of *sadae* (serving the great).

Compared with the invasion by the Japanese, the Manchu invasion lasted a shorter period of time and laid waste a smaller area of the country. Yet it worked a particular hardship on Korea in that it followed so shortly the invasion of the Japanese. There was no time to recover from the losses incurred by the latter before the Manchus attacked twice, despoiling the country even further. In particular, the damage in northwest Korea, along the route taken by the Ch'ing

---

[6]Ordinarily a tributary state in the Chinese system of international relations used for dating the reign titles of the state to whom it paid tribute. Korea, having at that time become a tributary of the Ch'ing dynasty, should have disregarded Ming reign titles, and especially so after the fall of the Ming in 1644.

armies, was enormous, ana there was great destruction in Seoul itself. Recovery from all these losses was beyond the strength of a government made up of officials absorbed in factional struggles.

The Deterioration of the Machinery of Government and the Introduction of Catholicism

The Yi Dynasty showed considerable advances over previous dynasties. The expansion of private agricultural estates, the arguments of Confucianists, and even the struggles of party factions were all signs of progress. Yet it was a progress not in the basic structure of society, but only within the bounds of the social relationships already in existence since ancient times and even such progress was quickly brought to a halt. The Japanese invasions which ravaged the whole land, and the Manchu invasions which followed before the wounds could be healed, hastened markedly the decline of the dynasty. This is shown directly in the startling decrease in land area controlled by the state, as a result of the Japanese invasions. According to the table below, government-controlled land in all provinces shrank to almost one quarter of earlier figures.

TABLE 2
Decline of Land Controlled by the State
(in thousands of kyŏl)

Province	Period before Japanese invasion	Kwanghae-gun period
Kyŏnggi	150	39
Chŏlla	440	110
Hwanghae	110	60
Ch'ungch'ŏng	260	110
Kyŏngsang	430	70
Kangwŏn	28	11
P'yŏngan	170	94
Hamgyŏng	120	47
TOTAL	1,708	541

This precipitous decline must undoubtedly be attributed not only to the devastation of the land through war and the flight of tillers from the fields, but also to fraud and deception practiced by officials, local government office clerks, and local men of influence. The disruption of the machinery of government brought about by the wars presented a golden opportunity to these men to enrich themselves, especially since the loss of land registers precluded any disclosure of their dishonesty. The figures above reveal the extent of material and human loss brought about by the Japanese invasion and the degree to which the machinery of government collapsed.

Since land provided the material basis of state power, it was imperative to regain control of it if the bureaucratic state was to be maintained. With this in view, a land survey was begun as soon as the Japanese armies had withdrawn, and, after that, repeated land measurements were taken. This produced some improvement, but a complete return to the prewar situation was never achieved. Even in 1726, at the beginning of the reign of Yŏngjo (1725-1776), known as a period of revival of state power in the latter half of the Yi Dynasty, the total land area of the eight provinces under government control was 1,220,000 *kyŏl*—far less than the 1,700,000 *kyŏl* before the Japanese invasions. Moreover, the 1,220,000 *kyŏl* included waste land and tax-exempt land, so that the area of government-controlled taxable land was not more than 830,000 *kyŏl*. The fact that the amount of waste land and tax-exempt land was relatively so large in the smaller over-all land area under government control indicates a decline in the power of the state.

The decrease in the amount of taxable land naturally resulted in financial difficulties. Finally it became impossible to pay officials their salaries or even to supply the military with essential provisions. It was necessary, therefore, for the government to consider new methods of levying taxes. At the beginning of the Yi Dynasty, the principal taxes were land taxes and taxes in kind. The taxes in kind, levied by the local government from the special local products made or grown by the peasant, were collected at central government offices. However, the items included in these taxes in kind and the period of their collection did not always coincide with the needs of the officials of the central government. Therefore it was the custom to sell products so collected to officially sponsored merchants, and thus finance the purchase of needed goods. This was inconvenient, and the officials attending the sales were dishonest; hence a system was devised of collecting rice rather than other taxes in kind and of purchasing necessities with rice. Payment in rice was initiated during Kwanghae-gun's rule (1609-1622), when financial difficulties became acute after the Japanese invasions. It was first tried in Kyŏnggi Province, and in succeeding reigns from the time of Injo its application was broadened until it was eventually carried on throughout the whole country. In the beginning, tax payments in rice were limited to the taxes in kind collected by the central government, but gradually the taxes in kind other than rice collected by the local government were also paid for in rice. Finally taxes in kind for both the central and local governments were made into one tax, payable in rice, which was assessed according to a nationwide land division. This new system was known as *taedong-pŏp* (law of great correspondence). Since this tax was introduced to replace taxes in kind, the latter should have disappeared, but actually necessary products formerly collected as taxes in kind continued to be requisitioned as occasion demanded. Thus the application of the *taedong* law really only resulted in the addition of a tax called *taedong-mi* (great correspondence rice), and taxes in kind continued.

The changes in the tax laws also affected labor service. At the beginning of the dynasty, labor service was in principle to be borne by freemen, Buddhist priests, unfree people, and slaves, and was used for public projects and warfare. Before long, however, cloth was collected in place of labor service, and the government began to pay people with cloth. After the Hideyoshi invasions, this method of payment was widely used, and farm households were taxed in cloth. But labor service still continued to be assessed, so the levy of cloth was simply an added burden for the farming population. It was even more difficult, however, to collect the cloth than it had been to collect the land taxes, for in order to obtain the cloth from all farmers, the government needed to know accurately the number of farm households. Officials and wealthy landowners, in order to avoid the imposition of this tax on their own unfree men and slaves, falsified reports on the size of the population, and owner-tillers hid in the homes of men of influence to evade the tax. This tax, therefore, was actually collected only from poor persons who had no protectors. Cloth assessments to pay for exemption from military service were even made on children and persons who had already died. As a result, the levy acquired the evil name of "white boned" or "yellow mouthed," that is "the color of the lips in death" cloth collection. Not only did it cause great suffering among the poor and encourage powerful men to falsify the figures of farm households, but it was unsuccessful because of its universal unpopularity. It became an issue within the government, until finally the assessment based on population was discontinued, and, from 1753 on, the cloth levy was made on the basis of land.

The change of payment in kind and labor service into *taedong* rice and cloth represents an improvement in taxation methods. But this improvement did not consist in an abolition of the old tax burdens; these were imposed just as before, and now new taxes were added to the old ones. This increase in taxes was due to the government's financial difficulties and not to a rise in farmer's level of subsistence, so that beyond the improvements in the form of taxation, there was no actual progress. This additional tax was identical with the *samsuryang* or "three hand" grain tax, imposed as a special wartime tax during the Hideyoshi invasions but which continued afterwards. These were attempts to try to bolster up, by means of taxes, the deteriorating power of the state.

To strengthen the bureaucratic state structure of the Yi Dynasty, it would have been necessary to question the basis of landholding, but this was inconceivable in view of the interests involved. The only possible subject for debate was the source of revenue. Yet even this presented difficulties, because the officials, dependent on the power of the state, were aware of their personal advantages and losses and were strongly opposed to any change that would be even slightly unfavorable to their interests. Each official was more concerned with his private gain than with the general interests of the state. Such a trend destroys a bureaucratic system of control, and in Korea it ushered in a period of quickening of graft on the part of officials and local government office clerks.

Enforcement of official discipline was constantly discussed. The king sent censors traveling in secret to all parts of the country to check on the dishonesty of the bureaucracy. Disguised, they lost themselves among the people in every community and acted as informers, reporting to the king on corruption or illegal action. In the maelstrom of vicious party factionalism, however, even their activities could not be impartial. The reestablishment of the declining and disintegrating bureaucratic state had become almost impossible.

Meanwhile, although all officials enjoyed a relatively privileged position, a division based on differences in economic status developed among them. Upper-class officials who held the highest offices in the royal household, the royal family, and the court, controlled vast tracts of land, mountains, streams, fishing places, and salt licks, and employed many free and unfree men. These officials often appropriated land attached to government offices and were able to live lives of luxury. The royal household and family were especially noted for enlarging their personal holdings in this way. They also monopolized ferries at river crossings making travel almost impossible for others.

Contrasted to these, there were officials who were excluded from power, and lower-class bureaucrats. Unlike their counterparts in previous dynasties, they lived in the country where, although deprived of power, they had special privileges. But they were discontented and resentful of the officials who held political offices from which power and wealth were derived. They formed factions which included well-known persons as members, and appealed to dissatisfied elements in the capital and countryside for support. They were constantly on the watch for opportunities to seize political power.

Among this group of ill-treated and disgruntled persons were offspring of high-class officials and their concubines. According to the family system of that time, the sons of concubines were in a different category than the sons of legal wives. They were given few opportunities to rise in the world, and in their discontent they would often join rebel and robber bands. Other recruits to these factions were groups of low-class officials who, even though they held official posts, could not hope to advance and were unable to live on their stipends. For them the status of an official was a source of pride, but their living conditions were unsatisfactory. The existence of such a large number of discontented elements indicates the increasing weakness and collapse of the bureaucratic system.

The luxury in which wealthier officials lived was much criticized by those who, though they had the status and training of officials, were excluded from such a life. They regarded with sympathy the peasants who lived in extreme poverty, and they blamed the bureaucratic system for creating these terrible conditions. Christianity, then transmitted from China, had a strong appeal for them. This religion had first entered Korea at the time of the Hideyoshi invasions, but its dissemination was delayed until Korean envoys to China brought it back to Korea together with Western learning. At first the interest of the Korean intelligentsia was focused primarily on Western astronomy, mathematics, and gunnery, and students of these subjects appeared among the Confucian scholars. Before long, however, many Koreans were converted to Christianity, and, by the latter part of the eighteenth century, it had spread to such an extent that the government prohibited it in 1786. The Yi Dynasty, which supported Confucianism as the highest teaching, regarded Christianity, in which ancestors were not worshiped, as a heterodoxy opposed to human morality.

In spite of the prohibition, Christianity spread rapidly. At the end of the eighteenth century, after the Chinese missionary Chou Wen-mu, who came from the Roman Catholic headquarters in Peking, arrived in Korea, the strength of the faith increased and the class of believers broadened to include not only the intelligentsia, but also people on the lower rungs of society. Against this growth of Christianity the Korean government took the most oppressive measures. In 1801, first Chou Wen-mu and Hwang Sayŏng, a Korean convert, were taken captive, and then other believers. The leaders of the movement were cruelly put to death on charges of high treason, and many of the Christian faithful were punished. Among them was the famous scholar Chŏng Yagyong (pen name: Tasan, 1762-1836). Although of relatively low official position, Chŏng was conversant with Chinese classics, histories, philosophy, and belles lettres. He was a master of the School of

Textual Criticism (sometimes called School of the Han Learning in China), and his empirical scholarship was a rare phenomenon in the academic world of his day. Furthermore, he was a bitter critic of the bureaucratic government of his time.

Even after this great persecution, men continued secretly to believe in Christianity. They brought into Korea Chinese and French missionaries and devoted themselves to the spreading of the faith. For a second time suppressive measures were adopted, and in 1839 many believers and foreign missionaries were put to death. Nevertheless, Christianity continued to spread in spite of all persecutions and flourished in the hearts of men who lived through such periods of anxiety and suffering.

The Desolation of Agricultural Villages

The farmers at the beginning of the Yi Dynasty were living better than in the past, and this probably contributed to the flourishing of the dynasty. But they were still bound by ancient social relationships and were entirely at the mercy of the officials. Consequently, when the state was beset with rebellions and devastating wars with foreign invaders, when the machinery of government became weaker and despotism intensified, the life of the farmer became extremely miserable. During the latter part of the Yi Dynasty, the agricultural village presented a bleak and wretched picture.

Even when the life of the farmer had been relatively comfortable during the early days of the dynasty, the level of production had been extremely low — so low that all food disappeared when there was a year of bad harvest. Thus, there was no agricultural development which could permit a division of labor, or economic development which could sustain any trade locally except by barter. Such trade as existed was the official business of the royal house and government offices, and dealt exclusively with the exchange among officials of goods exacted from the peasants. Such trading was conducted in the *yugŭijŏn* or "six markets" of Seoul and throughout the country. Peddlers called *pobusang* (swaddling-clothes carrying tradesmen) traveled from one town to another obviating the need for shops to be set up locally by merchants. There was hardly any circulation of money among the common people. This low level of trade in the villages, resembling a barter economy, was not due solely to the destitution of the farmers and the low agricultural output. A contributing factor was the control by the state of the major part of the handicraft production. There was no encouragement or opportunity for the common people to produce goods or develop any specialization. The industries managed by the state were using the labor of slaves or unfree persons under government control. The old slave-like relationships of the earlier dynasties remained for the most part unchanged in this sphere. This restriction on the activity and lives of the common people is indicative of the low level of development of the whole society.

In the wretched agricultural villages ignorance and superstition held sway, officials and landlords extorted at will, and government traders, officials, and wealthy landowners were lending money at high rates. Not only private individuals, but the government as well, lent grain in the spring to peasants without food, and in the fall would collect illegally high interests. The "ever normal granaries"

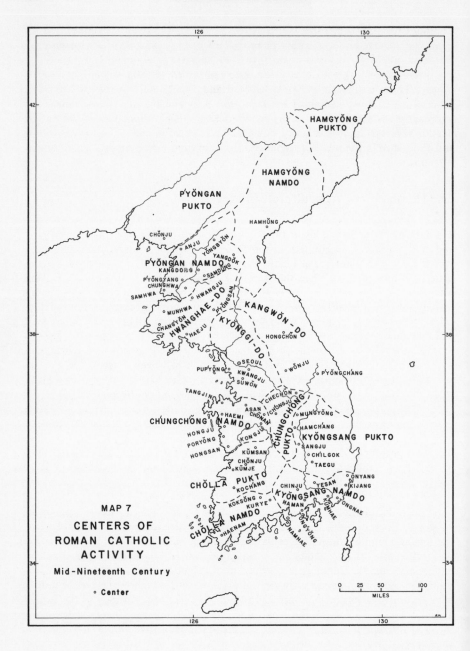

MAP 7

CENTERS OF
ROMAN CATHOLIC
ACTIVITY

Mid-Nineteenth Century

○ Center

that were ostensibly for the aid of the farmers became in fact nationwide institutions for obtaining high-interest rates. Under these conditions the chief aim of the farmers had to be the avoidance, as far as possible, of taxation and of the relentless extortion of officials. They hid their land, homes, and families and tried in every way to escape from government control. This was not possible through their own efforts, and so the help of powerful men had to be sought. To excape taxes, the farmers turned their land over to influential persons. Mainly as a result of this, in the latter part of the dynasty, land holdings of the royal house, the royal family, and important officials grew. By this time, family and village associations had become powerful. It was only by being a part of such an organization that poor farmers could exist. In order to live under the aegis of those of influence and be able to rely on the authority of such groups or family association, free men frequently lowered their status to that of unfree and gave up land which they had tilled for years. But there were limits even to this solution of the problem of livelihood. The royal family, officials, and wealthy landowners were unable to take in all who were beset by hunger, being themselves scarcely able to provide for those for whom they were already responsible. To be well off depended not on an increase in productivity, but on the acquisition of more land and labor which could be exploited. The wealth of those on the higher economic level involved the poverty of the poor. There was no hope of breaking this cycle, but only the prospect of misery endlessly breeding further misery.

This was the bleak and unsettling picture presented in the latter part of the Yi Dynasty. It was a time too of continuous disasters. Drought, flood, pestilence, epidemics, and plagues were numerous; mendicancy abounded; and death by starvation was a daily occurrence. Especially calamitous was the famine of 1671, during the reign of King Hyŏnjong, when the number of those who died from starvation and epidemics was greater than the number of those who perished in the Japanese invasions at the end of the sixteenth century. At the time of this famine, starving people openly broke into graves and ripped off the clothes from the dead bodies, and babies were abandoned on roads and thrown into irrigation ditches. The government promulgated a law for the gathering and care of abandoned babies. It urged the people to pick up such babies and permitted those who did this either to adopt them or make them slaves. This situation was not limited to the famine of 1671. Disasters succeeded one another throughout the land, even in Seoul. The reign of King Yŏngjo (1724-1776) is known as a renaissance period, but even then the spectacle of starving people eating corpses was common, and in the epidemic of 1749 the dead numbered five or six hundred thousand. In 1812, the twelfth year of the reign of King Sunjo, the number of people without food in P'yŏngan Province reached 900,000; in Hwanghae Province, 520,000; in Kangwŏn Province, 170,000; in Hamgyŏng Province 400,000; and in Kyŏnggi Province, 70,000. And in the next year there were 230,000 starving people in P'yŏngan Province; 300,000 in Hwanghae Province; 120,000 in Kangwŏn Province; 920,000 in Kyŏngsang Province; 180,000 in Ch'ungch'ŏng Province; and 690,000 in Chŏlla Province.

There was no way of helping this enormous number of starving people. Sometimes the government distributed rice gruel, but there was never enough to go around. When it became known that rice gruel would be given away in Seoul, hungry people would swarm in from the country side. Many of these people, unable to obtain food, died in Seoul of starvation, and the disposition of their bodies was a problem. The government proclaimed that the starving should try to eat pine needles, since the supply of rice gruel was insufficient. The people lost all hope of receiving help, but they were not passive. Time and again large groups of uprooted and aimless wanderers and beggars appeared in various parts of the country. In 1815, the fifteenth year of the reign of King Sunjo, the governor-inspector *(kwanch'alsa)* of Chŏlla Province reported that many persons were deserting their homes, that in extreme cases there were not even ten families remaining in a township *(myŏn)*, and that fertile fields had become waste land. To desert one's birthplace was common among farmers, but now the number of all peasants who left their homes and became wanderers rose enormously. Simply by wandering, however, they could not live. First they became beggars, then they obtained food by selling their daughters, then they abandoned their sons. Many died on the road. Some went to the mountains with the idea of carrying on fire-field agriculture, that is, clearing an area for planting by burning off the vegetation. As a result, forest fires increased and frequently spread to near-by villages and local government offices. Bold characters turned to banditry, attacking people in distress and robbing villages and towns. Robberies occurred even in Seoul in broad daylight. There were also incidents in which crowds gathered and destroyed the commercial establishments in Seoul. So-called *hwajŏk* (fire bandits) appeared on horseback carrying guns, and the sea coasts and rivers were infested with *sujŏk* (water bandits), pirates. Although such conditions were widespread, the most destructive incidents were the actions of unorganized mobs that ravaged and laid waste the countryside for a time and then dispersed.

Organized uprisings, however, did occur, and robber bands grew up from among the chronically starving, sick, and homeless people. During the reign of King Yŏngjo, these robber bands became known by such names as *Sŏgang dan* (Band of the West River) and *P'yesagun dan* (Band of the Four Abolished Counties, referring to northwestern Korea) — a band's name being given in accordance with its place of origin. These were not simply petty thieves, for they attacked government storehouses and took government goods. In addition to these bands, there were opposition movements among the peasants who resisted the imposition of taxes, seized requisitioned goods which had been taken from them, and agitated to expel government officials and local government office clerks. Even at the time of the Japanese invasions in 1592, popular uprisings against the extortion practiced by corrupt officials had occurred, but as disasters continued and the number of homeless, wandering persons increased, such uprisings became more frequent. Although these uprisings were often successful at first, they were put down in due course. These jacqueries were troublesome to the dynasty, but not dangerous to its existence.

The real threat to the dynasty came from the groups of discontented officials who were able to enlist the support of the peasant opposition. Although these officials were exploiters of the peasants, the latter depended on them for their livelihood and, in their misery, were easily incited to active resistance. These groups of officials, deprived of influence by the government, were discontent, like their counterparts in previous dynasties, and looking for an opportunity to seize power. They joined with other disgruntled elements in and out of office and were able to carry out large organized rebellions. A typical example of these is the one of Hong Kyŏngnae that broke out in 1811, the eleventh year of the reign of King Sunjo. It took place at a time when the country was full of starving, frightened, and homeless people, and Christians were being persecuted. It began in northwest Korea where discontented officials, who had been deprived of both political power and economic resources, organized the local government office clerks, merchants, and bold independent spirits of the area and chose as their leader Hong Kyŏngnae, a frustrated bureaucrat. Their rebellion was well planned, and careful provision was made for military equipment, banners, and communication with different districts. Its success was due not only to this, but to its inclusion of so many farmers as to make it almost a peasant uprising. At its peak, the rebel armies were in control of all the territory north of the Ch'ŏngch'ŏn River and, making Chŏngju their base, threatened the existence of the central government. It took the entire strength of the government forces and six months of fighting to recapture Chŏngju and put down this revolt. This was only the forerunner of many similar uprisings. In 1862, the thirteenth year of the reign of King Ch'ŏlchong, there were repeatedly serious uprisings in Kyŏngsang, Chŏlla, and Ch'ungch'ŏng provinces, none of which were successful.

Natural calamities, epidemics, famines, plagues, starvation, as well as robberies, rebellions, and peasant uprisings had become chronic. Neither from above nor below did ways for relieving these conditions present themselves. In the desolate agricultural villages, there was an all-pervading air of deep despair, an atmosphere which made the people receptive to the ideas of Christianity. Gradually this faith, at first confined to the intelligentsia, spread among the lower classes. For them, without hope in this world, this exotic teaching offered dreams of paradise. Its appeal was so great that it survived all attempts to suppress it. In the persecutions against the Roman Catholics, carried out in 1801, the first year of the reign of King Sunjo; in 1839, the fifth year of the reign of King Hŏnjong; and in 1866, the third year of the reign of King Kojong (also known as Yi T'aewang; assumed the title of Emperor in 1897) [1864-1907], large numbers of believers were put to death. Yet though Christianity provided a belief in which a future life made the present one more endurable, the wretched living conditions of the peasant in his desolate village were improved not at all.

VI

The Intrusion of the Great Powers in
Korea in Modern Times

Korea in Isolation

During this period of internal strife in Korea, of endless struggles between factions and hopelessness for the peasants, great changes were taking place in the outside world. The European nations and America, having begun to establish modern industrial societies for themselves, were now looking toward the East for expansion. Using the Opium War as a pretext, they forced China to open her ports in 1842, and in 1854 broke down the seclusion of Japan. The Far Eastern nations which had prided themselves on their ancient civilizations found themselves hard-pressed by the advance of England and France from the south, Russia from the north, and the United States across the Pacific Ocean. It was only a matter of time before this Western wave would reach Korea too.

The envoys who went yearly to China had been bringing news to Korea of this onslaught from the West. By way of China, Western natural science and Christianity had already entered Korea. But it was not until the first part of the nineteenth century that direct contact with the European nations and the United States was established. An English merchant ship arrived off the coast of Ch'ung-ch'ŏng Province in 1832 and sought to open up trade. This happened again the next year, and in 1845 soundings were taken off the coast of South Kyŏngsang and South Chŏlla provinces, and permission to trade was requested. The following year, 1846, a French warship appeared in the roadstead of Hongju, South Ch'ung-ch'ŏng Province; in 1865 a Russian warship arrived off the coast of Hamgyŏng Province at Kyŏnghŭng; in 1866 a French squadron occupied Kanghwa Island, at the mouth of the Han River on the approach to Seoul; in 1868 an American merchant ship, the *General Sherman*, sailed up the Taedong River in search of trade; and in 1871 an American squadron occupied Kanghwa Island in reprisal for her destruction.

Thus the ships of various Western nations appeared repeatedly off the coasts of Korea, but it was only when they occupied Kanghwa Island so close to the Korean capital that their presence became alarming to the court. The critical situation produced by this threat moved the government, disturbed already by the discontent of its population and by political factionalism, one step nearer to collapse. Korea, knowing how China, her suzerain, had suffered from the incursions of foreigners, hesitated to open up her country. She feared that to give up her policy of isolation would undermine the authority of the ruling official class by permitting a further spread of Christianity. This faith had continued to gain adherents even though prohibited by the government. Hence, Korea refused to open her doors to foreigners, strengthened her border defenses, and redoubled her efforts in the persecutions of Christians. Accordingly, in 1866, about 30,000 believers were executed, and an American ship, the *General Sherman,* sailing up the Taedong River seeking trade was attacked and destroyed by fire rafts. A French (1866) and later an American landing party (1871) occupied Kanghwa Island. They were vigorously attacked and both finally withdrew. This apparent military success confirmed the resolution of the government. The policy of excluding foreigners was firmly upheld, and in the capital cities of every province stone slabs were erected on which were inscribed this violent message: "The Western barbarians are invading and attacking Korea; if we do not fight we must make peace; those in favor of peace are traitors."

The Western nations were solely in search of trade. The temporary occupation of Kanghwa Island was only incidental. In the face of Korea's determined opposition and refusal to open her doors, they withdrew. This is in sharp contrast to the early opening of China and Japan in response to foreign pressure. But Korea's prolonged isolation cannot be attributed entirely to her strong stand and military defense. It is more to be explained by the attitude of the foreign powers to Korea, which was different from their attitude toward China and Japan. They were not motivated to conquer Korea by force of arms and acquire land there. It was not for that reason that they had occupied Kanghwa Island, but rather as retribution. (France had sought to punish the murder of French missionaries and the United States to punish the burning and destruction of the *General Sherman.* The incidents were closed when the debts of retribution were paid. The foreign powers, at that time, had more important problems on their hands. England, the leader in the aggression against Asia, was concerned with ruling India. The great Sepoy mutiny took place in 1857 and lasted until 1859. In the following years, England was busy pacifying the country and reestablishing a political system for India. Russia was concentrating her efforts on developing Siberia and the Maritime Province. France was engaged in controlling Annam, and the United States in opening up the American West after the Civil War. This left them neither time for, nor interest in, overcoming Korea's determined opposition to foreign trade.

The Opening of Korea

Korea could not preserve her isolation for long. Other nations were distracted from immediate advances on Korea, but a new and vigorous Japan now appeared on the scene. She herself had been forcibly opened up in 1854 by the United States. In 1868 the Meiji Restoration overthrew the Tokugawa Shogunate and an imperial government established. These changes set Japan on the way to modernization. After the Restoration, Western civilization was introduced and reforms were carried out. The trend, however, was not toward popular sovereignty, but rather toward clique government which continued to suppress agrarian uprisings and people's-rights movements. The old feudal militarists became bureaucrats and were given training in government-sponsored trade and industry. The foreign policy of the Meiji government included, together with reformist views, the idea of expelling the barbarians and attacking weak nations. This program was not simply the reactionary expression of a disgruntled military class, deprived of special feudal privileges, but had the general support of the liberals who were promoting the development of Japanese capitalism. An aggressive policy and jingoistic slogans such as "Enrich the nation and strengthen the military," were significant elements in Meiji policy. The weak nations against which aggression was aimed were those who had displayed their weakness during the incursions of the Western powers. Of these, Korea was the first to be chosen.

From the beginning of the Tokugawa period (1603), Japan had maintained peaceful relations with Korea. Even when the Tokugawa established their seclusion policy in 1633, these relations continued and were not interrupted until near the end of the period, when Japan was disturbed by many foreign and domestic problems. In 1867 the Tokugawa government, through the Sō clan of Tsushima, tried to send an envoy to Korea in order to explain the circumstances relating to the opening of Japan. When the Meiji government was established, a similar attempt was made to make known the Imperial Restoration and renew diplomatic relations. During this period, however, Korea was following a determined policy of isolation, and considered Japan as dangerous as the Western powers because Japan had been opened up by them. Consequently, the Japanese proposals were turned down. The reaction to this in Japan was a policy of force against Korea, advocated especially by disgruntled samurai who were leading a movement against the government. The clique government, instead of combating the idea of aggression against Korea, made use of it to divert the attention of the antigovernment group away from domestic affairs. Soon all classes in Japan were fired with the idea of a campaign to subjugate Korea. Opinions differed only in regard to when it should take place and who should lead it. The party supporting Saigō Takamori was in favor of an immediate invasion. As this party was put down by the government in 1873 the Korean project did not materialize, but it was evident that the idea was not displeasing to the government. It was, in fact, looking for an opportunity to carry out just such a campaign, but wished to do so with its own forces. The opportunity presented itself when in 1875 the Japanese warship *Unyō*, navigating off Kanghwa Island, was fired on by the Koreans. Public opinion in Japan was again inflamed. Warships and transports were immediately dispatched. Korea was forced to make a treaty opening up the country. This is known as the Treaty of Kanghwa, 1876. According to its terms, Korea was recognized as an independent nation; her tributary relationship to China was abolished; Pusan and two other ports were to be opened up; a Japanese legation was to be maintained at Seoul and consulates at each port; and the right to be tried by their own consular officials was granted to all Japanese living in Korea. This was the end of Korea's isolation. Japan had opened Korea by force as the Americans had opened Japan.

Korea, which had so stubbornly resisted the pressure of Western nations, acceded so easily to Japanese demands because of the political upheaval she was undergoing at home. The king's father, Yi Haŭng, better known by his title, Taewŏn-gun, who had upheld a policy of complete exclusion of the barbarians, had gone into retirement, and the opposing party, that of the Min family, came into power. Japan had taken into account this internal reversal in Korea, as well as the international complications which prevented Western powers from involving themselves there at that time, and noted too that China's power was being weakened by invasions. The abrogation of the latter's long-standing dominance over Korea by the Treaty of Kanghwa marks the beginning of the competition between China and Japan for control of the country, a competition which continued until the Sino-Japanese war (1894-1895). This competition now became the major factor affecting the Korean political situation.

The three ports, opened in accordance with the Treaty of Kanghwa, were Pusan (1876), Wŏnsan (1880), South Hamgyŏng Province, and Inch'ŏn (1882), Kyŏnggi Province. Large numbers of Japanese in Kyūshū, China, and Tsushima crossed over into Korea. They flooded Korea with Japanese goods, and their cheap cotton cloth in particular dominated the Korean market. On the other hand, rice and other foodstuffs were exported from Korea to Japan, so that dating from this early period Korea became a supplier of food for Japan. The level of production of goods in Korea remained extremely low, and the country became tied to the Japanese capitalist industrial market, a relationship which became another burden for Korea.

The Émeute of 1882 and the 1884 Incident

The rapid changes which swept over the world in the latter half of the nineteenth century included the Far East, but scarcely affected Korea internally. She was still largely occupied with factional strife, which became increasingly complex and bitter as the factions became involved with the foreign powers competing for the country.

When the warships of the Western powers first appeared in Korean waters, Taewŏn-gun was in control of the country. Although he was a member of the royal family, he had not become king, and had spent his early years in the capital's gay quarters. Then, taking advantage of internal quarrels in the royal palace, he placed his son on the throne (King Kojong; known as Yi T'aewang, 1864-1907), and, as the youthful ruler's father, seized power. He built up his own might by balancing one faction against another in the swirling party politics of the day and took advantage of his position to establish a strong party of his own. He planned the reconstruction of the magnificent Kyŏngbok Palace and the firm reestablishment of a strong bureaucratic state. To accomplish this, he relentlessly suppressed all opponents; he abolished the sŏwŏn, the headquarters of the factions, and confiscated their lands; he persecuted foreign missionaries and Christians who threatened the traditional order. It was he who had turned down the requests of foreign nations to open up Korean ports. In his antiforeignism and in his struggles with foreign powers, he stressed the need to attack and expel the "Western barbarians." The French and American occupations of Kanghwa Island and the rejection of the first Japanese request for trade occurred during the period of the Taewŏn-gun's dominance of the government. However, his forceful control of affairs aroused opposition in all classes. The large expenditures needed for armaments to "expel the barbarians" and the heavy expenses and enormous requisitions of labor and materials involved in reconstructing the Kyŏngbok Palace, all increased the burdens of the peasantry. A wave of hatred and resentment spread through the country. Officials who had been ousted by the Taewŏn-gun, and literati from the *sŏwŏn* whose lands had been confiscated, resisted the government of the Taewŏn-gun. Faced with such opposition, the Taewŏn-gun availed himself of the coming of age of his son King Kojong to retire in 1873.

Even after his retirement, the Taewŏn-gun wielded power through intrigue in the royal palace, but political leadership passed from the hands of his party to that of Queen Min. Persons who had been influential before were replaced, and the Min party filled all important government positions. At the same time, the former policies of the government were changed. At the insistence of the literati, some *sŏwŏn* were restored, and antiforeignism were softened to a policy of conciliation. It was during this period of change in foreign policy, brought about by the political reversal, that the Japanese efforts to open Korea were successful. At this time too a group of observers was sent from Korea to Japan (1881) to plan internal government reforms for Korea based on the reforms in Japan. From the beginning, however, the reform movement of the Min party was not intended to destroy the special rights of officials, nor to bring about a fundamental modernization of Korean society. Its significance lay rather in the fact that it was a means of opposing the policies of the Taewŏn-gun. For in Korea at that time, the social basis for modernization did not exist, nor was there a class of leaders interested in introducing basic changes. Consequently there was little prospect of the reforms persisting, and every prospect of opposition from the Taewŏn-gun party.

The revolt that occurred was not unexpected. It was triggered by dissatisfaction among the soldiers following reforms of the military system. The Min-controlled government had invited Japanese officers to Korea, had bought Japanese arms, and had been training a Japanese-style army. This had entailed the dismissal of many soldiers and officers of the old military forces. These reforms, which threatened their livelihood, were strongly resented by the military men. Tension increased among them until finally, incensed at receiving poor rations and no pay, they rose in arms. They were joined by other malcontents, and an uprising took place. The rebels attacked the residence of the Min family, destroyed the jail, stormed the barracks, killed the Japanese instructors, set fire to the Japanese legation, and entered the royal palace. Queen Min barely escaped with her life, and most leaders of the Min party were killed. This was the so-called "*émeute* of 1882."

The uprising was in essence a protest against the entering of the Japanese into Korea. The influx of Japanese and Japanese goods after the Treaty of Kanghwa and the introduction of Japanese-style reforms had created many problems in Korea. There was no true basis for modernization in Korean society, hence the opposition to the innovations could only take a conservative, even reactionary form. The Taewŏn-gun, the leader of the old conservative party, saw in this the chance he had been looking for to regain political power. Supported by the military, he placed himself at their head and took over the royal palace and control of his son. He replaced the new reform organization of the Min with the old system, dismissed the Min government officials, and attempted to reinstate the former uncompromising antiforeign policy.

Unfortunately for the Taewŏn-gun, Ch'ing China saw in the *émeute* an opportunity to reassert her authority over Korea and immediately took action. In the nineteenth century she had lost to Japan the dominant position in Korea which she had held for two hundred years as the suzerain of that country. During China's struggles against invading Western powers, the onset of the Taiping Rebellion, and other internal and external troubles, Japan had opened Korea and penetrated the country. But after China had carried out the government reforms of the so-called T'ung-chih Restoration period (1862-1874), she began to reassert her political position internally and externally and was ready to regain her lost power in Korea. In the economic sphere, Chinese merchants and commodities entered Korea in competition with Japanese traders and goods; and in the political sphere, in order to undermine the dominant position of Japan, China suggested to Korea that she open her ports to the Western nations. By acting as intermediary between Korea and the Western powers, China tried to reestablish her status as Korea's suzerain.

The *émeute* of 1882 gave China the perfect opportunity to intervene in Korea. The Ch'ing government dispatched an army of five thousand men ostensibly to help the Korean government. However, in suppressing the uprising in Seoul, they managed at the same time to capture the Taewŏn-gun. They sent him to China, took over the control of Korea, and reinstated the Min government which, being entirely dependent on China, abolished all Japanese-style reforms. The Chinese established the "Regulations for Merchants and Trade" with Korea; reasserted the former suzerain-tributary relationship; placed advisors in every department of Korean government and foreign affairs who were either Chinese or foreigners recommended by the Chinese, such as Paul George von Möllendorf and Robert Hall; and put military control in the hands of Yüan Shih-k'ai. In order further to impede Japanese penetration of Korea, China directed Korea to make commercial treaties with foreign nations. Such treaties were made with the United States in 1882, with England and Germany in 1883, with Italy and Russia in 1884, and with France in 1886.

The *émeute* of 1882 was a great blow to Japan. She sent troops to Korea, but the Chinese army already had the Korean political situation in hand, and Japan did not have the strength to oppose it. All she was able to obtain, through the Treaty of Chemulp'o of August 30, 1882, was punishment of those responsible for burning her legation, an indemnity for property destroyed, an apology, permission to have a legation guard, and the opening up of one more port.

In the midst of the international dealings involved in the advance of China into Korea and the withdrawal of Japan, Korea's bureaucracy split into two conflicting groups. The Min party, which had formerly opposed the conservative policies of the Taewŏn-gun, now became the conservative force dependent on China. Most important officials belonged to this group. It was called the *Sadae* (Serve the Great) party. Competing against it and opposed to the *sadae* policies of the Min was the Independence party whose supporters wanted Korea to be associated with Japan and, by learning from Japan's modernization, carry out reforms. The leaders of the Independence party, Kim Okkyun (1851-1893), Pak Yŏnghyo (1861-1939), and others, went to Japan. There they conferred with important persons and officials and planned to modernize Korea with Japanese help. In 1884 they determined to carry out a *coup d'état* with Japanese military backing, and supported directly by the Japanese troops stationed in Seoul. This appeared to be an auspicious moment, for China was then at war with France over Annam, and it was reported in Korea that she was being defeated. Presumably she would not have the strength to come to the aid of Korea. So the *coup* proceeded as planned. The palace was seized, ministers were killed, a new government was formed, and a reform platform proclaimed. Its contents included: policy of increasing national prestige; abolition of the policy of *sadae*; dealing with foreign nations on an equal basis; putting an end to clique despotism; employment of able persons in government service; and development of commerce and industry. In other words, the reform platform aimed at the modernization of Korea. It was an advance over the earlier reform movement of the Min.

Before these reforms could be carried out, however, the Independence party was overthrown. Contrary to expectations, a Chinese army began a counterattack and the Japanese troops retreated. Without them the further existence of the Independence party was hopeless since the movement was planned by only a segment of the bureaucracy and lacked popular support. The members of the party were either killed or fled to Japan. A government supporting the *sadae* policy was reestablished which, having wiped out the Independence party, became more conservative.

Due to this "1884 incident" the position of the Japanese in Korea deteriorated. At the height of the disturbance, the Japanese legation was again burned and Japanese nationals were killed. After the incident, feeling against the Japanese ran higher than ever within the government. In contrast, the influence of China, which controlled the Korean political situation through the Min government, increased. In order to combat this trend, the Japanese proposed that both Chinese and Japanese troops withdraw from Korea and, if in the future troops were dispatched to Korea, each nation would mutually inform the other. This was known as the Li-Itō (Li Hung-chang-Itō Hirobumi) Convention of 1885, also called the Treaty of Tientsin. After what had happened, however, even with the withdrawal of both armies, the position of the Japanese in Korea did not improve.

The Arrival of America and the European Powers in Korea, and Japanese Economic Penetration

Ch'ing China had succeeded in stopping the Japanese penetration of Korea, but in order to do this, the Chinese opened Korea to the Western nations. This move served its primary purpose, but resulted in the threatening of Chinese dominance in Korea. The activity of the Russians caused the most concern. In 1884, just when the Chinese were applying pressure on the Korean government, the Russian envoy Karl Waeber appeared on the scene. By ingratiating himself with von Möllendorf, the advisor to the government on foreign affairs recommended by the Ch'ing, he gained access to the palace. He established friendly relations with the royal family and court ministers and was soon in a position to influence policy. This was disturbing to the Chinese, already threatened by Russia's advance from Siberia. Russia's empire stretched from Europe to Asia, and now she appeared in Korea and was interfering with China's plan to reestablish and strengthen her old suzerain-tributary relationship with the country.

However, any plans Russia may have had for gaining control of Korea were blocked by the arrival of the British on the scene. At that time, Russia and Britain, the two great world empires, were competing with each other throughout the world. Even in Asia relations between them had become strained over the Afghanistan boundary problem. The movement of Russia southward from Siberia clashed with Britain's plans to penetrate into the Far East. Now the appearance of Russian influence in Korea made Britain apprehensive. In order to block Russia, England, in 1885, suddenly occupied Kŏmun Island (Port Hamilton) off the southern coast of Korea. This action took Russia by surprise, for the island was at the entrance of Tsushima Strait, on the principal route of the Russian Far Eastern fleet. Russia, through China and Korea, protested to England and threatened to occupy part of Korea to counter England's move. The Kŏmun Island incident was finally settled and, after two years of negotiations, the English forces were withdrawn. This clash between the two countries undoubtedly served to limit Russia's designs to penetrate Korea and perhaps obtain control of the country.

The power contest served also to give China an opportunity to reassert herself. She acted as an intermediary to resolve the Kŏmun Island incident, and then claimed that this role entitled her to a voice in Korean matters. However, she did not gain exclusive control over Korea, for other powers now freely interfered. Therefore when interests clashed, the Korean government no longer relied solely on the leadership of China, but followed the lead of the Western powers. Hoping to change this situation, the Chinese in 1885 sent back to Korea the Taewŏn-gun who had been interned at Pao-ting-fu in China. They also took control of the Korean customs, changed their Korean foreign-affairs advisors, interfered with the appointment of Korean diplomatic officials, and in other ways put pressure on the Korean government. However, these measures were not as effective as formerly, for now the strength of those in the Korean government who relied on Russia had greatly grown and the influence and control of China was correspondingly weakened.

The United States, Britain, Germany, Italy, France, and other Western nations appeared successively on the scene in Korea between 1882 and 1886. But because of the rivalry between England and Russia, a situation persisted in which no one country could gain predominance over Korea. Under these circumstances Japan, although she had failed politically in Korea, was again able to penetrate the country economically and seek opportunities for renewed political activity.

At that time, Korea's trade was developing rapidly. Imports expanded to eight times their original amount during the five-year period from 1877 to 1881, and in the seven-year period from 1885 to 1891 exports quadrupled. The major commodities in this growing trade were cotton-cloth imports and grain exports, the latter consisting mainly of rice and some soybeans. The chief countries exporting cotton cloth into Korea were China and Japan. A large portion of this cotton cloth was made in England, brought in by China along with cloth made by her own hand-loom cottage industry. On the other hand, the cloth imported from Japan was increasingly factory-made, the product of her modern spinning industry, a development as yet unknown in China. The principal consumer of the grain exports was Japan. With the growth of Japanese capitalism, a need for supplementary food supplies arose, and Korea became the major basic supplier. This relationship between Korea and Japan continued without change to 1945 when

Japan was defeated in the Second World War. Japanese capitalism had entered Korea with the aim of developing the country as a commercial goods market and a source of food supply. This explains why Japan's economic penetration of Korea was stronger than that of China, in spite of Japan's earlier political defeat and withdrawal from the country. The development of Japanese capitalism necessitated a reversal of the political withdrawal and required intensification of the drive for close economic relations. And, too, Japan was looking for an opportunity completely to wipe out her former failure.

The Tonghak Rebellion

In Korea at the end of the nineteenth century, this was the situation: a weak government under the aegis of foreign strength, the old official class still in power, and continuous internal factional strife, the factions allying themselves with competing foreign nations. Under such circumstances, there was little hope for a successful reform from above. This was clearly shown by the *émeute* of 1882 and the 1884 incident. Nor was there any hope of modernization from below. The peasants, who had been living under wretched conditions up to then, began to suffer even more as foreign countries penetrated Korea. In addition to the expenses necessary for the old bureaucratic state system, government expenditures were now increased by new burdens such as the purchase of armaments from abroad, the sending of diplomatic missions overseas, and the payment of indemnities to foreign nations. As modern industry had not yet appeared in Korea, there were no new sources of income and no method of increasing revenues except by raising the exactions on the peasantry. To make matters worse, after Korea was opened up the peasantry, from using a system that was almost barter were suddenly drawn into a commercial economy in which they became exposed to the intimidations of capitalism. Into a society where there had been few stores there suddenly was an influx from abroad of cotton-made products, pots, pans, farming implements, silk, linen, petroleum, dye stuffs, and salt. Cotton-cloth imports were especially large. The Korean farmer, now introduced to foreign goods, had no alternative but to give up his agricultural products in order to obtain this foreign merchandise. The export of these agricultural products became imperative, and they were what Japan, the principal supplier of the foreign goods, desired. In Pusan, Wŏnsan, and other open ports, Japanese-run grain stores were established. The owners of these stores sent representatives into the farming villages to buy grain, and the grain was then shipped to Japan. The rice and soy beans which the poor Korean farmers had grown, now became products to be brought to the Japanese grain markets, and the lives of the Korean peasants became tied in this way to Japanese commercial markets. The process of purchasing the grain was as follows: A loan was made to a farmer before harvest time in return for a promise to turn over a part or all of his harvest. It was a usurious method, whereby the poor farmer's wretched condition was exploited, and he was forced to sell his grain at a very cheap price. This was not fair trading, but it made possible the shipment of an enormous amount of grain to Japan. These exports caused such a severe food crisis in Korea that the government was forced to pass a law in 1889 prohibiting the shipment of grain to foreign countries. Japan, which needed the grain, opposed the law. This created a diplomatic problem between the two countries which continued for several years.

Meanwhile, an alarming new development was occurring – the lands of the peasants were falling into the hands of foreigners. Taking advantage of the farmers' ignorance of modern ownership rights and financial transactions, foreigners living in the ports, especially the Japanese, bought land at outrageously cheap prices or obtained it by making usurious loans. The living conditions of the Koreans grew progressively worse as this sort of foreign penetration of the country increased, so it was not surprising that antiforeign feeling emerged in Korea.

In 1888 rumors were rife of missing babies; it was said that foreigners had bought them and eaten them. A desire for revenge against foreigners swept the country, and reached such a pitch that the Japanese, American, English, German, and French legations forced the Korean government to take steps to suppress this movement. The United States, Russia, and France posted marines in Seoul to protect their nationals. This antiforeign attitude was a natural reaction to the domination of Korea by outside powers and its resultant pressure on the lives of the people. The Korean government, dependent solely on foreign support to maintain itself, strove to put down the antiforeign fever of the masses and tried to mollify the anger of the foreign nations.

The bureaucratic government of Korea was neither able to oppose foreign penetration of the country nor to carry out reforms itself. While trying to maintain its weakened authority, it was caught up in the vortex of foreign power politics and, not having the strength to solve the problems facing the country, could only strive to preserve itself. One group of progressives in the bureaucracy planned reforms for Korea, but as these reforms depended on the support of a foreign nation, the reformers could hardly be expected to oppose foreign penetration. It was among the wretched peasantry, despised by the officials for their ignorance, that opposition to such penetration was developing. This was the genesis of the Tonghak Rebellion, a large uprising comparable to the Taiping Rebellion and Boxer Rebellion in China.

The basis of the Tonghak Rebellion (1894) was the racial and cultural concept of Tonghak, a religion which bound together large numbers of adherents. The movement started from the teachings of Ch'oe Cheu (1824-1864). He was a scion of fallen nobility who had been distressed by the disturbed conditions in Korea, the decline in national strength, the misery of the people, and the flourishing of Christianity. He proposed to unify Confucianism, Buddhism, and Taoism and add the idea of a heavenly father, borrowed from Christianity. Such a religion, he believed, would be the salvation of the country. The words Tonghak, "Eastern Learning," by which the religion was known, were meant to contrast with Sŏhak, "Western Learning," to which Ch'oe attributed the breakdown of old Korean ways and customs. He began to spread his ideas about 1861 and rapidly attracted many followers from the dissatisfied fallen nobility and from the peasants who were discontented with their harsh living conditions and found hope in the new doctrine. The members of the sect were strongly critical of the current situation in Korea. The government consequently considered them heretics and made every effort to suppress the doctrine. Adherents were severely punished, and Ch'oe Cheu was beheaded. Nevertheless, in spite of all the government could do, the number of believers increased. In 1892, several thousands from every province in

Korea gathered in Poŭn County, North Ch'ungch'ŏng Province, and protested to the government against the persecutions of the Tonghak. Their representatives reached Seoul in 1893 and, prostrating themselves before the royal palace, begged for an end to the persecution. This petition stirred the people of Seoul. A rumor spread that Tonghak believers were massing to attack and kill the foreigners in the city, and foreign diplomats began preparing for defense. The government adopted a policy of strict prohibition of Tonghak doctrines and launched a nation-wide persecution against the believers. The Tonghak representatives, having failed in their petition to the throne, returned to Poŭn County. But by this time, about twenty thousand Tonghak supporters from all over Korea had assembled, had organized themselves, and had collected supplies. They built a stone fortress, trained soldiers, chanted Tonghak slogans, and raised a flag on which was written "Drive out the Japanese dwarfs and the Western barbarians, and praise righteousness." They were determined to attack and drive out the Japanese and the Westerners. The weak government, faced with this crisis, was hard put to find a solution. On the one hand, it gathered troops and tried to frighten the Tonghak followers, and, on the other hand, it recognized their sincerity and loyalty to the crown. Recognizing that the Tonghak leaders were demanding the expulsion of the "foreign barbarians" only in order to preserve Korean ways and customs, the government adopted a sympathetic attitude and was able to persuade the Tonghaks to disband as an act of loyalty to the royal house. Nevertheless, both the people and officials in Korea were profoundly shaken by the affair and there was a growing atmosphere of uneasiness.

The Tonghak movement attracted attention in all circles. Internally Korea was affected from the beginning. Externally the foreign powers evinced deep concern over the trend of affairs. A reaction began in every group associated with the Tonghak party. Originally the party had been made up of various divergent groups such as fallen nobility, dissatisfied Confucianists, and peasants, all of whom had different hopes and interests. They did, however, share one common aim in opposing the Japanese and Westerners and desiring to protect Korean customs and beliefs. Their program was extremely conservative and reactionary, and was also imbued with a violent ethnocentrism that sought to oppose by force any foreign penetration of the country. Since the Tonghak party was made up of such diverse interests, there were many paths it could have followed once it began to take political action. At the same time, there were many groups who could utilize it for their own purposes. First, among those closely associated with the Tonghak party were the fallen nobility and dissatisfied Confucianists from which the leaders of the group originally came. They now joined forces with the leader of the anti-Min party, the Taewŏn-gun. The latter had been taken to China at the time of the "*émeute* of 1882" but, after being pardoned, had been returned to Korea and was seeking an opportunity to overthrow the Min. The conservative program of the Tonghak party coincided with these plans of the Taewŏn-gun who imagined that the strength of the Tonghak movement would be useful in overthrowing the government. Secret negotiations were carried out between the Taewŏn-gun and the Tonghak leaders.

A second source of support for the Tonghak came from the Ch'ing ruler. He hoped that the Tonghak would precipitate a crisis of which China could take advantage. The Min government was then relying on Russian support and ignoring

China. If a situation arose which would justify China's intervention in Korea, China might be able in one blow to set up a Korean government which would completely follow China's dictates. Hence her secret encouragement of the Tonghak.

From still a third direction came wishes for Tonghak success. Japan, which the Tonghak aimed to drive out, believed an uprising would, to the contrary, give her a chance to reassert her position in Korea. Japanese partisans secretly joined the Tonghak party and encouraged its activity in the hope that Japan could profit from the ensuing unrest. At the same time, the Japanese government was keeping a careful watch on the position and moves of China.

Although internal and foreign interests were tied up with the Tonghak movement as described, it was the peasants who turned it into a formidable political force. They were the ones who had suffered most from the pressure of foreign nations which had penetrated Korea, as well as from the traditional methods of control. Peasant uprisings were occurring all over Korea at the time of the Tonghak Rebellion, although initially they were not connected with the Tonghak party. Many of these uprisings were suppressed, but, once the Tonghak Rebellion began, the wave of peasant discontent allied itself to the rebellion because of the sympathetic Tonghak religious and political creed. It was by absorbing the peasantry that the Tonghak party became a political force. Actually, the 1894 rebellion grew out of a peasant uprising in Kobu County in North Chŏlla Province. This uprising was a spontaneous outburst against the brutal rule of the chief county magistrate. Once it had occurred, the Tonghak leader, Chŏn Pongjun (1854-1895), put himself at the head of the peasantry, attacked government offices, issued a manifesto to the farmers, and collected "righteous troops" (ŭibyŏng). The manifesto spoke of reforming the bad government, driving out the foreigners, and improving the welfare of the people. These were all aims cherished by the peasantry. They joined the rebellion without misgivings for the movement, preserved strict military discipline, punished looting and acts of depredation, and maintained order. Thus the powerful movement spread over southern Korea. Local government troops were helpless before it, and local government offices one after another fell into Tonghak hands. Troops dispatched by the central government were likewise routed and scattered, and royal exhortations produced no results. The Korean government was in fact too weak to control the situation and, if matters had continued in this way, even Seoul, the seat of the government, would have been in danger.

The Tonghak Rebellion, however, was fated to fail because the Tonghak party lacked a nucleus of dedicated men to lead the peasantry and reverse the conservative trend. The leaders of the rebellion, for the most part, were men who were trying to come into power. There were also opportunists outside the party who used the disturbance to realize their ambitions and were ready to change their loyalties as conditions dictated. Especially significant was the fact that the progressives of that day were attempting to reform Korea with foreign support, and they never thought of uniting with the Tonghak party to try to bring about reform. They expected nothing from the Tonghak party and in no way depended on it.

Thus a situation existed where the defenders of Korean independence were also supporters of an antiforeign policy marked by extreme reactionary conservatism. Modernization was not to be expected from them, nor were they allied with those working toward this end. This fact, not surprising in view of the state of Korean society, undoubtedly contributed to the failure of the Tonghak Rebellion.

The Sino-Japanese War and the Reforms of 1894

The Korean government, unable alone to put down the Tonghak Rebellion, sought Chinese help. This was the event for which China had been waiting. She had been watching the movement closely and secretly encouraging it. Now she seized the opportunity to send troops openly to Korea. But China was not the only nation hoping to profit from the troubled conditions in Korea. Japan, shut out of the political scene there since the *émeute* of 1882 and in need of more markets for her modern industries, was hoping more than ever for a chance to reestablish herself in that country. So when China sent troops to Korea at the request of that government, Japan sent some also. While the Chinese were trying to decide what their position would be toward Japan and how they would subjugate the Tonghak, the Japanese army entered Seoul and by its armed presence, dominated the political scene in Korea.

As soon as foreign intervention occurred in Korea, the Tonghak Rebellion was crushed. When there was no more danger of internal unrest, the Korean government requested the withdrawal of the Chinese and Japanese armies. China, finding it difficult to make either war or peace with the Japanese, proposed a simultaneous withdrawal of troops from Korea. Russia, the United States, Britain, and the other powers, fearing Japan would have sole control over Korea, likewise urged the withdrawal of all troops. However, because of the tension between Russia and Britain at that time, the request of the foreign powers was not backed by military pressure and thus did not intimidate Japan. In view of the international situation, Japan dared not only to establish strong control over Korea, but even to provoke war with China. This stand of the Japanese brought about the outbreak of the Sino-Japanese war in August 1894. It was to be the decisive struggle between recently modernized Japan and the huge old Ch'ing Empire. Japan, which had fostered a policy of militarism and military training since the Meiji Restoration, was able to defeat the Chinese armies quickly and remove all Chinese influence from Korea.

Japan then set about getting rid of the Min government and establishing a pro-Japanese government in Korea. Kim Koengjip and other progressives were placed in office and, with the backing of Japanese power, they embarked on a reform program. The political situation in Korea was complicated, for at the head of the pro-Japanese progressives appeared the Taewŏn-gun. He had long been the leader of the antiforeign conservative groups, and he was among those associated with the Tonghak party which had urged the expulsion of the Japanese from Korea. Consequently one would not have expected any association between the pro-Japanese progressives and the Taewŏn-gun. Nevertheless he became their leader because both the progressives and the Taewŏn-gun were strongly opposed to the Min, and also the progressives were still weak and needed support. Japan, guiding this patchwork government, sponsored a Korean reform program known as the reform of 1894. This reform extended to every field of economic activity, politics, society, and culture, and was an attempt to modernize old Korea all at once. It included, to speak only of its more important features, the following: the equality of common people and *yangban* before the law; the destruction and abolition of registers of public and private slaves; the prohibition of the sale of human beings; the ending of the unfree class status for tanners, actors, station keepers, and members of particular occupations; the recognition of widows' remarriage; the abolition of the custom of commoners standing at attention or making obeisance when government ministers passed by; the abolition of child marriage; the abolition of entire-family responsibility for crimes committed by any individual member; the abolition of punishment by beating; the abolition of arrest and punishment by officials other than proper legal and police officers; the abolition of the old system of examination for office; the establishment of a new law for selecting officials; the recognition of the right of public opinion and discussion; accountability of officials for illegal actions; the abolition of concurrent appointment to official position in both the palace and outside government offices; the introduction of the collection of taxes in metallic currency; the prohibition of extortion within the palace and other government offices; the abolition of distinctions of superiority for civil officials and inferiority for military officials; a program of sending students abroad and of inviting foreign advisors to Korea.

A reform on such a scale was obviously needed in Korea, but difficult to put into effect. The society was so backward that many persons still had slave or unfree status. No internal force to encourage reform had yet developed. Only a strong government could modernize the country, and such strength could not be expected from the progressives. It could only be founded on Japanese support. Actually in spite of what appears at first glance to have been a rapid advance, little progress was accomplished.

While an attempt was being made to carry out the described reforms, the Japanese army drove the Chinese army out of Korea. With Japan's military position thus strengthened, the expectations of the progressive party in Korea rose. There was now little reason to continue the Taewŏn-gun in his powerful position, and he was removed. Pak Yŏnghyo, who had been criminally indicted in the 1884 incident, was now included in the cabinet, and the pro-Japanese and progressive character of the government became more pronounced. In January, 1895, the Korean king proclaimed the *"Fourteen articles of Hongbŏm"*[1] which contained provisions for the following: separation of palace and government expenses; prohibition of the royal family and queen from interfering in the government; clarification of the division of power between all government offices; observation of the regulations concerning tax collection; reforms in the disbursement of revenues and in the system of local government; actual recruitment of soldiers; establishment of a civil and criminal law code; and a system for raising qualified men to office irrespective of background. This proclamation followed the line of the reforms of the previous year and further strengthened them. In particular, it aimed at eliminating the interference of Queen Min and the Taewŏn-gun in the government, as

---

[1]*Hongbŏm* (Chinese pronunciation: *hung-fan*) is the title to a section of the Confucian classic known as the *Shu-ching* (Book of History). This section of the *Shu-ching* deals with the ideal pattern of government.

well as separating Korea from China, and making her dependent on Japan.

The Sino-Japanese war ended in a Japanese victory, and in April, 1895, the Treaty of Shimonoseki was concluded between Japan and China. Japan obtained from China the Liaotung Peninsula, Formosa, the Pescadores, and an indemnity of twenty thousand gold taels, together with a promise that various ports on the Yangtse River would be opened up to her. The Chinese threat to Korea was removed, and Japan was recognized as having a dominant position in both Korea and South Manchuria. Japan's forceful policy had succeeded, and it seemed as if her plan to gain complete control of Korea might now be realized.

The Struggle between Japan and Russia

The joy of the Japanese at their victory in the Sino-Japanese war was dissipated in less than a week after the signing of the Treaty of Shimonoseki because of the so-called Three Power Intervention by Russia, France, and Germany. These powers, especially Russia, had planned to intervene earlier in Korea, immediately before the Sino-Japanese war, but had failed to act. Now, however, that Japan had defeated China and was trying to establish herself firmly in Korea and Manchuria, Russia persuaded Germany and France to join with her in strongly opposing such activities. Faced with such a coalition, Japan had no alternative but to accept bitterly the three-power request and return to China the most prized of the fruits of her victory, the Liaotung Peninsula.

The Three Power Intervention was the spark that set off the so-called "second partition" of the Far East by the powers. China, whose weakness had been exposed by her defeat at the hands of the Japanese, became the object of savage Western aggression. In 1896, on the heels of the Three Power Intervention, Russia obtained in Manchuria the rights to mines and railroads and police power, and in 1897 leased Port Arthur and Ta-lien (Dairen). France obtained special rights and privileges in South China in 1896, and leased Kuang-chou Bay in South China in 1899. Germany obtained special rights and privileges in the Shantung Peninsula and occupied Chiao-chou Bay (also known as Kiaochow Bay) in 1897. In order to counter this three-power advance into China, England leased Weihaiwei and the Chiu-lung (Kowloon) Peninsula in 1898. The United States, in an effort to limit the aggression of the powers, announced the "open-door policy" for China in 1899, but took Hawaii and the Philippines in the Pacific. Finally, Japan too, in order not to be left out by the other powers, obtained from them in 1898 a promise that Fukien Province would not be divided but would be left to her.

This race for special privileges was felt also in Korea. The rights and profits connected with mines and railroads in Korea passed into the hands of foreigners. The contest between the foreign powers to obtain such rights aggravated the political competition between the powers in Korea. This, together with the old factional strife, caused discord in the royal palace. First, when Japan backed down at the time of the Three Power Intervention, the power of the Korean progressive party associated with the Japanese was shaken, and the strength of the Russian-oriented party of Queen Min increased. In order to stage a come-back, the progressive party approached the Japanese minister, General Viscount Miura Gorō and other Japanese, as well as the Taewŏn-gun, and had a group of soldiers surround and enter the royal palace. Queen Min was killed in this disturbance (October, 1895), and the pro-Russian party was swept out of office. Soon afterward, however, the pro-Russian party connived with the Russian minister, Karl Waeber, to seize the king, spirit him out of the royal palace, and move him to the Russian legation. At the same time, pro-Japanese Korean officials were put to death and, overnight, in February 1896, a pro-Russian government was established in Korea. After that, the king resided in the Russian legation for about a year. During this period, Korean politics were completely dominated by Russia.

TABLE 3

CONCESSIONS AND CONCESSIONAIRES IN KOREA, 1896-1900

Year	Rights or privileges granted	Concessionaires
1896	Building of Inch'ŏn-Seoul railroad	American
1896	Exploitation of Kyŏngwŏn and Chongsŏng mines in North Hamgyŏng Province	Russian
1896	Exploitation of gold mines at Unsan in North P'yŏngan Province	American
1896	Building of Seoul-Ŭiju railroad	French
1896	Exploitation of forests in the Yalu River basin and on Ullŭng Island	Russian
1897	Exploitation of Tanghyŏn gold mines in Kŭmsŏng County of Kangwŏn Province	German
1898	Building streetcar lines in Seoul	American
1898	Building the Seoul-Pusan railroad	Japanese
1900	Exploitation of the Ŭnsan gold mines in North P'yŏngan Province	German
1900	Exploitation of the Chiksan gold mine in South Ch'ungch'ŏng Province	Japanese

The Korean government for several years was dominated by either Japan or Russia, and much of the natural resources of Korea fell into foreign hands. To counter these conditions, an independence movement developed in Korea. Sŏ Chaep'il (known in the West as Philip Jaisohn, 1863-1951), Yun Ch'iho (1864-1946), and others who had studied in the United States were the principal leaders of the intellectual group who formed the famous Independence Club. They sought to popularize ideas of liberty, civil rights, and independence, and fought against the sale and transfer of concessions in Korea to foreigners. When the government tried to set up a palace guard of foreign mercenaries in 1898, the Independence Club opposed the plan and finally forced it to be abandoned. Later during the same year, under the auspices of the Independence Club, a large meeting was held of the so-called Manmin Kongdong Hoe (Popular Cooperative Society). Besides members of the club, the meeting included students, city dwellers, coolies, and even government clerks and Confucianists. It attacked the pro-foreign attitude of the government and, at the same time, demanded among other things freedom of speech and public trials for major criminals, and presented a list of these proposals to the king. The government, although recognizing the justice of the proposals, dismissed the government clerks who had participated in the meeting and formed as a counterpoise a government organization known as the Imperial Association. Itinerant merchants and peddlers *(pobusang)* were forced into the Imperial Association. The members of these opposing groups clashed in the streets of Seoul, and the city was thrown into an uproar by the disturbance. Because of such incidents, the Independence Club was suppressed by the government and its activities ceased. The club differed from earlier progressive movements in that it emphasized not only reform, but also freedom and independence. It represented not just a political party or segment of the intelligentsia seeking to gain political power, but had support from every element of society. Its program and activities are a significant indication of the growth of a broadly based Korean popular movement. However, it too failed because foreign influence in Korea was still stronger than internal opposition to it.

Of all foreign countries, Russia was the one most strongly entrenched in Korea. Having built up controlling power in Manchuria, Russia tried to gain control by force of the Korean court, a matter of considerable concern to Japan. The penetration of the latter into the Asiatic mainland had been stopped by the Three Power Intervention but, with continually increasing industrial development after the Sino-Japanese war, Japan's desire for expansion became even more compelling than before and her attention reverted to Korea. Consequently, a clash of interests between Russia and Japan over Korea was nearly inevitable. However, as Japan did not feel confident that she could compete with Russia in actual power, she first compromised and attempted only to establish a power base. In a series of conventions, in 1896, 1897, and 1898, it was agreed that neither nation would interfere in Korea's internal affairs, and Russia promised not to hamper Japanese industrial and commercial activities in that country.

Russia was willing to make this compromise with Japan because she wished Japan to recognize the Russian position in South Manchuria where she was then concentrating her attention. Russia, however, did not intend to turn Korea over to Japan. Therefore, immediately after the Japanese-Russian conventions, Russia occupied whaling stations facing the Sea of Japan, and in 1899 tried to take over

Mokp'o in South Chŏlla Province and Masan in South Kyŏngsang Province as naval bases for her Far Eastern fleet. To oppose this, Japan took control of the three ports of Masan, Kunsan in North Chŏlla Province and Sŏngjin in North Hamgyŏng Province, and in the Masan region bought up property to block the Russians from obtaining land there.

In 1900, while Japan and Russia were struggling against each other in Korea, the popular uprising known as the Boxer Rebellion, directed against foreign penetration, broke out in China. To put down the rebellion, the foreign powers dispatched troops to China, while Russia took advantage of the situation to send a large army into Manchuria. Even after the suppression of the rebellion the army was not withdrawn. Thus Russia was in a position to press down on the Far East from the north, a situation disturbing to Britain, Russia's enemy. At this time, Britain was clashing with the Russians in Afghanistan, and with Russia's ally, France, in China, and was also threatened by the world-wide advance of a newly arisen Germany. In view of this global conflict of interests, Britain chose Japan to become her ally in the Far East. In 1902 the Anglo-Japaneses alliance was concluded.

Japan, which had been unable alone to oppose Russia, now entered the international struggle counting on British support against Russia. Japan's anti-Russian policy became more pronounced. She demanded that the Russian army in Manchuria be withdrawn and that Russia recognize Japan's position in Korea. Russia refused to withdraw her army from Manchuria, and tried in Korea to establish the thirty-ninth parallel as the dividing line between the spheres of influence of the two nations. A clash between Russia and Japan was unavoidable, but now it was no longer simply a Russian-Japanese conflict, but a world-wide conflict of imperialistic interests which took the form of a Russian-Japanese struggle over Korea and Manchuria. The Russo-Japanese war broke out in February 1904 and lasted to 1905. Due to serious internal troubles, Russia, thought to be one of the most powerful nations in the world, was surprisingly defeated by Japan, a newcomer on the world scene.

The Japanese Annexation of Korea

In 1897 the name for Korea, Chosŏn, was changed to Empire of the Great Han (Taehan Cheguk), and the king was called the Kwangmu Emperor of the Great Han. In spite of this flourish, the Korean government was scarcely able to maintain itself in the vortex of foreign conflicts over the country. When Japan defeated Russia, and Japan's controlling position in Korea was confirmed, the *raison d'être* for an independent Korean government disappeared. The trend of Korean political affairs after the Russo-Japanese war was toward establishing as firmly as possible Japan's exclusive domination of the country, the ultimate end of which was annexation.

In January 1904, Russian, American, British, and Italian troops entered Seoul. This was when the clouds of the Russo-Japanese war were threatening and conditions in the country were unstable. Korea, thinking Russia would be victorious, announced its neutrality, but on February 9, Japanese troops landed at Inch'ŏn and immediately entered Seoul. When the tide of war turned in favor of

Japan, Korea became pro-Japanese. Then, on February 23, under Japanese military pressure, Korea began unlimited cooperation with the Japanese army and signed the so-called Japanese-Korean Protocol which included a clause stating that "places and facilities necessary for military operations will be made available." Following this, on May 18, Korea abrogated all her agreements and treaties with Russia. On August 23, she entered into the First Japanese-Korean Convention at which she agreed to use advisors recommended by the Japanese government in the Ministries of Finance and Foreign Affairs, and agreed to consult with the Japanese government over the making of treaties and other important matters concerned with foreign countries. When it became clear that Japan was to be decisively victorious, a new Anglo-Japanese Alliance was concluded. This took place in August 1905. A month later, after a Japanese victory, a peace treaty between Japan and Russia was signed at Portsmouth, New Hampshire. Now Japan's predominant political, economic, and military position in Korea was internationally recognized. In November of the same year, Japan advanced her position in Korea one step further: All matters relating to foreign affairs in Korea were to be directed and supervised by the Japanese Foreign Office in Tokyo; Korea was not to make any agreements or treaties with foreign countries unless Japan acted as intermediary; and a Resident General representing the Japanese government was to reside in Korea and control the foreign affairs of the country. This was known as the Second Japanese-Korean Convention. According to its provisions, a Residency General was established in Seoul on February 1, 1906, and Itō Hirobumi was appointed the first Resident General. He was empowered to give direct orders to Korean government offices on matters important to the Japanese. His control was not limited to foreign affairs alone, but extended to Korean internal affairs also. Then, since Japan had acquired control of Korean foreign relations, all diplomatic agencies of foreign countries in Korea were abolished. Accordingly, the British, American, Chinese, German, French, and Belgian ministers left Seoul in March 1906.

Now, in fact, Korea had become part of Japan. Within the country, however, there was tremendous opposition to this state of affairs, and this feeling was strong also in the royal palace. In June 1907, a secret envoy of the Korean emperor appeared at The Hague in Holland at the opening of the Meeting for International Peace. He disclosed the sufferings of Korea under the Japanese and sought international pressure to rid Korea of Japanese oppression. But his plea was unsuccessful. It produced, in fact, the opposite result. Japan took it as a pretext to exert more pressure than ever on Korea. The emperor was forced to abdicate, the army was disbanded in July 1907, and in December of the same year the Revised Japanese-Korean Convention was established whereby internal reforms, codifying laws, appointment and dismissal of high officials, and important administrative acts all required the approval of the Resident General. In July 1909, the administration of justice and prisons was placed in Japanese hands, as were also police duties in June 1910. The Japanese military police (kempei) and the Japanese police (keisatsu) now openly displayed their power.

Although Korea was now in effect a Japanese protectorate, Japan was still not satisfied. She considered even nominal independence might be dangerous and so, to make sure that Korea would be dominated completely, she determined to make that country an integral part of her empire. In August 1910, the treaty annexing Korea to Japan was concluded, and Korea came under absolute Japanese control. For centuries Korea had observed the ritual of "serving the great" (*sadae*) toward Chinese dynasties, but during that time she had still been able to determine her own destiny. Even in the midst of foreign incursions, she had maintained her independence at least in name. But now she was actually deprived of her sovereignty. Both in name and in fact, she became part of the Japanese empire. From 1910 until August 1945 Korea did not exist as a nation.

While these changes were taking place, Korea was also suffering from economic and social aggression. The early intrusions of the Japanese were greatly accelerated after the beginning of the Russo-Japanese war under strong pressure from Japan. Reform of the Korean monetary system was the responsibility of the Daiichi Bank, control of the railroads and communication facilities was in the hands of the Japanese government, and money necessary to set up the Korean Bank and local financial associations was loaned by the Japanese government. With help from the same source, the Oriental Development Company (Tōyō Takushoku Kaisha) was established to exploit agriculture. Under the direction of the Resident General, experimental stations were organized for agriculture, forestry, fisheries, mining, commerce, and industry, and an administration under a modern legal system was established. The school system was modernized and the old *sŏdang* type education abolished. Family and population registers, which formerly had been inaccurate, were now carefully checked by the military and civil police; the number of households was found to be 2,742,263, and the population 12,934,282. The land survey was especially significant. Under the old system of land relationship, there were no owners in the modern sense. Now, overnight, ownership rights were assigned, and, with the idea of dividing the land according to modern legal practice, a large-scale land survey was begun in 1910. This extensive undertaking continued until after Korea was annexed, and it resulted in the loss to Korean farmers of a very large amount of land. In this and other ways the modernization of Korea by the Japanese protectorate government brought additional suffering and new hardships to the population. The rapid changes produced in Korean society, as is always the case with colonies, benefited the controlling colonial power and ignored the local victims of the modernization.

The forceful military, political, economic, and social take-over of the country by the Japanese naturally aroused in the Koreans considerable opposition and disquiet. The reason Japan annexed Korea and refused even to recognize her as nominally independent lay in the militaristic character of Japanese capitalism. At the same time the Japanese government felt that even a nominal independence was a constant threat and would continue to be one until annexation eliminated all resistance.

From the beginning some Koreans, believing that their best hope lay in the power of the Japanese, organized movements allied to that power and dependent on it. When Itō Hirobumi was killed by a Korean in 1909 at the railway station in Ha-erh-pin (Harbin), Manchuria, the Japanese took the assassination as a pretext to extend by force their control over Korea. At this time Song Pyŏngnyak, Yi Yonggu, and other Koreans formed a society called the Ilchinhoe. It gained more than a million members who upheld the idea that Korea could best avoid being considered a nation of underdeveloped people by proclaiming her reliance on the benevolence of the Japanese emperor. This society was very active in hastening the annexation of Korea. Among the political figures of the day were many who allied themselves with Japan in the hope of thereby improving their positions. It is also true that they drew into their movement a large number of farmers who were politically unaware. The Japanese directed the activities of this group and tried to help it broaden its power. Most Koreans, however, were opposed to annexation from the start and were unhappy over Japanese domination of the country. The strong opposition of the Korean court to the Japanese is clearly revealed by the emperor's sending of the secret envoy to The Hague in 1907. It is significant too that D. W. Stevens, a Japanese-appointed American advisor on foreign affairs attached to the Korean government, while on leave from Korea, was killed by Koreans in San Francisco in 1908; Itō Hirobumi was assassinated at Harbin in October of the next year; and Prime Minister Yi Wanyong, chief pro-Japanese Korean, was stabbed in December. All these were expressions of the anti-Japanese feelings of the Koreans.

The group who felt the deepest antagonism to Japan were the old class of officials and the *yangban*. They included pro-Russian and pro-American officials who had lost power as a result of the domination of the country by Japan; persons who had lost their privileged positions in the earlier abortive Japanese reforms; and individuals who, proud of their authority as officials, did not relish humbling themselves before the Japanese. There were many such persons among the royal family and high bureaucracy. Although they often had diverse objects in mind, they all stood by the Yi royal family and shared the common aim of opposing the Japanese in order to preserve an independent Korea. Some of them at the time of the annexation committed suicide, others planned the assassination of Japanese or pro-Japanese Koreans, and still others assisted the anti-Japanese so-called "righteous troops" *(ŭibyŏng)* and anti-Japanese intellectuals.

A second important group of opponents to the Japanese were the intellectuals influenced by the old Independence Club. They included the Great Han Self-strengthening Association (Taehan Chagang Hoe), the Friends of the West Study Society (Sŏu Hakhoe), the North Hamgyŏng Province Encouragement of Learning Society (Hambuk Hŭnghak Hoe), the Youth Society (Ch'ŏngnyŏn Hoe), and similar organizations. These published newspapers such as the *Cheguk sinmun* and the *Hwangsŏng sinmun,* opposed the *Ilchinhoe,* spread anti-Japanese propaganda, and attacked the government. Koreans in the United States, Hawaii, and Vladivostok also published newspapers stressing the same ideas as the intellectuals in Korea. Other publications in the capital which criticized Japan and attacked her policies in Korea were the *Korean Daily News,* published by an Englishman, Ernest Thomas Bethell; the *Taehan maeil sinmun,* also published by Bethell, in mixed Chinese and *ŏnmun*; and the *Corean Review,* published by an American, Homer Hulbert.

The unemployed soldiery composed a third group who harbored strong anti-Japanese feelings. Previously, the mass discharge of soldiers had provoked the *émeute* of 1882, but the incident had been limited to the city of Seoul. In contrast to that, the present movement was nation-wide. When in 1907, under pressure from the Resident General, the Korean army was disbanded, two divisions of the Seoul city guards rose in rebellion and exchanged fire with the Japanese army. Following this, the Kanghwa detachment of the Suwŏn area defense unit fled, taking its arms with it. As the rebellion spread, troops that had already been disbanded rose up throughout the country. With the exception of North Hamg-yŏng, North P'yŏngan, and South Kyŏngsang provinces, the uprising was nation-wide, and in Kyŏnggi, Kangwŏn, and Ch'ungch'ŏng provinces, it was especially vigorous. The "righteous troops" partisans were active until after the annexation.

The rebellion could not have spread to such an extent had it not been associated with the people of the countryside. Nevertheless, while this was a large-scale opposition movement, its leaders were officials and *yangban* who cherished their former authority, and its main strength came from the unemployed soldiery. Consequently spontaneous peasant activity in its behalf was weak and, besides, it had no connection with the intellectual group. For these reasons, the "righteous army" movement was directed mainly toward restoring the former dynasty, and inevitably took the form of a conservative, antiforeign movement.

Each of the movements described threatened Japanese control of Korea to some extent and so contributed to the Japanese decision to annex the country. Actually, in the face of the strong Japanese military strength such movements had little chance of success, and their ultimate and successive suppression was inevitable. Yet the hopes and activities of the Koreans for independence resolutely continued. What is more, in spite of Japanese repression, a truly strong Korean independence movement developed.

VII

Korea Under Japanese Rule

Military Administration

When Japan annexed Korea she created the position of Korean Governor General in whose hands rested the full control of the country. The Governor General was personally appointed by the emperor, and only generals and admirals were eligible for the position. He was directly responsible to the emperor and had absolute authority to control Korean military and civil affairs. The army minister, General Terauchi Masatake, was appointed first Governor General, and it was he who put into effect the so-called "military administration." He united the regular police and the military police *(kempei)*; made the director of the military police the chief of police affairs; and appointed heads of the military police as chiefs of police in every province, putting, in this way, security entirely in the hands of the military police. This arrangement, along with the decree that only a general or admiral could serve as Governor General, was characteristic of the government of Korea. Under the military administration, Korean mutual aid societies, political associations, even meetings of any large groups of people outside their homes, were forbidden. The publication of newspapers in the Korean language was prohibited. There was no method by which Koreans might express themselves politically. Educators and nonmilitary officials had to wear Japanese-style uniforms, and to carry swords. It was by force alone that Korea was to be subjugated, and military government, the roots of which were strong in Japan, displayed itself with surprising frankness in Korea. The regime continued uninterrupted until it aroused the nation-wide opposition of Koreans as a result of the incident of March 1, 1919, and even after that, though changed in form, it continued as the basic policy for the governing of Korea.

It was because Japan anticipated Korean opposition to her rule that she installed the military government as the most effective means of suppressing it. During this administration, the Japanese carried out many basic projects in preparation for a more complete exploitation of the country. All these measures were necessary to give Japan adequate control over Korea as a colony, but they were deeply upsetting to Korean society and speeded up the disintegration of the old social structure. Basic construction projects were begun for roads, railways, harbors, water transport and communications, and new currency and monetary systems developed. The old system of weights and measures was replaced by Japanese standards.

The land survey was the most ambitious and important task attempted by the Japanese. It was begun immediately after the annexation and was not completed till nine years later, in 1919, at a cost of twenty million yen. By the survey, modern land-ownership rights were established for the first time in Korea. Previously, vast lands had simply been attached to the royal house, to palaces, to government offices, to *sŏwŏn*, and to *yangban* families. In general, the official class had the controlling power over these lands, but did not actually administer them. This was left in the hands of land agents known as *saŭm*. The officials merely collected a revenue from the harvests. There were innumerable *saŭm* between the peasant and the official, each able to exploit his position as middleman. Thus it was not always clear who held the authority to tax. Those who tilled the soil, and whose families in many cases had tilled it for generations, had no claim to the land. They were either slaves or common people without rights. They did not own the land on which they worked, but neither was it clear who owned it. The concept of land ownership simply had not developed. There were no adequate documents or records to which to refer for a title, and no clear boundaries between different areas. The units of measurement were of every sort. In some cases land was owned communally by villages and whole families. All this presented a problem for the Japanese even before annexation. They could easily take the land from the Koreans by unscrupulous methods, but there was no possibility of establishing ownership, and this made unrestricted buying and selling of land extremely difficult. In 1906 orders were issued requiring that all ownership of land and buildings be proved and registered, but this did not produce adequate results. It was vitally important for Japanese capitalism, if it were to control Korea, that there should be firm ownership of land and free disposition of it. To this end, the detailed and exhaustive land survey was undertaken. The question remained as to what basis of land ownership should be recognized. It was solved by the requirement that owners of land claim their rights within a certain time limit. If they failed to do so, their land was placed in trust with palaces and government offices. The land which peasants tilled became government domain, and communal lands of villages and families were transferred into the hands of influential individuals or became government land. Many managed cleverly to obtain lands to which they were not legally entitled. The amount of wooded and arable land which fell to the government was enormous, and some of the *yangban* class became big landholders. The peasantry, on the other hand, lost whatever might have been considered their traditional land rights. The land survey established modern ownership rights by force, and the Japanese were guaranteed title to their property, but most peasants were deprived of the basis of their livelihood. Those who lost their wooded or arable land either established a new tenant relationship with the landowners, or were forced to desert their villages and could only wander about unemployed. The land which slipped out of the hands of the peasants was usually collected by the government, and part of it was sold cheaply to the Oriental Development Company, to other Japanese land companies, and to Japanese immigrants. In this way, large Japanese agricultural estates grew up under state protection.

Although now land in Korea had become a commercial commodity and the modern concept of ownership had been established, the production relationships did not change. The old tenancy system of a slavelike peasantry and overseers equivalent to officials, now reappeared within the new association of tenant and owner. The only change was that now it was more profitable and convenient for the new landowners to collect their high rents in the form of finished products from the tenants rather than in rice or cloth as in the past.

A huge army of indigent persons grew up in Korea, for their land was gone and there was no modern industry to absorb them. At this point, Japan had neither time nor money to develop an industry in Korea because Japan had its hands full developing her own industry which experienced a phenomenal growth during the First World War supplying the allies with war goods. She was importing agricultural products, especially foodstuffs from Korea, and exporting industrial products to Korea. Her complete control of Korea's economy through trade, after annexation, made it possible for her to promote more forcefully in that country a typical colonial economy.

The March First Movement and the Change in Administration Policy

Only a few months after the land survey was completed a serious disturbance took place in Korea. This was the March First movement, significant in the history of the Japanese administration of Korea and in the history of the development of the Korean nationalist movement. It is also sometimes known as the *Manse* (10,000 years, i.e. Long live Korea) incident. After the Japanese annexation, Korea's society rapidly disintegrated. The Japanese land survey, other reforms, and the importation of Japanese goods into what had previously been a barter economy, caused many farmers to go into debt and lose their land, and in some cases even brought about the ruin of members of the *yangban* class. New economic opportunities sufficient to absorb these impoverished persons were not available. Farmers who had been badly off in the past became desperate, and crowds of wretched people without means of livelihood appeared in farming villages. The number of those who abandoned their homes and wandered about unemployed increased. They went into the mountains and practiced fire-field agriculture or, in many cases, drifted off to Manchuria, Siberia, and to the United States, China, and Japan.

Opposition to the Japanese rule burned fiercely among the Koreans in spite of the fact that manifestations were severely suppressed under the Japanese military administration. Just at that time, the First World War ended and revolutions occurred in Russia and other countries. The doctrine of national self-determination, proclaimed by President Wilson of the United States, spread among the oppressed peoples throughout the world. The doctrine appealed especially to the Korean people who had lost their fatherland. The independence movement first developed among Koreans living abroad and gradually extended to the masses in Korea itself. In January 1919, the former ruler of Korea, Yi T'ae-wang (Kojong) died, and it was rumored that a Japanese physician had poisoned him. The death of Yi T'aewang, a symbol of the former Yi Dynasty in Korea, galvanized the independence movement into action. The first day of March, 1919, two days before his funeral, was chosen as the day for the public announcement of an independence proclamation. Landowners, capitalists, religious representatives, intellectuals, well-known men from every walk of life signed the proclamation. It stated that Korea, through the kind help of the powerful nations of the world, hoped to gain independence. The proclamation did not call for a violent struggle. In fact, the movement had recourse to only two methods in its efforts to achieve independence, namely to make petitions to foreign powers and to shout in the street "Long live the independence of Korea." There were no plans for an armed uprising. The leaders of the independence movement believed that through the good will of foreign nations alone independence could be gained. On March 1, the leaders advised the Japanese authorities by telephone that the movement was about to begin and asked them to deal with the matter calmly. The leaders were quickly arrested, but the independence proclamation was announced in Seoul and other cities, and demonstrators marched shouting *manse* (a cheer, pronounced *banzai* in Japanese). The Japanese military police used gunfire against the demonstrators and called even the army and navy for help. From the Japanese point of view, the fact that the Koreans even shouted for independence was considered insubordination, and the use of large mass parades was adjudged the height of rebelliousness. Vicious fighting broke out between the Koreans and the Japanese in the cities, and soon in the country also, to which the movement rapidly spread. Throughout the nation people joined the movement and took part in the mass parades – old men, young men, women, and children of all classes. In March and April, when the movement was at its height, it is estimated that about 500,000 people actively joined in the demonstrations, and the members of the movement numbered over a million. All over Korea resounded the cry: "Long live independence." There were disturbances at 618 places and a total of 848 such instances altogether. Forty-seven township offices, three military police posts, and twenty-eight regular police stations were damaged, as well as seventy-one post offices, court houses, customs houses, schools, and other public buildings. The number of dead and wounded were: 166 Japanese officials and military police; 29 Japanese civilians; and 1,962 Korean rioters. Held for investigation were 19,525 persons, including 471 women, and 10,441 persons, including 186 women, were prosecuted. The independence movement was not limited to Korea, but developed also in Harbin and Chien-tao (Manchuria), in Hawaii, and in any place where a Korean colony existed. In Chien-tao, Manchuria, in particular, it was strong; there, Koreans attacked the Japanese consulate.

But even this surprisingly large independence movement was suppressed and ended in failure. The foreign support on which the leaders had counted did not materialize. The "calm meeting" with the Japanese had been out of the question. Shouts of *manse* were no match for Japan's military power. In spite of the popular nation-wide support for the movement, it had neither strong native capitalist nor worker backing, since both groups were undeveloped. It was only an expression of the general dissatisfaction of the Koreans with Japanese rule and had no centrally organized body to sustain it. The drive for independence continued, nevertheless, but gradually ceased to be a vigorous popular movement. Later the exiled leaders assembled in Shanghai and elected Yi Sŭngman (Syngman

Rhee) (1875-1965) president of the Provisional Government of the Republic of Korea *(Taehan Minguk Imsi Chŏngbu)*. They gave verbal support to the movement for independence within Korea, but it became a movement of only a group of politicians. The "Korean Independence" slogan no longer could arouse the people. They recognized that it was unrealistic and unrelated to the daily economic problems of the country. The foreign powers had not come to their aid as expected, and the Koreans relapsed into an attitude of bitterness and despair. However, from among them a new independence movement with a different basis began to emerge.

The March First movement failed, but it had engendered enormous nationistic feeling in Korea and had inspired the people to more and braver action than could have been expected by its leaders. It served to awaken the Japanese to the enormous force which was threatening them and was being held in check only by their military might. Though the movement was crushed this time, the Japanese realized that in the long run their military administration would be unequal to the task. Therefore the Japanese changed their policy. They replaced the Governor General and adopted a "cultural rule policy." At first this was rather limited in scope, but the fact that it was established at all was due to the force of the March First movement.

Admiral Saitō Makoto was called out of retirement to become Governor General, and the rule that only an active army or navy officer could fill this office was abolished in principle, but in practice the office was confined to active or retired officers. The military police were replaced by regular police, and government officials and teachers were no longer required to wear uniforms and carry swords. Within certain limits, the expression of opinion by Koreans was allowed, and publication of newspapers in Korean such as the *Chosŏn ilbo* and the *Tonga ilbo* was permitted. Also, certain influential Koreans were allowed to take part in local and national politics and, although this was on an extremely circumscribed scale, it did provide Koreans with an avenue for political expression.

The change from a policy of military rule to cultural rule occurred at a time when Japan needed Korea economically. For some time, Korea had been a basic source of Japan's food supplies, but the rapid development of Japanese capitalism during the First World War caused a serious food crisis in Japan, especially in 1918 and 1919 when the price of food skyrocketed. In 1918 there were rice riots throughout Japan, and the importance of Korea increased. Now it was no longer enough to transport Korean-grown rice to Japan; there was need for a positive plan to increase rice production in Korea to meet Japan's food deficit.

The first plan for increasing rice production covered the fifteen-year period from 1920-1935; it required the expenditure of 168,000,000 yen and the improvement of 420,000 *chŏngbo*[1] of land. It was an attempt on a large scale to increase rice production by 9,200,000 *sŏk*. In 1925 the plan was changed to call for an investment of 325,000,000 yen and an increase of rice production of 8,160,000 *sŏk* in the period from 1926 through 1938. Although these results were not achieved as planned, Korea became, nevertheless, Japan's key food-supplying area. The amount of rice shipped to Japan went up enormously. This increase

---

[1] A *chŏngbo* is a Japanese land measure *(chōbu)* equal to 2.45 acres.

benefited Japan but was of little benefit to Korea. In fact, in Korea, in spite of a growing population, consumption of rice declined yearly, and there were serious food shortages which were made up by the importation from Manchuria of various inferior types of grain such as millet. In 1912, the imports of Manchurian millet were a mere 15,000 sŏk, but in 1930 they had reached 1,720,000 sŏk. In order to ship rice to Japan, Koreans had to cut down on their rice consumption and subsist on millet.

TABLE 4
KOREAN RICE PRODUCTION AND RICE EXPORT
(IN SŎK)

Year	Rice production	Export
1912	11,600,000	500,000
1915	14,100,000	2,300,000
1918	13,700,000	2,200,000
1924	15,200,000	4,600,000
1930	13,700,000	5,400,000
1931	19,200,000	8,400,000
1932	15,900,000	7,600,000
1933	16,300,000	8,700,000

Putting into operation this plan for increasing rice production resulted in a serious change in Korea's economy. Rice became the principal commodity to be supplied to Japan, and a single-crop agriculture was established. Korean commercial and credit operations, as well as transportation and other related activities, were organized around rice production, and industry was centered in the field of rice-polishing and the production of rice wine. The entire self-sufficient Korean economy of the country areas disintegrated. Korea now had a colonial economy, tied exclusively to Japan.

Such an economy was inevitably sensitive to changes in conditions outside the country. In 1929 and 1930, a world-wide agricultural panic occurred. Japan, caught in the panic, now considered the growth of Korean agriculture and the importation of Korean grain dangerous to herself in that it aggravated the depression in Japan. She placed a limitation on Korean rice imports, and the whole program of increasing the production in Korea became a critical issue. Finally, Japan abandoned the rice-production program altogether in 1934. This was a severe blow to Korea which had shifted to a single-crop economy. Since the program had been instituted originally only for the benefit of Japanese capital, such an outcome could not be wholly unexpected.

In the process of increasing rice production, great strides forward had been made in the technical aspects of Korean agriculture. Seed quality was improved, land was developed, planting techniques had advanced, and progress was made in the use of agricultural equipment. Enormous agricultural estates, using large-scale water control and irrigation techniques, also had come into being. But still the production of rice was carried out as before on the basis of the old tenancy system with high-rate tenancy payments, payments in kind in white milled rice, and the fixing, control, and rebate of assessments under the *saŭm* system. The tenancy payments thus obtained became the major source of the rice supplied to Japan, and even the rice remaining in the tenants' hands was exchanged for Manchurian millet and sent to Japan. Japan demanded more rice than even the increased production made available and more was supplied her than permitted any adequate meeting of local need. This caused the failure of many farmers and their miserable standard of living. In the process of increasing rice production, tenancy of the old tenant-landlord relationship type increased considerably. The following table shows the decline in the number of owners and part-owners tilling their own land, and the extraordinary increase in the number of tenants. One can deduce from it that filling the stomach of the prewar Japanese with white rice was accomplished only at the price of victimizing the Korean farmer.

TABLE 5
RELATION OF LAND OWNERSHIP TO TENANCY, 1919-1930
(IN PERCENT)

Year	Nonfarming landlords	Farmer- owners	Owner- tenants	Tenants	Fire-field agriculturalists
1919	3.4	19.7	39.3	37.6	0
1924	3.8	19.5	34.5	42.2	0
1928	3.7	18.3	31.9	44.9	1.2
1930	3.6	17.6	31.0	46.5	1.3

The Manchurian Incident and the Advance of Korean Industrialization

During the period of increased rice production, the mining industry in Korea was gradually developing. At the time of the First World War, Japan had been busy producing goods to fill the orders of the Allies and had no time to establish industries in Korea. After the end of the war and the wartime prosperity, however, the value of Korea as a profitable market for investments became apparent. At the request of Japanese capitalists, the restrictive Korean corporation laws were abolished in 1920, the policy for setting up corporations changed from the former one of regulation to "free enterprise" and to complete liberty granted in establishing companies. In the same year, the system of tariffs and custom duties was revised, and the customs regulations of Japan were made applicable to Korea. The boundaries within which Japanese tariffs were in effect now included the area from the Straits of Korea to the Yalu River. Japanese capitalists and commercial manufacturers in Korea came to have a much freer hand than ever before, and from this time on Japanese capital actively penetrated the country and Japanese companies were set up in many places. In the early 1920's, however, few industries were established that required large capital investments. On the whole, investment was in small-scale commercial activities, food-processing industries, land or agriculture. The only significant exception was that the basis was laid for the generation of hydroelectric power in northern Korea. Formerly the generating of hydroelectric power in Korea was regarded as unpromising because of the low rainfall and high percentage of bare mountains, but, following an investigation which lasted from 1922 to 1926, it became clear that northern Korea held a huge potential for electricity, if the channel-diversion method for hydroelectric generation were used. In 1926, the Korean Hydroelectric Company (Chōsen Suiden Kabushiki Kaisha) run by Noguchi Jun (1873-1944) and his Japan Nitrogen Corporation, was set up to start on generation of electric power on the Pujŏn River system, a headwater tributary of the Yalu River in north Korea, and in 1927 the Korean Nitrogen Fertilizer Company (Chōsen Chisso Hiryō Kabushiki Kaisha) was formed to use the electricity generated by the Korean Hydroelectric Company. The chemical industries established on the basis of this electrical power were on a large scale not only for Korea, but also for Japan, and, due to them, it was proved that the establishment of heavy industry in Korea was technically feasible.

From 1929 on, Japanese capitalism was caught up in the world depression and, if Japan were to overcome her economic difficulties, it was necessary for her to develop an investment market which would be capable of producing high profits. The value of Korea became apparent to Japanese capital now because of its plentiful supply of electricity and its advantageous labor market. Labor in Korea worked for long hours at low wages.

This movement of capital to Korea was speeded up by the Manchurian "incident" of 1931 and the establishment of the Japanese puppet state of Man-chou-kuo. The incident served as a pretext for establishing a garrison state in Japan, heightened the value of Korea's strategic raw materials, and led to the continued development of industry and mining in Korea. Besides, with the rapid rise in the value of gold, after Japan and other nations went off the gold standard, an unprecedented gold rush occurred in Korea. Now too, Japanese capital, which found its activities paralyzed by the rigid economic controls in Japan and Manchuria, discovered a relatively unfettered market in Korea and proceeded to move into it.

At this time, the Korean one-crop economy, which had developed because of the program for increasing rice production, was suffering severely from the impact of the world agricultural panic. In order to improve the situation, a movement for reviving agricultural villages was pushed. However, because agricultural conditions in this period were so hopeless, it was considered more promising to utilize Japanese capital to foster the growth of Korean industry. Under the so-called liberalization policies of General Ugaki Issei, the Governor General, various inducements, much criticized at the time, were given to attract Japanese capital to Korea. Encouraged in this way, Korean industry grew astonishingly within a period of a few years. This change is evident in the following breakdown of the comparative value of Korean production from 1925 to 1936, calculated in yen.

A HISTORY OF KOREA

TABLE 6
GROWTH OF KOREAN INDUSTRY, 1925-1936

Product	1925		1931		1936	
	Yen	Percent	Yen	Percent	Yen	Percent
Agricultural	1,213,510,000	72.7	702,855,000	63.1	1,208,911,000	51.8
Forestry	53,486,000	3.2	59,413,000	5.3	118,064,000	5.1
Fisheries	85,825,000	5.1	77,562,000	6.9	164,003,000	7.0
Mining	20,876,000	1.3	21,741,000	2.0	110,429,000	4.8
Industrial	295,204,000	17.7	252,924,000	22.7	730,806,000	31.3
TOTAL	1,668,901,000	100.0	1,114,495,000	100.0	2,332,213,000	100.0

The next table indicates the changing relative importance of different industrial activities in Korea from 1930 to 1936, showing in particular the development of the chemical industry. (See Table 7.)

These various industries grew up in Kyŏnggi Province, in South Chŏlla Province, in North and South Kyŏngsang provinces, in Hwanghae Province, in South P'yŏngan Province, and in North and South Hamgyŏng provinces. In contrast to southern Korea where light industry predominated, heavy industry was concentrated in northern Korea. The chemical industry in Hamgyŏng Province was especially outstanding. Hitherto this area had been known as "outer Korea," an unopened section of the country, but now, due to the plentiful electric power there, it became the largest center of industry in northern Korea. The progress of the chemical industry which centered in the cities of Hŭngnam and Wŏnsan, in South Hamgyŏng Province, was typical of the advance of all Korean industry. Cities like Hŭngnam which had earlier been villages where only a few fishermen and their families lived, suddenly were transformed into large industrial centers with populations in the tens of thousands. The industrialization of northern Korea radically changed the Korean economic picture. With southern Korea concentrating on rice production and light industry, the economic significance of heavy industry in northern Korea was very great, and Korea became divided into two major industrial areas.

But northern Korea was now important not only economically, but also had come to have great strategic value. From the beginning, Korea had played a significant role in relation to Japan's Asiatic continental policies, and the most important continental land route had gone through Seoul to An-tung and Mukden (Feng-t'ien), the so-called An-feng railroad. After the Manchurian incident and the establishment of Man-chou-kuo, Japanese continental policy, especially toward the Soviet Union, became still more aggressive. Now besides the An-feng railroad, it was essential to open up a route in the north connecting the sea of Japan, northern Korea, and Manchuria. Together with the development of a railroad network in eastern Manchuria, the building of harbors and railroads in North and

TABLE 7
CHANGE IN CHARACTER OF KOREAN INDUSTRY, 1930-1936

Industry	1930				1936			
	Production Value (Yen)	Percent	Number of Workers	Percent	Production Value (Yen)	Percent	Number of Workers	Percent
Spinning	33,674,000	12.8	19,011	22.7	90,378,000	12.7	33,830	22.8
Iron and steel	15,263,000	5.8	4,541	5.4	29,365,000	4.0	6,787	4.6
Machine tools	3,328,000	1.3	2,854	3.4	7,398,000	1.0	7,939	5.3
Ceramics	8,348,000	3.2	5,366	6.4	19,032,000	2.7	8,269	5.6
Lumber and construction	7,037,000	2.7	2,629	3.1	19,230,000	2.7	4,906	3.3
Chemical	24,676,000	9.4	4,720	17.5	162,462,000	22.9	41,972	28.2
Printing	8,184,000	3.1	4,146	4.9	12,426,000	1.8	6,273	4.2
Food processing	142,054,000	57.8	27,055	32.3	320,580,000	45.2	32,617	21.9
Gas	6,432,000	2.4	525	0.6	39,988,000	5.6	812	0.5
Others	4,068,000	1.5	3,052	3.7	10,002,000	1.4	5,394	3.6
TOTAL	253,064,000	100.0	73,899	100.0	709,861,000	100.0	148,799	100.0

South Hamgyŏng provinces was speeded up. The so-called "argument for northern Korean routes" was discussed, and was considered to have strategic merit.

During this period, the incident of February 26, 1936, occurred in Japan. In an uprising in Tokyo, fanatical army officers assassinated a number of Japan's more moderate leaders. Following this the military atmosphere in Japan became more pronounced, and strategic war industries grew rapidly in Manchuria. Japan's demands on the Korean economy also increased, and in March 1937 she put into effect the Heavy Industry Control Law. The rapidly developing state of national emergency in Japan and Manchuria spread to Korea through the mandatory application of this law, and the expansion of Korean industry was spurred on under control laws which applied equally to Japan and Korea. But this industrialization of Korea did not bring about the development of Korean-owned industry, for nearly all large industries were Japanese enterprises, established for the most part with the capital of the big *zaibatsu* (cartels) such as the Mitsui, Sumitomo, Noguchi, and Mitsubishi. It was only through the investment of such monopolistic capital that Korea could be industrialized and turned into a military supply base.

The China Incident, the Pacific War, and the Transformation of Korea into a Military Supply Base

The China Incident, really an undeclared war between China and Japan, occurred in July 1937, and after this Japanese demands on Korea increased. The reintegration of the Korean economy, begun as a result of the Manchurian Incident, was now pushed a step further. The following table presents a percentage breakdown of the total value of production in Korea for 1936 (the year before the China Incident) and for 1939.

TABLE 8
SHIFT IN KOREAN PRODUCTION, 1936-1939
(IN PERCENT)

Products	1936	1939
Agricultural	52	42
Forestry	5	5
Fisheries	7	8
Mining	5	6
Industrial	31	39
TOTAL	100	100

The table shows that by 1939, the relative value of mining and industrial output together had increased and was greater than that of any other single economic activity in Korea. Besides, among all industries in 1939, the chemical industry ranked first, having replaced food-processing which had been the most important in 1936. The table below compares the relative value of the production of various industries in 1936 and 1939. Percentages have been rounded off to the nearest half or whole percent.

TABLE 9
COMPARISON OF VALUE OF PRODUCTION BY INDUSTRY, 1936-1939
(IN PERCENT)

Industry	1936	1939
Spinning	12.5	13.0
Iron and steel	4.0	9.0
Machine tools	1.0	4.0
Ceramics	2.5	3.0
Chemical	23.0	34.0
Lumber and construction	3.0	1.0
Printing	2.0	1.0
Food processing	45.0	22.0
Gas	5.5	2.0
Others	1.5	11.0
TOTAL	100.0	100.0

The 1936 value of the production of the chemical, machine tool, and iron and steel industries, constituting so-called heavy industry, added together amounts to only 28 percent of the value of total industrial production in Korea; by 1939, however, this figure had risen to 47 percent, indicating what phase of industrialization had been emphasized as a result of Japanese needs for military supplies. In considering this change, it should be borne in mind that the value of over-all total production in Korea rose from 2,300,000,000 yen in 1936 to 3,900,000,000 yen in 1939. Furthermore, the program for increasing rice production in Korea, abandoned in 1934 due to the world agricultural depression, was reinstituted after the China Incident because of the growing food shortage, and production was scheduled to reach 20,000,000 sŏk per year. In spite of this rise in agricultural production, the increase in heavy industry outstripped the increase in all other industries since Japanese demands were greatest in this sector of the economy.

This development was a result of the Japanese military situation, not brought about in response to Korea's own needs. Consequently, the former semiautonomous position of Korea vis-à-vis Japan could not continue. Korea became regulated by the Japan-Korea-Manchuria Resource Mobilization Plan, centered in Japan. The program for the development of Korean industry was set up by the Japan Planning Board; the National Mobilization Law of Japan included Korea and imposed on her mandatory Japanese wartime mobilization conditions. The desires of the Koreans were completely ignored.

At the same time, Korean transportation and communication facilities took on a more pronounced military character, expanding far beyond the needs of the Korean economy. This was due to the fact that the fighting on the Asiatic continent indicated the urgency of increasing military transportation in Korea. New railroad lines were built, and the double-tracking of trunk lines was speeded up. Other types of land, sea, and air transport services were rapidly expanded, and direct communication facilities between Japan, Korea, and Manchuria were increased.

These conditions of wartime mobilization inevitably led to mobilization in Korea on all fronts — social, political, cultural — and with it began the so-called Unification of Japan and Korea (Naisen ittai-ka) movement, and the Transformation into Imperial Subjects (Kōmin-ka). In the past, education in Korea had been divided into two major systems, one providing elementary schools, middle schools, and girls' schools for the Japanese, and the other providing common schools, higher common schools, and higher girls' common schools for the Koreans. As a result of a reform in the educational ordinances in 1938, this division was abolished and all schools followed the regular Japanese system. As a basic educational policy the three principles of Clarifying the National Polity, Japan and Korea as One, and Training to Endure Hardship were sponsored, and Koreans were expected to have a sense of duty as imperial Japanese subjects. In October 1937, immediately after the China Incident, the "oath of imperial Japanese subjects" was drawn up, and in the elementary schools of Korea the students recited daily at morning meetings the following sentences: "We are subjects of the empire of Greater Japan. We unite our hearts in striving to give loyalty and service to the emperor. We will learn to endure hardships and be strong upright citizens." High-school students and those in higher educational institutions, as well as non-students, were forced to recite aloud phrases similar to these at morning meetings, ceremonies, and other occasions. In order to speed up the transformation of Koreans into Japanese subjects, it was decided to popularize the Japanese language, and, from 1938 on, elementary schools were used as centers for associations established throughout the country for the purpose of studying Japanese. In the schools themselves the use of Korean was forbidden, and newspapers in Korean were abolished.

To nourish the "Japanese spirit," so-called "exercises for imperial subjects" were introduced to provide training in the rules of "military way" (budō); the system of exercises was extended to schools, young men's associations and government offices, and even the population in general. In addition, at every school there were "love the country" days, when Shintō shrines were visited and there were flag-raising ceremonies. After September 1939, all these observances were combined, and were celebrated together on the first of each month throughout the country, a day which was called the Day of Service for the Rise of Asia. In addition, bowing in the direction of the emperor's palace, silent invocations at mid-day, the wearing of Japanese-type uniforms by Korean civil servants, and similar measures designed to transform Koreans into imperial subjects were energetically put into practice. In addition, Koreans were forcibly encouraged to alter their names, giving them a Japanese style, or were even required to discard completely their traditional Korean family names. By September 1940, 80 percent of the total population, that is 16,000,000 persons, had changed their names. Koreans were made to visit Shintō shrines as if their own clan deities were there; each home was provided with a "god stand" known as the Great Imperial Shrine of the Sun Goddess (Amaterasu Kōdai Jingu); and Shintō shrines were built in all communities.

It was not only along these spiritual lines that Korea was mobilized. After the undeclared war against China began, Koreans were included in the front lines, in accordance with a system for army volunteers. The celebrations when these troops were sent away, and home front service, were taken as opportunities to inculcate in the Korean masses a spirit of militarism and hatred against China. There was also a labor and service mobilization in Korea for increasing production of military supplies and for providing Japanese troops with entertainment and billets.

This trend toward total mobilization also caused widespread anti-Communist measures to be taken. Immediately after the China Incident, in order that the official position be clearly understood, associations were formed throughout Korea, but principally at military posts, to discuss public affairs. In 1938 the Korean Anti-Communist Association (Chōsen Bōkyō Kyōkai) was set up with the Civil Administrator of Korea (Seimu Sōkan)[2] as president. There was an allied branch in every province with local branches at police stations. Anti-Communist associations were organized even in villages, factories, and companies; and cultural and religious organizations were required to establish anti-Communist cells.

In 1940, all these organizations, following the example of the Imperial Rule Assistance Association (Taisei Yokusan-kai) in Japan, were unified into the People's United Strength Movement, which joined with the Korean Government General to undertake the mobilization and training of Koreans. This movement was in fact a transplantation of the Imperial Rule Assistance Association of Japan, but in Korea it was divested of its political characteristics. It stressed instead the Unification of Japan and Korea and the Transformation of Koreans into Imperial Subjects. The whole organization of the movement was built up around administrative bodies, and strongly increased the concentration of power from above.

Korea was no longer just a commercial market, a source of raw materials, or an investment market for Japan. She had become an integral part of the Japanese empire. Korea, known as the "continental front-line military supply base," was in fact the base for Japanese Asiatic continental policy. In this context, Korean traditions and special characteristics, as well as Korean ideas and desires, counted for nought. Everything in Korea had to be subordinated entirely to Japanese strategic military needs. Korean economic growth, the spectacular industrialization of the country, the Unification of Japan and Korea, the Transformation of

---

[2] After the Governor General (Sōtoku) the Civil Administrator (Seimu Sōkan) was the ranking official in Korea during the period of Japanese rule.

Koreans into Imperial Subjects, and all similar developments had been brought about simply to fill such needs.

This trend became even more pronounced after 1941 when Japan entered the war in the Pacific. In 1942 a draft law was put into effect in Korea. The old system of volunteers was changed to a system of conscription, a further indication of the great demands Japan was making on Korea. The mobilization of students, conscription, military training, and other measures, identical with those in force in Japan, were applied in Korea to a colonial population that had no voice whatever in the matter. Opposition to such measures in Korea was much stronger than in Japan, but as there were no means of expressing it under a system of absolute military control, resentment seethed deeply in the hearts of Koreans.

Korean Nationalist Movements after the March First Movement

The March First Movement brought about a change in Japanese administrative policy in Korea from a military administration to one based on a so-called cultural policy in which the integration of Koreans and Japanese was advocated. From this time onward, the Korean economy, society, and culture made surprising progress at the strong insistence and pressure of the Japanese. Especially following the Manchurian Incident in 1931, the Korean economy changed completely as it was adapted to growing military demands. While Korea was experiencing its "industrial revolution," changing from an agricultural to an industrial economy, the integration of Korea with Japan was proceeding apace through the development of such activities as the Japan and Korea Unification movement. But what did the Korean people actually obtain from Japanese rule over Korea?

Without doubt, the government, the society, the economy, and the culture of Korea developed extraordinarily during the period of Japanese domination. In place of the former *yangban* rule, an organized government of civil servants was established. In areas which previously had not been opened up, large-scale industries were established. Vast agricultural estates with excellent irrigation facilities came into being. Modern communication and transportation services were set up, and large cities developed. Schools were built everywhere, the magnificent Imperial University was established, and an excellent palace of fine arts and museum were constructed. In particular, the enormous hydroelectric generating facilities constructed in north Korea were impressive. When one considers all these things, it would seem natural even today, after Japan's defeat in the Second World War, that there would be people in Korea who would acknowledge the benefits of the Japanese administration. Actually, it is highly questionable whether Koreans profited from these excellent facilities, and whether the living standards of the Koreans were raised by them. One must not forget the great numbers of destitute persons during the period when Japan was in control. In January 1934, at a consultative meeting of the principal leaders of the rural village reconstruction movement, Governor General Ugaki Issei spoke of the fearful misery of the Korean peasantry. He stated that every spring the number of wretched farmers lacking food and searching for bark and grass to eat, approached 50 percent of the total peasant population. These were the words of the Governor General, so the real situation was worse; even the Governor General was forced to recognize the terrible plight of the Korean farmer.

Large numbers of destitute persons existed also during the Yi Dynasty, and the Japanese administration was unable to change this situation. But, worse than that, the development of Korea under the Japanese constantly created a new destitute population. Words in current use at the time such as the "spring and autumn poor," "uprooted wanderers," "stowaway," "fire-field agriculturists," and "dwellers in earth mounds" indicate the seriousness of the conditions. As the words signify, there were constantly people suffering from starvation, groups of Koreans who in desperation crossed over to Japan and Manchuria, peasants who penetrated mountain forests and practiced a primitive fire-field agriculture, and persons who lived in earth caves on the outskirts of large cities like Seoul. By 1939, when Korean industry had made great strides forward, there were 570,000 *chŏngbo* of fire-fields, and 340,000 households or about 1,870,000 persons living off fire-field agriculture — a really extraordinary fact. The rapid capitalist development of Korea had thus created a large number of primitive agriculturalists. And these victims, born of the progress of Korea, were the foundation upon which such progress was first built.

The modernization of Korea, which began with the land survey, created many small tenant farmers. In 1939, 68 percent of the paddy fields and 52 percent of the dry fields in all Korea were tenant-cultivated, and 53.6 percent of all farm families were full-term tenants. When one adds the part-time tenants to this, the percentage of tenancy rises to 77.2 percent. In southern Korea, the main rice-producing area, 70 percent of the farm families were full-time tenants and, together with the part-time tenants, the figure for tenancy reaches 94 percent. In other words, the great majority of the peasantry were becoming tenants. At the same time, the tenant-landlord relationship was a harsh one, preserving the conditions of the past, and the livelihood of the peasants remained in jeopardy. The existence of destitute farmers, illegal emigrants, fire-field agriculturists, and the like, was made inevitable by this land situation. But since under Japanese control a land reform could not be expected, it was natural that the wretched condition of the Korean farmer should persist during the period of Japanese administration.

The rice which the Japanese ate was grown by these poverty-stricken farmers. The rice which the farmers turned over to the landlords for their high-rate tenancy payments and the rice which they sold to the rice merchants in order to buy cheap millet, all became a major part of the Japanese diet. The food-supply policy of Japan was set up, predicated on such conditions. The plan for increasing rice production in Korea not only failed to change this situation, but even aggravated it.

The poverty-ridden Korean farm villages were, at the same time, an important foundation for the industrialization of Korea inasmuch as they provided a source of plentiful, cheap labor accustomed to harsh conditions such as long hours and low wages. This labor pool was highly valued by Japanese capitalists, for it made possible large colonial profits. An ample supply of labor in all fields, much cheaper than the so-called cheap labor market of Japan, and the ability to oppress this labor force much more severely than was possible in Japan — these were important factors in the attraction of Japanese capital to Korea during its industrialization.

The Japanese administration introduced much that was new in Korea and built a great deal. In doing so, it made victims of many in the very heart of society. It produced a small number of Koreans who depended on Japanese power and, at the same time, a large number of Koreans who disliked Japanese control. The Japanese tried through the Unification of Japan and Korea and the Transformation into Imperial Subjects to take away from Koreans their national consciousness, but they could not remove the resentment from their hearts. The resistance movement of the Koreans against the Japanese continued to be strong, up to the time of Japan's defeat and withdrawal from Korea in 1945.

The nationalist movement in Korea which had died down for a while after the failure of the March First movement, gradually grew up again in a new form. It differed from the March First movement, which had been simply a demonstration for national independence, relying on the aid of foreign nations, for now they developed into movements associated with socialism and the class struggle. The leaders of the March First movement had included landowners and capitalists, while now the main supporters of the new movement were workers, farmers, students, and intellectuals. These organizations did not include any active nationalistic capitalists, such as often appeared in other colonial countries, because there was little opportunity for such a group to develop under Japanese control. The few small Korean capitalists who did establish themselves were able to exist only on Japanese sufferance. Tenant and labor disputes, student organizations, ideological campaigns, incidents involving the Communist Party, and similar organizations, events, and activities characterized the new nationalist movement.

These movements reached their high-water mark about 1930. In 1920 there were 15 tenant disputes involving 4,040 persons; in 1923, 176 disputes involving 3,973 persons; in 1930, 726 disputes involving 13,012 persons; and in 1931, 667 disputes involving 10,282 persons. Labor disputes followed the same pattern. Originally Korean labor consisted mainly of miners and construction workers, and there were few factory workers. This was especially true before the Manchurian Incident; due to paternalistic control, labor organization was impeded. In 1917 there were only 8 strikes involving 1,148 persons, but in 1920, 81 strikes involving 4,599 persons, and in 1923, 72 strikes involving 6,041 persons. After 1925 labor disputes intensified and became organized. Major labor disturbances took place, such as a general strike in Wŏnsan in 1929 and a general strike in Seoul the following year.

The labor disputes were not simply spontaneous occurrences, but were politically motivated as part of the Korean struggle against Japanese imperialism. Immediately following the March First movement, some of the Korean nationalists in Shanghai became dissatisfied with the old movement and approached the Russian Communist Party. In 1920 they established in Shanghai a Korean Communist Party (Koryŏ Kongsandang) which opposed the Provisional Government of the Republic of Korea (Taehan Minguk Imsi Chŏngbu) that had been formed there from among the supporters of the March First movement. This new trend in political thought occurred not only in Shanghai but spread among the Korean younger generation within Korea and abroad, and, in place of the former nationalists, the Socialists and the Communists became powerful. In 1922, the Seoul Young Men's Association (Seoul Ch'ŏngnyŏn Hoe) was formed, and in 1923 the North Star Society (Puksŏng Hoe) was founded among Korean students in Tokyo, both of which were active in fostering Socialist and Communist ideas. Shanghai and Tokyo became the two main centers for the ideological movement of the Koreans, and from these two centers revolutionary ideas were introduced into Korea until, in 1925, the Korean Communist Party (Chosŏn Kongsandang) was established in Korea itself. With this a revolutionary movement within Korea began in earnest, reaching its height in 1930. The previously mentioned tenant and labor disputes were encouraged as an important aspect of this movement.

In 1925 the Peace Preservation Law was put into effect to oppose this movement and, in the same year, the first Communist Party members were arrested. On June 10, 1926, the Communist Party tried to stage a new March First movement and to instigate a nationwide independence march on the occasion of the death of Yi Ch'ŏk (Sunjong) the last king of the Yi Dynasty. Before the demonstration could take place, however, it was discovered and occasioned the second arrest of Communist Party members. After this, too, the Communist Party was struck hard blows, for in March 1928, the third wholesale arrest of its members took place, and again a fourth round-up of Communists was carried out in August of the same year. After each police action, however, the Communist Party was reconstituted, and continued to encourage and lead tenant and labor disputes.

One group of Communists formed the New Foundations Society (Sin'gan Hoe) in 1927 which was made up of writers and educators, including Korean nationalists and reformers. This society was legally organized and provided a broad united front. Laborers, students, and intellectuals were deeply influenced by it. The large-scale student disturbance of 1929 was the greatest product of its efforts. This was triggered by a clash between Japanese and Korean high school students on commuter trains in Kwangju, South Chŏlla Province. This dispute developed into a nationwide movement of students who demanded the abolition of colonial discriminatory treatment. The movement continued through 1930, and grew into a huge disturbance in which 54,000 students participated involving 194 schools. This was the largest nationalist uprising since the March First movement, but its character was different in that it was carried out by students explicitly as a protest against Japanese imperialism.

Labor and tenant disputes occurred constantly encouraged by this student movement. This was the period around 1930 when Korean popular movements reached their apogee and during which all Korea was gripped by an air of tension. The struggle for national independence, bound now to the daily problems of the people, extended throughout the whole of Korea. This was the time, too, when Korea became enveloped in the wave of the world financial panic, when farm villages which had become producers solely of rice suffered hard times, and when depressed economic conditions, characterized by emigration, legal and illegal, and unemployment, became prevalent. Under these circumstances leftist movements spread and grew strong. To counteract these, the authorities, on the one hand, sponsored rural village reconstruction and self-help movements, and on the other, severely suppressed leftist organizations, rounded up and imprisoned Communists and instigators of labor disputes, and did not hesitate to close schools in which there were serious strikes.

With the outbreak of the Manchurian Incident in 1931, the strategic importance of Korea increased. The measures adopted for dealing with labor disputes and radical movements became more stringent. It was no longer possible for political opposition to express itself publicly as had been allowed earlier. Also the trend toward thought control in order to resist communism was accentuated. Among the Koreans themselves, divisions and differences appeared, and in 1931 the *Sin'gan Hoe* was dissolved. An underground group of Communists, however, involved largely with the peasantry and labor, continued its activity. Futhermore, the rapid advance of industry from this period on caused a great increase in the number of industrial workers, from 250,000 in 1933 to 300,000 in 1935, to 520,000 in 1937 and to 690,000 in 1938. After the China Incident in 1937 and the outbreak of the war in the Pacific in 1941, the number of Korean workers again took a sharp upturn. This increase broadened the base for Communist activity, but agitation was quickly suppressed by Japanese military force. There was no possibility of organizing resistance, for at the slightest sign of danger all disturbances were nipped in the bud. Despite this, Korean opposition to Japanese rule burned more strongly than ever.

During this period Korean political activities were carried on by groups outside Korea. They included the Northeast Anti-Japanese United Army *(Tongbuk Kangil Yŏn'gun)* of Kim Ilsŏng,[3] which was based on support from Koreans in Manchuria; Kim Ku's nationalist party, the United Association of Movements for the Revival of Korea *(Han'guk Kwangbok Undong Tanch'e Yŏnhaphoe)* which was allied with the Chinese Nationalist Government *(Kuomintang)* in Ch'ung-ch'ing (Chungking); and Syngman Rhee who had American backing. The anti-Japanese movement in Manchuria of Kim Ilsŏng was the strongest of these. The vast majority of Koreans who were outside of Korea lived in Manchuria. From the latter years of the Yi Dynasty, displaced Koreans had gone to Chien-tao, Manchuria, but during the period of Japanese administration of Korea the number of Koreans migrating there had greatly increased. In 1936 there were approximately 870,000 Koreans there. This group had strong anti-Japanese feelings, and frequently caused major disturbances after the March First movement. The Chien-tao area became the base for ceaseless anti-Japanese activity and was looked upon by the Japanese as a den of "rebellious Koreans." Kim Ilsŏng organized these Koreans living in Manchuria, armed them and, throughout the entire Second World War, kept up a struggle against the Japanese. To Koreans who could not carry out anti-Japanese activities within Korea itself, this movement was considered most courageous. This made it possible for Kim Ilsŏng to become the leader of North Korea at the end of the war.

---

[3] The Northeast Anti-Japanese United Army, in Korean the *Tongbuk Kangil Yŏn'gun,* more properly known by its Chinese name *Tung-pei K'ang-jih Lien-chün,* was in fact a Chinese Communist controlled army that fought the Japanese. Kim Ilsŏng as well as other Koreans participated in the anti-Japanese activities of this group, but it was primarily Chinese and not Korean oriented. Kim before 1945 was alien to the Korean Communist movement and to Korean Communists, rather advancing through the ranks of the Chinese Communist revolutionaries in Manchuria. His name, Kim Ilsŏng, appears to be a pseudonym, through which he inherited the credit due to other Korean revolutionaries with the same name. See Suh, Dae-sook, *The Korean Communist Movement,* (Princeton: Princeton University Press, 1967), 253-93, for a documented analysis of Kim's pre-1945 activities, including his participation in the Northeast Anti-Japanese United Army.

VIII

The Liberation and the Tribulations
of the Korean People

Korea Liberated and Divided

The defeat of Japan on August 15, 1945, brought to an end the Japanese administration of Korea. Independence, which had for so long been a cherished desire of
the Koreans, could now become a reality. Already in the Cairo Declaration of
November 27, 1943, China, the United Kingdom, and the United States announced that "mindful of the enslavement of the people of Korea [we are]
determined that Korea shall become free and independent," and in the Potsdam
Declaration of July 20, 1945, this was reiterated. Thus the intention of liberating
Korea and granting it independence had been publicly proclaimed to the world in
common statements of the democratic nations, and its realization was looked forward to. With the defeat of Japan, it became an actuality.

By mid-1945 the defeat of Japan was considered imminent, but Japan's leaders surrendered before complete internal collapse occurred. Although by this time
the people of Japan were extremely dissatisfied with the prosecution of the war,
they had neither the strength to end it nor had they expressed their opposition to
it when one group of Japan's ruling class brought about the surrender. Consequently the reform of Japanese society after the war was carried out without
internal upheavals and under the aegis of foreign nations. This profoundly influenced Japan's postwar development. Korea, likewise, was occupied by foreign
nations following the war, and the reform of Korean society was initiated by these
occupying powers, but, because the Korean environment was unlike the Japanese,
the effect of this on Korea was much more profound than it was in Japan.

Japan left Korea not because she was directly forced to do so by Korean opposition, but because she was defeated by outside nations. Even though the dissatisfaction and resentment of the Koreans against the Japanese was very deep, any expression of it had been prevented by Japanese military control, and the Koreans had not
had the strength to overthrow Japanese control. All political activity in Korea had
been completely suppressed, hence when Japanese control was removed, there was
no organized authority to step into the breach. When the Japanese left, the social,

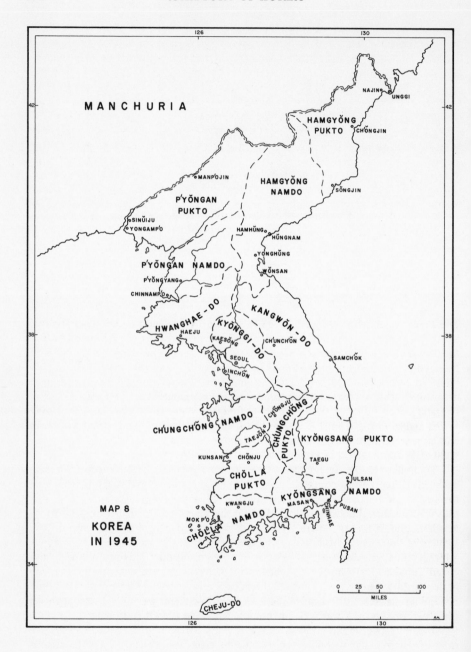

MANCHURIA

NAJIN
UNGGI

HAMGYŎNG
PUKTO
CHŎNGJIN

MANP'OJIN

HAMGYŎNG
NAMDO
SŎNGJIN

P'YŎNGAN
PUKTO

SINŬIJU
YONGAMP'O

HAMHŬNG
HŬNGNAM

YONGHŬNG

P'YŎNGAN NAMDO
WŎNSAN

P'YŎNGYANG

CHINNAMP'O

HWANGHAE-DO
KANGWŎN-DO

HAEJU
KYŎNGGI-DO
KAESŎNG
CH'UNCH'ŎN

SEOUL
SAMCH'ŎK
INCH'ŎN

CH'UNGCH'ŎNG NAMDO
CH'ŎNGJU
CHUNGCH'ŎNG
PUKTO
KYŎNGSANG PUKTO

TAEJŎN

KUNSAN   CHŎNJU
TAEGU

CHŎLLA
PUKTO
ULSAN

KYŎNGSANG NAMDO

MAP 8
KWANGJU
MASAN
PUSAN

KOREA
IN 1945
MOKP'O
CHINHAE

CHŎLLA
NAMDO

0   25   50   100
MILES

CHEJU-DO

economic, and political machinery in Korea simply collapsed. The Japanese had monopolized the higher positions in all government offices, and their sudden withdrawal made the task of reorganization extremely difficult. In the midst of the resulting confusion, there was intense political activity. Political organizations sprang up in cities and farm villages; hundreds of Communist Party members, released from jail, began operating in the open; and every shade of opinion, from Communist to nationalist, was loudly expressed. Only one desire was shared by all: to establish as quickly as possible a unified political authority; to restore political, economic, social and cultural institutions; and to build an independent nation for the people. In accordance with this desire, the Committee for the Preparation of Korean Independence *(Kŏn'guk Chunbi Wiwŏnhoe)* was formed with wide popular representation, and under its sponsorship the Korean People's Republic *(Chosŏn Inmin Konghwaguk)* was born. However, in spite of this state of political activity, no unifying political party or individual developed. No political activity had been allowed under the Japanese, so now there was nothing to serve as a nucleus of the republic and give it direction. As a result, numerous factions formed and fought one another and concerted action was hardly possible.

It was into this atmosphere that Koreans who had been active politically outside Korea returned home. Syngman Rhee, one of the important persons in the March First movement, Kim Ku who had spurred on the cause of Korea in Chungking, and other such respected persons were greeted with great anticipation, but their return did not strengthen the unity of the people. On the contrary, it deepened the rift between Communists and nationalists, and finally, in February 1946, the Korean People's Republic, which had been organized after so much trouble, was dissolved.

It was not, however, only the internal conditions which made the uniting of Korea difficult. International rivalry was an even greater obstacle. The united front which Soviet Russia and the United States had maintained during the Second World War rapidly disintegrated after their common enemies disappeared, and soon the two nations came into direct conflict over Korea. Russia declared war against Japan on August 8, 1945, and immediately began an attack on Manchuria. At the same time she crossed the frontier in northern Korea and advanced into the country. Now, too, the United States initiated its occupation of Japan in the latter part of August and sent troops into Korea, announcing the formation of a military government in Korea on September 9, 1945. Thus Korea was again occupied. The American and Soviet armies had merely replaced those of the Japanese. For the sake of military convenience alone, the thirty-eighth parallel was made the dividing line between the areas of operation of the two armies, and it was agreed that each would occupy its own sphere. It was not long before this arbitrary dividing line came to have very important political connotations. It became the boundary on either side of which quite different groups became powerful, and diametrically opposed political policies were carried out. The thirty-eighth parallel became a point of contact between two fiercely conflicting worlds. This was only a segment of the contest between the two great orbits of power, the United States and Soviet Russia, a contest which rapidly heightened in intensity after the defeat of Japan, and influenced the civil wars in the Far East, that is, in China and Indo-China. It was because the armies of the two countries came face to face across the thirty-eighth parallel that Korea became one of the most explosive areas on the globe. This obviously made it very difficult to achieve Korean unity.

Nevertheless, unification remained the main national aspiration of all Koreans. Even though political parties were split up within the country, no party could renounce this aspiration, nor could the United States and Russia ignore it. Also, since there was a world-wide cry for peace, Korean unification was generally considered desirable. Since the principle of Soviet-American cooperation had not yet been destroyed, the problem of Korean unification was taken up at the meeting of foreign ministers in Moscow in December 1945. There it was decided that a trusteeship over Korea by the four great powers, the United States, England, China, and the Soviet Union, would be set up for a period of five years or less. On the basis of this agreement a joint American-Soviet conference was to be held in March 1946, in order to discuss the establishment of a provisional Korean government. It seemed now as if the day for the unification and independence of Korea was fast approaching.

But these expectations were betrayed by the question of the qualifications of the political parties and organizations which were to participate in the conference that would establish the provisional Korean government. The Russians insisted that only those political parties which had supported the trusteeship decision of the Moscow meeting of foreign ministers be permitted to take part, and that those who had opposed the decision be excluded. The United States disagreed, and argued that the principle of freedom of speech required that all parties be allowed to participate. To have followed the Russian proposal would have excluded the rightist political parties which had opposed the trusteeship decision of the meeting of foreign ministers. To have followed the American stand would have made possible the participation of representatives of the many rightist splinter parties at the conference. Therefore the decision as to who could take part was crucial not only for the makeup of the conference, but for the kind of future government for Korea. As the Russians and Americans were unable to compromise, the first joint conference broke up in May 1946. One year later, in May 1947, another joint conference was held, but it too ended in failure. Apparently no solution to the problem could be reached by direct negotiations between the Soviet Union and the United States, the two nations occupying Korea. In September 1947, therefore, the United States laid the problem before the General Assembly of the United Nations, and there both nations resumed their arguments. Ultimately, a so-called American plan was approved in spite of the opposition of the Soviets. It called for the formation of the United Nations Temporary Korean Commission, with general elections to be held under its supervision, and the founding of a united government. In accordance with this decision a general election was held in May 1948, in June a National Assembly was established, and in July a constitution was promulgated. Syngman Rhee was inaugurated, and the Republic of Korea (Taehan Minguk) came into being. It was first recognized by the United States (January 1949) and then by Nationalist China, France, Britain, and the Philippines.

In this way a government in Korea was set up which was recognized by the United Nations commission, by the United States, and by other nations supporting her stand. But this did not in any way solve the Korean problem. The Korean general election had been held only in South Korea, and the Republic of Korea controlled only this area. Furthermore, the political situation was extremely unstable in South Korea. And lastly, north of the thirty-eighth parallel, a government had grown up which was completely different from that in the South.

Originally the handling of the Korean problem had been one aspect of an important common world-wide policy for the Soviet Union and the United States. After occupying Korea, however, each nation followed its own policy, planting and nurturing its power in the area under its control. During the period when the joint conferences were held, a North Korean People's Committee *(Puksŏn Inmin Wiwŏnhoe)* led by Kim Ilsŏng was established in North Korea (February 1946). Following this, an epoch-making land reform was carried out in North Korea (March 1946), and there were put into effect labor laws (May 1946), laws giving equal rights to men and women (July 1946), and laws for the nationalization of major industries (August 1946). In addition, the North Korean Democratic People's Front *(Puk-Chosŏn Minjujuŭi Minjok Chŏnsŏn)* was formed in July 1945, as well as the powerful North Korean Labor Party *(Puk-Chosŏn Nodongdang)* whose nucleus was the Communist Party.

On the other hand, in American-dominated South Korea, a democratic council was formed in February 1946 as an advisory body to the military government, and in December of the same year, an interim legislature was established. So, although the Soviet Union and the United States held joint conferences for the sake of unifying Korea, at the same time, in keeping with their individual global policies, they promoted their different respective spheres of influence and strove to bring about Korean unification along their own lines.

These activities of both nations became even clearer after the breakdown of the joint conferences. The United States, in spite of Soviet opposition, formed a government in South Korea under the aegis of the United Nations and recognized it as the only legitimate government in Korea. In response to this, in October 1947 the People's Committee in North Korea decided to draw up a constitution, and in February of the following year a draft constitution was announced. In August a general election of the Supreme People's Assembly was held. In September, the Supreme People's Assembly convened, the constitution was accepted, and the Democratic People's Republic of Korea *(Chŏson Minjujuŭi Inmin Konghwaguk)* was formally established, with Kim Ilsŏng chosen as prime minister. In October 1948, the Democratic People's Republic of Korea was recognized first by the Soviet Union and later during the same year by various nations of the Soviet block.

In this way, the thirty-eighth parallel became the dividing line between two separate Korean governments supported by two opposing world camps. Liberation from Japanese domination, in spite of the hopes of the Korean people, had brought about a division of Korea.

The Desire for Unification

For a people who had the same language, customs, and culture and who had existed for centuries within the same political and economic framework, it was unnatural to be split up and attached to two conflicting world orbits, and to have the thirty-eighth parallel, which had no geographical *raison d'être*, become an impassable barrier. The Koreans longed for the unification and the independence

of their fatherland more than anything else, and this national desire transcended
political parties and factions, save for a small group of politicians. The independence of the Korean people had been the major aim of all popular movements
both before and after the March First movement. Although opinions had been
divided regarding the method of attaining independence and the kind of organization that should exist afterward, no popular movement was possible in Korea
which ignored independence. Now this foremost desire of the Koreans had been
betrayed. Therefore the formation of a unified independent Korea continued to
be the chief popular demand of the Koreans.

The Committee for the Preparation of Korean Independence *(Kŏn'guk Chunbi Wiwŏnhoe)*, which appeared immediately after the defeat of the Japanese, had
been created in response to this demand. The committee finally was unable to
accomplish anything, and a tendency to divisiveness appeared which became more
marked after its failure. The drive for unification, however, did not end, but grew
even stronger as the trend to division increased. A general election in Korea was
planned for May 1948 in accordance with the decision of the United Nations, but
it could be carried out only in South Korea. This unilateral election could only
widen the North-South separation in the country, and a cry was raised for general
elections throughout both North and South Korea. In response to this, a conference of political leaders for unification was held in North Korea at P'yŏngyang in
April 1948, attended by Kim Ku, Kim Kyusik, and many other representatives of
political parties in South Korea. Kim Ku was a well-known leader of anti-Japanese
and independence movements. He was in exile in Chungking during the Second
World War, and was spoken of as a nationalist with extreme rightist views. Kim
Kyusik was head of the South Korean interim legislature until February 1948, but
resigned because he was opposed to unilateral elections in South Korea. He was a
liberal who had received his education in the United States. These men were
typical of the participants in the April conference who, though voicing many
different shades of opinion, were united in an effort to achieve Korean unification.

The response to the appeal for unification, above and beyond parties and
factions, was so great that in June, following the unilateral May elections in South
Korea, another conference for unification was held in North Korea at which
political leaders from the North and South discussed future action. In August of
the same year, at the insistence of the North Korean group, elections were held
for representatives of the Supreme People's Assembly, and at the same time
underground elections were held even in South Korea, in spite of attempted harsh
suppression by the authorities. It is reported that 6,730,000 persons cast ballots in
South Korea, and representatives from South Korea were elected. The election
was not just a Communist stratagem which deceived the people in South Korea
for, although this plan for unification originated in North Korea, right-wing politicians had also participated, and large masses of people were moved by it because
unification was a common demand of all Koreans. Consequently, a popular front
linking both North and South Korea, the Democratic Front for the Unification of
the Fatherland *(Choguk T'ongil Minjujuŭi Chŏnsŏn)*, was established in June
1949. It included all political parties or organizations of North Korea, as well as
many participants from South Korea.

With the formation of the Democratic Front, the work for unification was intensified. In its formatory meeting it had been decided that in September general elections should be held throughout North and South Korea, that the supreme legislative body set up on the basis of this general election should choose a constitution, that a new government should be set up on the basis of this constitution, and that the existing governments and armies of both North and South Korea should be disbanded. Though these declarations appealed strongly to South Koreans, the South Korean government would not accede to the plan. On June 7, 1950, the Democratic Front for the Unification of the Fatherland proposed to the people and to political parties and organizations in South Korea that a general election be held in North and South Korea from August 5 to August 8, and that a supreme legislative assembly be opened at Seoul on August 15. To prepare for these events, it was suggested that from June 15 to June 17, a popular consultative assembly of North and South Koreans hold meetings at Haeju (slightly above the thirty-eighth parallel) or at Kaesŏng (just below the thirty-eighth parallel). Three special envoys were dispatched to South Korea to make known these aims, but the South Korean government rejected the proposals and declared that all South Koreans who accepted and complied with the North Korean overtures would be considered traitors and punished. Furthermore the three special envoys from North Korea were imprisoned. Hence the efforts at unification by the Democratic Front came to nothing.

After that, on June 19, 1950, the North Korean government presented a plan for unification to the South Korean national assembly. This plan included proposals that the national assemblies of North and South Korea set up a united government for the whole country, that the united government adopt a new constitution under which nationwide elections would be held, that the army and police be unified into a single force, that the existing military and police forces in North and South Korea be disbanded, and that Syngman Rhee, Yi Pŏmsŏk (at that time prime minister of the South Korean government), Kim Sŏngsu (head of the rightist Democratic Nationalist Party), and six others be imprisoned as national traitors. These proposals naturally were unacceptable. It was only a few days after that, on June 25, that civil war in Korea broke out, and with this all chances for peaceful unification vanished.

Independence had been the wish of all Koreans during the period of Japanese domination, and now, after the defeat of Japan, the one desire of all the Korean people was unification. Not only did the Koreans strive continuously for it, but efforts to achieve unification of the country were made by the powers outside of Korea. Examples of this are the Moscow meeting of foreign ministers, the joint American-Soviet conferences, and the organization of the United Nations Commission on Korea. Yet all these hopes and projects ended in failure, not only dashing the hopes of the Koreans, but also causing serious economic repercussions. North Korea, with its heavy chemical industries and its inexhaustible hydroelectric supply, was separated from South Korea, the granary of the country. In South Korea, electricity was often not available, and in North Korea, grain had to be imported from Manchuria. If North and South Korea could have been united, an improvement in the economy of the whole country would definitely have resulted.

Two Koreas

The principal factor which prevented the unification of Korea was the conflict between two world ideologies. The liberation from Japan was realized through the occupation of the country by American and Soviet armies, so that the process of liberation coincided with a phase of occupation. This was the basic cause of the division of Korea, and the people of Korea wanted very much for the occupying armies to withdraw. In December 1948, the Russian armies left North Korea, and, following that, in June 1949, the American armies were withdrawn. Now military control of Korea disappeared, but both countries continued actively to sponsor cultural, political, military, and economic projects in their respective spheres of influence, and the clash between the United States and the Soviet Union over Korea persisted. In view of the antagonistic relations between these two world powers, a solution to the problem of Korean unification was practically unattainable.

The Soviet Union and the United States not only made Korea the stage for their own rivalry, but they also brought about a deep internal conflict within Korea. The country became divided not simply along geographical lines, it also was split into two Koreas that adopted completely divergent political, economic, and cultural aims. This development of two opposing and conflicting tendencies among the Korean people greatly complicated the unification of the country.

After the defeat and withdrawal of the Japanese from Korea, those who spoke out for unification and who led the movement to unite the nation were mainly North Koreans or supporters of the North Korean regime. From immediately after the end of the war, when the Committee for the Preparation of Korean Independence was established, until the formation of the Democratic Front for the Unification of the Fatherland in 1949, leftist parties were always at the center of activities for unification, and various other parties cooperated with them. Consequently the South Korean government, which had adopted a platform of opposition to communism, guarded against unification movements, suppressed those in South Korea, and rejected the appeals for unity from North Korea because unification movements were not accepted at their face value but feared as fronts for revolutionary and destructive activities.

The original movement for unification was only an extension of the independence movement, the latter having simply changed its characteristics after the Second World War. Therefore it was natural that the movement for unification should be heir to the traditions of the nationalist movement, including its revolutionary character. Needless to say, after the failure of the March First movement, the mainstream of Korean nationalist activities was influenced by the left. During the period of Japanese administration, there had been little opportunity for the development of native Korean capitalism. The majority of the people had become paupers, and political activities had been suppressed. Under these circumstances, a moderate nationalist movement could not develop, and it was inevitable that Korean nationalism would be led by radicals and leftists. This revolutionary character of the Korean nationalist movement during the period of Japanese rule continued after the liberation. Immediately .following the end of the Second World War, people's committees were organized rapidly throughout Korea, and when the American army landed in Korea (September 1945), attempts were being made to organize the committees on a national scale. Although there was a tangle of internal divisions and conflicts among the people's councils, on the whole they followed a clearly leftist line.

The occupation of Korea by American and Soviet armies began in this atmosphere, which of course was advantageous to the Russians. They fostered the leftist current as the driving force for the rebuilding of North Korea, and, with this as a foundation, brought about many reforms and innovations. Such changes as land reform and the nationalization of major industries were rapidly carried out, and a strong government organization was established based on the Communist Party. Resistance to these abrupt changes occurred, and more than a million persons fled from North to South Korea. But while the innovations created many enemies, they also made allies of those who benefited from them, and these persons were organized under the authority of a strong controlling body. With this powerful political force, a planned reconstitution of every phase of economic and cultural life went ahead at a rapid pace. In mining and manufacturing, North Korea utilized the enormous hydroelectric power and the installations of the heavy chemical industry left behind by the Japanese, as well as the abundant mineral resources of the North (in 1945, 92 percent of all Korea's electric power, 90 percent of her metallurgical industry, and 82 percent of her chemical industry were in North Korea), and achieved results far surpassing those attained during the Japanese period. For example, the total production goal in 1950 was 230 percent of production in 1944. Agricultural output also increased due to the land reform, to the use of mechanization, and to improved techniques. The problem of food shortages which had always existed up to that time, was overcome, and in 1949 self-sufficiency in food became possible. In the cultural field too, school construction, adult education, and a campaign against illiteracy were vigorously pursued, and the theatrical, literary, and artistic activities of villages, factories, and private organizations were stimulated. All these innovations and developments naturally received full support from the Soviet Union. Also, the victory of the Communists in neighboring China helped North Korea materially and ideologically, and North Korea's growth was aired and propagandized in South Korea.

In the midst of this growth in North Korea proposals for peaceful unification of Korea were made. Although they emanated from North Korea, they were in keeping with the popular feeling and consequently even anti-Communist nationalists heeded the call.

In South Korea, conditions were entirely different from those in the North. The first thing that the American occupation army did was to curb the activities of the radical masses and to try to lead them along a different line. To accomplish this, a military government was established and, at the same time that revolutionary activities were being curbed, the power of anti-Communist groups was fostered. It was not, however, an easy task, for under Japanese rule even moderate political movements had been outlawed or destroyed, now making it difficult to find political forces on which the Americans could rely. There had always been people who worried over the activities of the radical elements, but the majority of these were unpopular pro-Japanese individuals, conservative landlords, and usurious capitalists, none of whom could command a broad popular following. Furthermore, there were strong conflicting factions among anti-Communist politicians which made it difficult to unite the anti-Communist forces. Besides, the

Korean capitalists and entrepreneurs were so weak that it was not easy for them to pull together the chaotic economy. In the midst of these mounting obstacles, Syngman Rhee, who had returned to Korea from the United States in 1945, was chosen to take charge of the political situation.

The major effort of those in control of South Korea was directed toward maintaining order. The stabilization of the political situation and the reconstruction of the economy were not possible until internal security had been guaranteed. The struggle to do this absorbed approximately 60 percent of the budget during the 1949 fiscal year. The fact that the major part of the budget was spent in this way impeded the development of South Korea, and was one of the chief causes of the ensuing inflation. The seriousness of the security problem in South Korea is evident from the frequent occurrence of farm and labor disturbances, of ideological disputes, and of the activities of guerrilla bands. In April 1948, uprisings took place on Cheju Island, in opposition to the general elections being held in South Korea. In October of the same year, troops at Yŏsu and Sunch'ŏn that were meant to put down the uprisings on Cheju Island, mutinied. From that time on guerrilla activities expanded everywhere in South Korea and continued unabated throughout the whole of 1949. The South Korean government used strong punitive measures against them, such as forcefully moving families from guerrilla areas, thus creating desolate uninhabited regions, and trying in many other ways to bottle up guerrilla action. All the energies of the government were concentrated on maintaining order. The losses incurred through April 1950 were as follows: 36,000 persons killed; 11,000 persons wounded; 45,000 homes burned completely; 4,000 homes partly burned; 61,000 families, involving 316,000 persons, sustaining damages; and 78,000 families, comprising 432,000 persons, displaced. Cheju Island in particular suffered heavily, and 27,000 persons out of a population of 250,000 were killed; 39,000 homes were completely destroyed.

Under these circumstances there was little hope for constructive work. A land reform had been expected since the advent of the American military government, but, because of the strong influence of the landlords, it did not materialize and the old landlord-tenant relationships continued as before. This, combined with a lack of fertilizer (most of the fertilizer in Korea was produced in North Korea) caused agricultural production to decline below the level of that in the Japanese period. Industry also became stagnant because of the scarcity of electrical power and raw materials, the deterioration of technical skills, and poor management. Production in 1948 declined to 20 percent of that in 1940. This drop in production, together with the increase in military expenditures, brought about a serious inflation, which in turn heightened social unrest. The economy of South Korea after the liberation was such that even with American aid, amounting to $550,000,000 by the end of 1949, it was supported with difficulty.

It was in this atmosphere of instability in South Korea that North Korea ceaselessly made overtures for the unification of the country. Kim Ku and Kim Kyusik were foremost among the political figures in South Korea who tried to come to an agreement with North Korea, but the South Korean government rejected the North Korean proposals and, going still further, punished as traitors those who advocated the unification of North and South Korea. In June 1949, seven members of the National Assembly, including the vice-chairman, were imprisoned for "plotting" with North Korea, and Kim Ku, the grand old man of the

Korean independence movement, was assassinated. After this, the movement to unite North and South Korea outwardly disappeared from the political scene in South Korea.

This undesirable stituation in South Korea became a problem even in the United States. In January 1950, the American House of Representatives voted against the bill for economic aid to South Korea. This was a serious matter for South Korea, suffering as she was from serious inflation, stagnation in industry, and unstable political conditions. Secretary of State Dean Acheson declared that without economic assistance South Korea would collapse in two or three months. As a result of his pleading for the passage of the aid bill, a $100,000,000 appropriation was approved in March 1950. Shortly before this, on January 26, a Japanese-American-Korean military agreement had been concluded. The South Korean government was not satisfied with the agreement and asked for more military aid, but the United States did not accede to their request. Then a conflict occurred between President Rhee and the South Korean National Assembly, and President Rhee announced that the general elections previously scheduled for May would be postponed. Finally, in the face of no progress being made in the National Assembly in their deliberation over the budget for the 1950 fiscal year, Secretary Acheson, on April 7, issued a warning stating that if the South Korean government neglected to take anti-inflationary measures and did not carry out the general elections, the United States would reduce economic aid to South Korea.

Because of this warning, the budget for the 1950 fiscal year was approved during the last ten days of April, and on May 30, general elections were held in South Korea. In the elections, the candidates of the existing government and opposition parties lost heavily and, out of 210 assemblymen elected, 130 were independents. Among them were men who had connections with North Korea and who believed in the unification of North and South Korea. Thus the elections were clearly unfavorable to the existing South Korean government.

In the beginning of June when South Korea was enshrouded in an air of uneasiness after the general elections, the Democratic Front for the Unification of the Fatherland made new proposals for peaceful unification. Shortly after this, the North Korean government, addressing itself to the newly elected South Korean National Assembly, also called for the establishment of a united Korean government under the aegis of the legislatures in North and South Korea, and demanded the imprisonment of President Syngman Rhee and eight other persons in South Korea as national traitors. The Korean conflagration began immediately thereafter.

Civil War

The civil war which began in Korea on June 25, 1950, rang down the curtain on peaceful unification of the country. It indicated the extraordinary difficulties involved in unification and made clear the world-wide character of the Korean problem. The world situation, as a result of this civil war, rapidly deteriorated, and increasingly severe tension was readily apparent. The solution of the Korean problem was no longer subject solely to the wishes of the Korean people, but seemed to be manipulated by outside world powers. The Korean people who had for so long suffered under the domination of a foreign power, did not even have time to taste the joys of liberation before their country was again made the stage for another international conflict. This was the inevitable result of Korea's liberation having taken place during a period of mounting tension between two world powers. It was an unforeseen and incalculable misfortune for the Korean people that the long-prayed-for independence and longed-for peaceful unification should end in war and bring about the destruction of homes, devastation of rice fields, and death and hardship to many millions. Although the American and Russian occupation of Korea freed the Korean people from a condition of slavery and should have brought them independence and freedom, it only shattered their dreams and laid waste their country.

One of the major consequences of the Second World War has been that the peoples of Asia, held for so long in colonial servitude, have risen to throw off imperialist colonial domination and to gain freedom and independence. This gigantic movement throughout Asia cannot be stopped, and it gives us occasion to reflect on the unfortunate present condition of Korea. The lesson finally made clear by the carnage in Korea is that management of Korean affairs by the Koreans themselves will be more felicitous for the Koreans than foreign intervention or direction, and one can expect that the Koreans will develop their capacity to achieve this end.

Conclusion

The history of Korea from its beginnings to the present day is a history of suffering and destruction caused by foreign oppressions and invasions. The periods when Korea was entirely free from foreign pressure were very short, so that a comparison with Japanese history is meaningless. This explains why Korea has evolved so unevenly. Time and again Korea's development was retarded by the recurrence of these destructive foreign invasions just when the first signs of progress had appeared. By the end of the nineteenth century, Korean society had advanced to a stage requiring the emancipation of the servile classes. Such progress was made step by step and, though it was often interrupted, at times even to the point of retrogression to earlier less-advanced ways of life, the Korean people managed to overcome these setbacks and to continue on the path of progress. While this process of development has had many individual features, it has basically been along the same lines followed by the other peoples of the world.

Korean history, being so much a story of hardships brought about by foreign nations, has caused the Korean people to nurture a fierce resentment against external enemies. Although the ruling class in Korea has frequently compromised or given in before such enemies, among the common people a tradition of not surrendering has grown up. The acts of ancient heroes who defended the country against foreign invaders have been given a mystical aura in popular legends passed down among the peasants. No matter how inaccurate or spurious these legends may be, they have delighted the hearts of the peasantry. They are the traditional heritage of a people molded in adversity. In the modern period, the traditions have taken many new forms and had a wide-spread rebirth as foreign aggression repeatedly recurred. Events such as the Tonghak Rebellion, the activities of the "righteous army," the March First movement, and the Kwangju students' riots were all outwardly different and are variously described, yet through each one runs strongly a hostility toward foreign oppressors. Every time such events oc-curred, the accomplishments of men of old who had defended the country against foreign attack were recalled in a mystical and heroic light.

With the defeat of Japan in 1945, it became possible for Korea to attain her long cherished independence. The words "Korean" and "Korean nation" now evoked a sense of pride as they had never done during the Japanese era, and one may consider the Second World War was a dividing line that marks a great change in the status of the Korean people.

How will Korea's present tribulations affect the traditions of the Korean people? For an answer to these questions, we must not only observe the world-wide situation as it relates to Korea, but we must also watch the actions of the Korean people themselves.

Appendix

Chronological List of Rulers and Dynasties

ANCIENT KOREA (2333 B.C.-108 B.C.)

Largely legendary until about 200 B.C. Tan'gun is a semidivine mythical figure; Ch'i-tzu (Kija) was said to be a scholar from China who founded a dynasty that reigned until 194 B.C.; Wei-man (Wiman) was a usurper from China. He and two successors ruled Korea until 108 B.C.

A. Period of Tan'gun 檀君 (2333 B.C.-1122 B.C.)

B. Period of Ch'i-tzu 箕子 (1122 B.C.-194 B.C.)

C. Period of Wei-man 衞滿 (194 B.C.-108 B.C.)

CHINESE COLONIES (108 B.C.-313 A.D.)

Introduction of Chinese culture into Korea and gradual cultural and political development of the Sam Han and other Korean tribes.

A. Period of Four Prefectures (108 B.C.-82 B.C.):

Lo-lang (Nangnang) 樂浪 ;

Lin-t'un (Nimdun) 臨屯 ;

Hsüan-t'u (Hyŏndo) 玄菟 ;

Chen-fan (Chinbŏn) 眞番 .

B. Period of Two Prefectures (82 B.C.-204 A.D.):

Lo-lang; Hsüan-t'u.

C. Period of Three Prefectures (204-313):

Lo-lang; Hsüan-t'u;
Tai-fang (Taebang) 帶方 .

THREE KINGDOMS AND UNIFIED SILLA (313-935; traditional dates: 57 B.C.-935 A.D.)

A. Karak 駕洛 (42?-562)
A small state in the basin of the Naktong River ruled by the Kim 金 Dynasty; absorbed by Silla in 562.

T'aejo	太祖	(42-199)
To Wang	道王	(199-253)
Sŏng Wang	成王	(253-291)
Tŏk Wang	德王	(291-346)
Myŏng Wang	明王	(346-407)
Sin Wang	神王	(407-421)
Hye Wang	惠王	(421-451)
Chang Wang	莊王	(451-492)
Suk Wang	肅王	(492-521)

Yang Wang 讓 王 (521-532)

Mal Wang 末 王 (532)

B. Paekche 百 濟 (18 B.C.?-660 A.D.)

Ruled by a Puyŏ 扶 餘 clan.
Generally in close alliance with Japan. Occupied by T'ang China and Silla in 660; defeated by Silla in 663.

Onjo Wang 温祚王 (18 B.C.-28 A.D.)

Taru Wang 多婁王 (28-77)

Kiru Wang 己婁王 (77-128)

Kaeru Wang 蓋婁王 (128-166)

Ch'ogo Wang 肖古王 (166-214)

Kusu Wang 仇首王 (214-234)

Saban Wang 沙伴王 (234)

Koi Wang 古爾王 (234-286)

Chaekkye Wang 責稽王 (286-298)

Punsŏ Wang 汾西王 (298-304)

Piryu Wang 比流王 (304-344)

Ke Wang 契王 (344-346)

Kŭnch'ogo Wang 近肖古王 (346-375)

Kŭn'gusu Wang 近仇首王 (375-384)

Ch'imnyu Wang 枕流王 (384-385)

Chinsa Wang 辰斯王 (385-392)

Asin Wang 阿莘王 (392-405)

Chŏnji Wang 腆支王 (405-420)

Kuisin Wang 久爾辛王 (420-427)

Piyu Wang 毗有王 (427-455)

Kaero Wang 蓋鹵王 (455-475)

Munju Wang 文周王 (475-477)

Samgŭn Wang 三斤王 (477-479)

Tongsŏng Wang 東城王 (479-501)

Munyŏng Wang 武寧王 (501-523)

Sŏng Wang 聖王 (523-554)

Widŏk Wang 威德王 (554-598)

Hye Wang 惠王 (598-599)

Pŏp Wang 泫王 (599-600)

Mu Wang 武王 (600-641)

Ŭija Wang 義慈王 (641-660)

P'ungjang Wang 豐璋王 (660-663)

C. Koguryŏ 高句麗 (37 B.C.?-668 A.D.)

Ruled by the Ko 高 Dynasty.
The years 313 to 552 were the period of Koguryŏ dominance in the peninsula; thereafter, the kingdom gradually declined and was finally overthrown by T'ang China and Silla.

Tongmyŏngsŏng Wang 東明聖王 (37 B.C.-19 B.C.)

Yurimyŏng Wang 琉璃明王 (19 B.C.-18 A.D.)

Taemusin Wang 大武神王 (18-44)

Minjung Wang 閔中王 (44-48)

Mobon Wang 慕本王 (48-53)

T'aejo Wang 太祖王 (53-146)

Ch'adae Wang 次大王 (146-165)

Sindae Wang 新大王 (165-179)

Kogukch'ŏn Wang 故國川王 (179-197)

Sansang Wang 山上王 (197-227)

Tongch'ŏn Wang 東川王 (227-248)

Chungch'ŏn Wang 中川王 (248-270)

Sŏch'ŏn Wang 西川王 (270-292)

Pongsang Wang 烽山王 (292-300)

Mich'ŏn Wang 美川王 (300-331)

Kogugwŏn Wang 故國原王 (331-371)

Sosurim Wang 小獸林王 (371-384)

Kogugyang Wang 故國壤王 (384-391)

Kwanggaet'o Wang 廣開土王 (391-412)

Changsu Wang 長壽王 (413-491)

Munja Wang 文咨王 (492-519)

Anjang Wang 安藏王 (519-531)

Anwŏn Wang 安原王 (531-545)

Yangwŏn Wang 陽原王 (545-559)

P'yŏngwŏn Wang 平原王 (559-590)

Yŏngyang Wang 嬰陽王 (590-618)

Yŏngnyu Wang 榮留王 (618-642)

Pojang Wang 寶藏王 (642-668)

D. Silla 新羅 (57 B.C.?-935 A.D.)

Ruled variously by the Pak 朴, Sŏk 昔, and Kim 金 families, although principally by the last. The years 552 to 660 were the period of Silla dominance among the Three Kingdoms, and after 660 the peninsula was united under Silla's rule. The period of united Silla is generally divided into three phases – greatness (660-780), decline (780-887), and disintegration (887-935).

Hyŏkkŏse Wang 赫居世王 (57 B.C.-3 A.D.), Pak

Namhae Wang 南解王 (4-24), Pak

Yuri Wang 儒理王 (24-57), Pak

T'alhae Wang 脫解王 (57-80), Sŏk

P'asa Wang 婆娑王 (80-112), Pak

Chima Wang 祇摩王 (112-134), Pak

Ilsŏng Wang 逸聖王 (134-154), Pak

Adalla Wang 阿達羅王 (154-184), Pak

Pŏrhyu Wang 伐休王 (184-196), Sŏk

Naehae Wang 奈解王 (196-230), Sŏk

Chobun Wang 助賁王 (230-247), Sŏk

Ch'ŏmhae Wang 沾解王 (247-261), Sŏk

Mich'u Wang 味鄒王 (262-284), Kim

Yurye Wang 儒禮王 (284-298), Sŏk

Kirim Wang 基臨王 (298-310), Sŏk

Hŭlhae Wang 訖解王 (310-356), Sŏk

Naemul Wang 奈勿王 (356-402), Kim

Silsŏng Wang 實聖王 (402-417), Kim

Nulchi Wang 納祇王 (417-458), Kim

Chabi Wang 慈悲王 (458-479), Kim

Soji Wang 炤知王 (479-500), Kim

Chijŭng Wang 智證王 (500-514), Kim

Pŏphŭng Wang 法興王 (514-540), Kim

Chinhŭng Wang 眞興王 (540-576), Kim

Chinji Wang 眞智王 (576-579), Kim

Chinp'yŏng Wang 眞平王 (579-632), Kim

Sŏndŏk Yŏwang [Queen] 善德女王 (632-647), Kim

Chindŏk Yŏwang [Queen] 眞德女王 (647-654), Kim

Muryŏl Wang 武烈王 (654-661), Kim

Munmu Wang 文武王 (661-681), Kim

Sinmun Wang 神文王 (681-692), Kim

Hyoso Wang 孝昭王 (692-702), Kim

Sŏngdŏk Wang 聖德王 (702-737), Kim

Hyosŏng Wang 孝成王 (737-742), Kim

Kyŏngdŏk Wang 景德王 (742-765), Kim

Hyegong Wang 惠恭王 (765-780), Kim

Sŏndŏk Wang 宣德王 (780-785), Kim

Wŏngsŏng Wang 元聖王 (785-798), Kim

Sosŏng Wang 昭聖王 (799-800), Kim

Aejang Wang 哀莊王 (800-809), Kim

Hŏndŏk Wang 憲德王 (809-826), Kim

Hŭngdŏk Wang 興德王 (826-836), Kim

Hŭigang Wang 僖康王 (836-838), Kim

Minae Wang 閔哀王 (838-839), Kim

Sinmu Wang 神武王 (839), Kim

Munsŏng Wang 文聖王 (839-857), Kim

Hŏnan Wang 憲安王 (857-861), Kim

Kyŏngmun Wang 景文王 (861-875), Kim

Hŏn'gang Wang 憲康王 (875-886), Kim

Chŏnggang Wang 定康王 (886-887), Kim

Chinsŏng Yŏwang [Queen] 眞聖女王 (887-897), Kim

Hyogong Wang 孝恭王 (897-912), Kim

Sindŏk Wang 神德王 (912-917), Pak

Kyŏngmyŏng Wang 景明王 (917-924), Pak

Kyŏngae Wang 景哀王 (924-927), Pak

Kyŏngsun Wang 敬順王 (927-935), Kim

E. Later Paekche (892-936)

Proclaimed officially in 900; destroyed by Koryŏ.

Kyŏnhwŏn Wang 甄萱王 (892-935)

Sin'gŏm Wang 神劍王 (936)

F. Later Koguryŏ (901-918)

Called Majin 摩震 (904-910) and T'aebong 泰封 (910-917); destroyed by Koryŏ.

Kungye 弓裔 (901-918)

KORYŎ KINGDOM (918-1392)

Established by Wang Kŏn 王建 and ruled by the Wang 王 dynasty (except from 1375 to 1389). After 950, the rulers of Koryŏ were vassals of one of the Chinese dynasties or sometimes of a non-Chinese foreign prince; in this list the principal dynasty or other foreign power to whom a Koryŏ king was vassal is named after his dates of reign.

A. Period of Establishment (918-997)

T'aejo 太祖 (918-943)

Hyejong 惠宗 (944-945)

Chŏngjong 定宗 (946-949)

Kwangjong 光宗 (950-975), Sung 宗

Kyŏngjong 景宗 (976-981), Sung

Sŏngjong 成宗 (982-997), Sung and Khitan 契丹

B. Period of Prosperity (998-1122)

Mokchong 穆宗 (998-1009), Sung and Khitan

Hyŏnjong 顯宗 (1010-1031), Sung and Khitan

Tŏkchong 德宗 (1032-1034), Sung and Khitan

Chŏngjong 靖宗 (1035-1046), Sung and Khitan

Munjong 文宗 (1047-1083), Sung and Khitan

Sunjong 順宗 (1083), Sung and Khitan

Sŏnjong 宣宗 (1084-1094), Sung and Khitan

Hŏnjong 獻宗 (1095), Sung and Khitan

Sukchong 肅宗 (1096-1105), Sung and Khitan

Yejong 睿宗 (1106-1122), Sung and Khitan

C. Period of Decline (1123-1374)

  I. Control by Influential Nobles

    Injong 仁宗 (1123-1146), Chin 金

    Ŭijong 毅宗 (1147-1170), Chin

  II. Presumptuous Control by Generals (1171-1259)

    Myŏngjong 明宗 (1171-1197), Chin

    Sinjong 神宗 (1198-1204), Chin

    Hŭijong 熙宗 (1205-1211), Chin

    Kangjong 康宗 (1212-1213), Chin

    Kojong 高宗 (1214-1259), Chin

  III. Relations with the Yüan 元 Imperial House (1260-1374)

    Wŏnjong 元宗 (1260-1274), Yüan

    Ch'ungnyŏl Wang 忠烈王 (1275-1308), Yüan

    Ch'ungsŏn Wang 忠宣王 (1309-1313), Yüan

    Ch'ungsuk Wang 忠肅王 (1314-1330), Yüan

    Ch'unghye Wang 忠惠王 (1331-1332), Yüan

    Ch'ungsuk Wang 忠肅王 (1332-1339), Yüan

    Ch'unghye Wang 忠惠王 (1340-1344), Yüan

    Ch'ungmok Wang 忠穆王 (1345-1348), Yüan

    Ch'ungjŏng Wang 忠定王 (1349-1351), Yüan

    Kongmin Wang 恭愍王 (1352-1374), Ming 明

D. Period of Disintegration (1375-1392)

    Sinu 辛禑 (1375-1388), Northern Yüan

Sinch'ang 辛昌 (1389), Ming

Kongyang Wang 恭讓王 (1389-1392), Ming

CHOSŎN KINGDOM (1392-1910)

Ruled by the Yi Dynasty, which was established by the revolt of General Yi Sŏnggye 李成桂 (T'aejo) against the last of the Wang monarchs. The Yi monarchs were vassals of the Ming Dynasty until 1623, and of the Ch'ing Dynasty from 1623 to 1895.

A. Period of Establishment (1392-1400)

    T'aejo 太祖 (1392-1398)

    Chŏngjong 定宗 (1399-1400)

B. Period of Greatness (1401-1494)

    T'aejong 太宗 (1401-1418)

    Sejong 世宗 (1419-1450)

    Munjong 文宗 (1451-1452)

    Tanjong 端宗 (1453-1455)

    Sejo 世祖 (1456-1468)

    Yejong 睿宗 (1469)

    Sŏngjong 成宗 (1470-1494)

C. Period of Internal Disorganization (1495-1567)

    Yŏnsan-gun 燕山君 (1495-1506)

    Chungjong 中宗 (1506-1544)

    Injong 仁宗 (1545)

    Myŏngjong 明宗 (1546-1567)

D. Period of Exhaustion (1568-1724)

    Sŏnjo 宣祖 (1568-1608)

    Kwanghae-gun 光海君 (1609-1623)

    Injo 仁祖 (1623-1649)

    Hyojong 孝宗 (1650-1659)

Hyŏnjong 顯宗 (1660-1674)

Sukchong 肅宗 (1675-1720)

Kyŏngjong 景宗 (1721-1724)

E. Period of Revival (1725-1800)

Yŏngjo 英祖 (1725-1776)

Chŏngjo 正祖 (1777-1800)

F. Period of Decline (1801-1910)

Sunjo 純祖 (1801-1834)

Hŏnjong 憲宗 (1835-1849)

Ch'ŏlchong 哲宗 (1850-1863)

Kojong 高宗 (Yi T'ae Wang 李太王) (1864-1907); assumed the title of emperor in 1897; Japanese protectorate established in 1906.

Sunjong 純宗 (Yi Wang 李王) (1907-1910)

GOVERNMENT GENERAL (1910-1945)

Korea subject to Japanese rule and administered by a governor general who was appointed by, and responsible only to, the Japanese crown. All governors, except Admiral Viscount Saitō, were generals of the Japanese Army.

Terauchi Masatake 寺內正毅 (1910-1916)

Hasegawa Yoshimichi 長谷川好道 (1916-1919)

Saitō Makoto 齊藤實 (1919-1927)

Ugaki Issei* 宇垣一成 (1927)

Yamanashi Hanzō 山梨半造 (1927-1929)

Saitō Makoto 齊藤實 (1929-1931)

Ugaki Issei 宇垣一成 (1931-1936)

---

*Acting governor general

Minami Jirō 南次郎 (1936-1942)

Koiso Kuniaki 小磯國昭 (1942-1944)

Abe Nobuyuki 阿部信行 (1944-1945)

POSTWAR KOREA

South Korea

United States Occupation (1945-1948) Lieutenant General John R. Hodge, commanding general

Military Governors:

Major General Archibald V. Arnold (1945)

Major General Archer L. Lerch (1946-1947)

Brigadier General Charles G. Helmick (acting) (mid-summer, 1947)

Major General William F. Dean (1947-1948)

Republic of Korea

Presidents:

Syngman Rhee (August, 1948-April, 1960)

Hŏ Chŏng 許政 (acting) (April, 1960-August, 1960)

Yun Posŏn 尹譜善 (August, 1960-March, 1962)

Chang Toyŏng 張都暎 Chairman, Supreme Council for National Reconstruction (SCNR) (May, 1961-July, 1961)

Pak Chŏnghui 朴正熙, Chairman, SCNR (July, 1961-December, 1963)

Pak Chŏnghui (since December, 1963)

North Korea

Soviet Military Occupation (1945-1948)

Guard Colonel General Ivan Chistiakov,
commander of the Soviet forces on entry
into Korea.

The Democratic People's Republic of
Korea

Premier:

    Kim Ilsŏng金日成(since Septem-
ber,1948)

Glossary

Note: (K), (J), (C) indicate that the word is Korean, Japanese, or Chinese.

p.   person

p.n.   place name

l.w.   literary work

c.t.   civil title

m.t.   military title

Aejang 哀莊 (K): Silla King.

Aeno 哀奴 (K): p.

ajŏn 衙前 (K): c.t., clerk. See *sŏri.*

Amaterasu Kōdai Jingu 天照皇大神宮 (J): Great Imperial shrine of the Sun Goddess.

An-feng 安奉 (C): The railroad connecting An-tung and Feng-t'ien (Mukden).

Ansan 安山 (K): p.n.

An-tung 安東 (C): p.n., Manchuria.

Ashikaga 足利 (J): Japanese shogunate (and family) (1336-1568).

Asuka 飛鳥 (J): Japanese period about 552-664 A.D.

banzai 萬歲 (J): See *manse.*

budō 武道 (J): "martial way," includes Japanese fencing, archery and the use of the *naginata* (glaive).

ch'ach'aung 次次雄 (K): the Korean title for the second ruler of Silla, may mean shaman.

chang 莊 (K): estate.

Ch'ang 昌 (K): Koryŏ king. See Sinch'ang.

Chang Pogo 張寶高 (K): p. See Kungbok.

Changan 長安 (K): a short-lived Korean state founded by Kim Hŏnch'ang.

Chang-ch'eng 長城 (C): p.n., Manchuria.

Changsu 長壽 (K): Koguryŏ king.

changwŏn 莊園 (K): manor.

Chao-hsien 朝鮮 (C): see Ch'i-tzŭ Chao-hsien-kuo.

Chao-hsien-kuo 朝鮮國 (C): see Chi-tzu Chao-hsien-kuo.

Cheguk sinmun 帝國新聞 (K): a newspaper.

Cheju Island 濟州 (K): p.n.

Chemulp'o 濟物浦 (K): p.n., present-day Inch'ŏn, Kyŏnggi Province.

Ch'en 陳 (C): Chinese Dynasty (557-588 A.D.).

Chen-fan 眞番 (C): Commandery founded in Korea by Han Dynasty.

Chep'o 薺浦 (K): p.n., South Kyŏngsang Province.

Ch'i 齊 (C): Chinese dynasties; Southern Ch'i (479-501 A.D.) Northern Ch'i (550-576 A.D.).

Chiaōchou Bay 膠州 (C): p.n., Kiaochow Bay.

Chien-tao 間島 (C): p.n., Manchuria.

Chiksan 稷山 (K): gold mine, North Ch'ungch'ŏn Province.

chim 朕 (K): royal "we."

Chi'min yao-shu 齊民要術 (C): l.w., Essential Skills for the People.

Chin 晉 (C): Chinese dynasty (265-317) Western Chin; Eastern Chin (317-419 A.D.).

Chin 金 (C): dynasty founded by the Jürchen (1115-1234).

Chin, Later 後金 (C): see Later Chin.

Ch'in 秦 (C): Chinese dynasty (221-207 B.C). Also the state founded by a Tibetan people in the fourth century.

Chin Han 辰韓 (K): Han tribes in southern Korea which occupied present-day North Kyŏngsang Province in the Three Kingdoms period.

Chindan Hakhoe 震檀學會 (K): Chindan Society.

Ch'ing 清 (C): Manchu Dynasty (1636-1912).

chin'gol 眞骨 (K): true bones, a designation of members of the highest class of Silla aristocracy.

ching-t'ien-fa 井田法 (C): "well-field" law. Fields divided into nine units, hence resembling the character, ching 井 (well). Eight families tilled the outer fields and cultivated in common the center field for the lord.

Chinhŭng 眞興 (K): Silla king.

Chinhwŏn 甄萱 (K): p.

Chinju 晉州 (K): p.n., South Kyŏngsang Province.

Chinsŏng 眞聖 (K): Silla queen.

chipsasŏng 執事省 (K): ministry of management.

Ch'ip'yŏng yoram 治平要覽 (K): l.w., Basic Survey for Governing Peacefully.

Ch'i-tan 契丹 (C): see Khitan.

Ch'i-tzu 箕子 (C): p., also Kija (K).

Ch'i-tzu Chao-hsien-kuo 箕子朝鮮國 (C): also Kija chosŏn-guk (K). The state founded allegedly by Ch'i-tzu in the third century B.C.

Chiu-lung Peninsula 九龍 (C): p.n., Kowloon Peninsula.

ch'ŏ 處 (K): estate.

Cho Chun 趙浚 (K): p.

Cho Kwangjo 趙光祖 (K): p.

Cho Minsu 曹敏修 (K): p.

Cho Wich'ong 趙位寵 (K): p.

chōbu 町步 (J): 2.45 acres. See chŏngbo.

Ch'oe 崔 (K): family name.

Ch'oe Cheu 崔齊愚 (K): p.

Ch'oe Ch'unghŏn 崔忠獻 (K): p.

Ch'oe Ch'ungsu 崔忠粹 (K): p.

Ch'oe Hang 崔沆 (K): p.

Ch'oe U 崔瑀 (K): p.

Ch'oe Ŭi 崔竩 (K): p.

Ch'oe Yŏng 崔瑩 (K): p.

Choguk T'ongil Minjujuŭi Chŏnsŏn 祖國統一民主主義戰線 (K): Democratic Front for the Unification of the Fatherland.

Ch'ojŏn 草田 (K): p.n., North Kyŏngsang Province.

chŏkko 赤袴 (K): red trousers, the distinguishing mark of a ninth century Silla bandit group.

Ch'ŏlchong 哲宗 (K): Yi king.

Chŏlla 全羅 (K): Province in Korea.

chŏllang 銓郎 (K): c.t., selection officer.

chŏn 典 (K): department.

Chŏn Pongjun 全琫準 (K): p.

chŏng 停 (K): military garrison.

Chŏng Chungbu 鄭仲夫 (K): p.

Chŏng Mongju 鄭夢周 (K): p.

Chŏng Tojŏn 鄭道傳 (K): p.

Chŏng Yagyong 丁若鏞 (K): p., penname, Tasan.

ch'on'gaek 佃客 (K): p., tenant farmer.

chŏngbang 政房 (K): administrative chamber.

chŏngbo 町步 (K): 2.45 acres, a Japanese land measure, chōbu.

Chŏngbuk 清北 (K): Pure Northerners, Yi Dynasty party faction.

Ch'ŏngch'ŏn (River) 清川 (K): p.n.

Ch'ŏnghae-jin 清海鎮 (K): p.n., present-day Wan 莞 Island in South Chŏlla Province.

Chŏngjong 定宗 (K): p.,Koryŏ king.

Chŏngju 定州 (K): p.n., North P'yŏngan Province.

Ch'ŏngnam 清南 (K): Pure Southerners, Yi Dynasty party faction.

chŏngni 丁吏 (K): slaves who accompanied their masters when they rode on horseback.

Ch'ŏngnyŏn Hoe 青年會 (K): Youth Society.

Ch'ŏngsŏ 清西 (K): Pure Westerners, Yi Dynasty party faction.

Ch'ŏngsobuk 清小北 (K): Pure Small Northerners, Yi Dynasty party faction.

Chongsŏng 鍾城 (K): p.n., Hamgyŏng Province.

chŏngsŭng 政丞 (K): c.t., minister of state.

chŏnho 佃戶 (K): tiller, tenant farmer.

chŏnjang 田莊 (K): paddy estates.

Chŏnju 全州 (K): p.n., North Chŏlla Province.

ch'ŏnmin 賤民 (K): despised people, who by virtue of their low social status were unfree, although many were not chattel. The group as a whole suffered from legal disabilities, although the social acceptance among commoners varied widely. Ch'ŏnmin included: slaves, serfs, shamanesses, female entertainers, butchers, basket makers, sandal makers, menial servants in government service and certain holders of low official offices. In the Yi period monks and nuns were classed as ch'ŏnmin.

chŏnsigwa 田柴科 (K): paddy land and woods by class, rice land and firewood land allotted to those in the service of the government.

Ch'ŏrwŏn 鐵圓 (K): p.n., (Silla), modern. 鐵原

Ch'ŏrwŏn 鐵原 (K): p.n.

Chōsen 朝鮮 (J): Korea.

Chōsen Bōkyō Kyōkai 朝鮮防共協會 (J): Korean Anti-Communist Association.

Chōsen bunka-shi 朝鮮文化史 (J):l.w. Cultural History of Korea.

Chōsen Chisso Hiryō Kabushiki Kaisha 朝鮮窒素肥料株式會社 (J): Korean Nitrogren Fertilizer Company.

Chōsen gakuhō 朝鮮學報 (J): Journal of the Academic Association of Koreanology in Japan.

Chōsen koseki zufu 朝鮮古蹟圖譜 (J): l.w. Album of Korean Antiquities.

Chōsen rekishi chiri 朝鮮歷史地理
(J): *Korean Historical Geography.* (Journal)

Chōsen Suiden Kabushiki Kaisha 朝鮮
水電株式會社
(J): Korean Hydroelectric Company.

Chōsen-shi 朝鮮史 (J):l.w. *History of Korea.*

Chōsen-shi gaisetsu 朝鮮史概説
(J): l.w. *Introduction to Japanese History.*

Chōsen-shi Kenkyūkai 朝鮮史研究會
(J): Korean History Study Society.

Chōsen-shi no shirube 朝鮮史のしるべ
(J): l.w. *Introduction to Korean History.*

Chōsen-shi nyūmon 朝鮮史入門(J): l.w.
A Guide to the Study of Korean History.

Chosŏn 朝鮮 (K): Korea.

Chosŏn Kongsangdang 朝鮮共産黨
(K): Korean Communist Party.

Chosŏn ilbo 朝鮮日報 (K): a newspaper.

Chosŏn Inmin Konghwaguk 朝鮮人民共和國
(K): Korean People's Republic.

Chosŏn Minjujuŭi Inmin Konghwaguk 朝鮮
民主主義人民共和國(K): Democratic
People's Republic of Korea.

Chou 周 (C): Chinese dynasty
(c. 1028-257 B.C.) Northern Chou (557-579
A.D.).

Chou Wen-mu 周文謨(C): p.

chu 州 (K): district.

Chu Hsi 朱熹 (C): p.

Chu Yüan-chang 朱元璋 (C): founder of
the Ming Dynasty. See Hung-wu.

Ch'uang-hai 滄海 (C): Commandery
founded by the Han Dynasty in northern
Korea.

Chukchu 竹州 (K): p.n.

Chumong 朱蒙 (K): a diety wor-
shipped as the ancestor of the Koguryŏ
people.

chun 郡 (C): commandery.

Ch'un-chiu 春秋 (C): Spring and Au
tumn, period in the late Chou Dynasty from
the eighth to the fifth century B.C.

Chungbuk 中北 (K): Middle Northern
ers, Yi Dynasty party faction.

Ch'ung-ch'ing 重慶 (C): p.n. Chungking.

Ch'ungch'ŏng 忠清 (K): province in Korea

Chungjong 中宗 (K): Yi king.

Ch'ungjŏng Wang 忠定王 (K): Koryŏ king.

Chungking 重慶 (C): see Ch'ung-ch'ing

Ch'ungnyŏl Wang 忠烈王 (K): Koryŏ king

chün-t'ien-fa 均田法(C): "equal field" law
During the T'ang Dynasty each male or
reaching adulthood was supposed to be
given by law about fifteen acres of land and
in return he paid taxes in kind.

chut'ong 州統 (K): district abbot.

Daiichi Bank 第一 (J): First Bank.

Dairen (C): see Ta-lien.

Feng-t'ien 奉天 (C): p.n.,Mukden, Manchuria.

Fu-chien 福建 (C): Chinese province,
Fukien.

Fukien (C): see Fu-chien.

Fukuda Tokuzō 福田德三 (J): p.

Fu-shun 撫順 (C): p.n., Manchuria.

Fu-yu 扶餘 (C): see Puyŏ.

Haein (sa) 海印寺 (K): Haein (Buddhist)
Temple.

Haeju 海州 (K): p.n., Hwanghae
Province.

Ha-erh-pin 哈爾濱 (C): p.n., Harbin, Manchuria.

Hakata (Bay) 博多 (J): p.n.

Hambuk Hŭnghak Hoe 咸北興學會 (K): North Hamgyŏng Province Encouragement of Learning Society.

Hamgyŏng 咸鏡 (K): Province in Korea.

Hamun (sa) 咸恩寺 (K): Hamun (Buddhist) Temple.

Han 漢 (C): Chinese dynasty. Former Han (206 B.C.-8 A.D.). Later Han (23-220 A.D.).

Han 韓 (K): Korean tribes that occupied southern Korea in the period of the Three Kingdoms.

Han River 漢 (K): p.n.

Handang 漢黨 (K): *Han* party, Yi Dynasty party faction.

Han'guk Kwangbok Undong Tanch'e Yŏnhaphoe. 韓國光復運動團體聯合會 (K): United Associations of Movements for the Revival of Korea.

Han'guk-sa 韓國史 (K): l.w. *History of Korea.*

Han'guk-sa sillon 韓國史新論 (K): l.w. *New View of Korean History.*

hangŭl 한글 (K): the present name of the script invented at the command of King Sejong. It contained 17 consonants and 11 vowels when it was proclaimed in 1446; various modifications reduced these to 14 consonants and 10 vowels. Words are written in syllable clusters.

hanja 漢字 (K): Chinese characters.

Hansŏng 漢城 (K): p.n., modern Kwangju, Kyŏnggi Province.

hansŭng 飯僧 (K): "rice priest."

Hanyang 漢陽 (K): p.n.,Seoul.

Happ'o 合浦 (K): p.n., modern Masan, North Kyŏngsang Province.

Harbin 哈爾濱 (C): see Ha-erh-pin.

Hatada Takashi 旗田巍 (J): p.

Hideyoshi (J): see Toyotomi Hideyoshi.

hoep'i 廻避 (K): "avoid returning," principle of not appointing officials to posts in their native districts.

Hŏnan 憲安 (K): Silla king.

Hŏndŏk 憲德 (K): Silla king.

Hong Kyŏngnae 洪景來 (K): p.

Hŏn'gang 憲康 (K): Silla king.

Hongbŏm 洪範 (K): *Hung-fan* (C), title of a section of the Confucian Classic, *Shu-ching (Book of History).*

Hongju 洪州 (K): p.n.,South Ch'ungch'ŏng Province.

Hŏnjong 憲宗 (K): Yi king.

hŏpch'ik 險側 (K): title of lesser chiefs of Han tribes in the Three Kingdoms period.

Hot'ae 好太 (K): Koguryŏ king. See Kwanggaet'o.

Hot'ae-wang-bi 好太王碑 (K): stele erected in 414 to commemorate the successful campaigns of King Kwanggaet'o of Koguryŏ.

hsien 縣 (C): prefecture. See *hyŏn* (K).

Hsien-pi 鮮卑 (C): a steppe people on the northern periphery of China active in eastern Mongolia and southern Manchuria in the third century A.D.

Hsin 新 (C): Chinese dynasty. Actually the reign of Wang Mang (8-23 A.D.).

Hsü Ching 徐兢 (C): p.

Hsiung-nu 匈奴 (C): a barbarian people inhabiting the steppes north and west of China from approximately the fourth century B.C. to the beginning of the Christian era. Some authorities have identified them as the Huns.

Hsüan-t'u 玄菟 (C): commandery founded in Korea by the Han Dynasty Chinese.

Hsü-chou 徐州 (C): p.n.

Hung-fan 洪範 (C): see *Hongbŏm*.

Hŭngnam 興南 (K): p.n., South Hamg-yŏng Province.

Hung-wu 洪武 (C): reign title (1368-1398) of Ming Dynasty founder, Chu Yüan-chang. (q.v.)

Hŭngyang 興陽 (K): p.n., South Chŏlla Province.

Hunmin chŏngŭm 訓民正音 (K): l.w., *Proper Phonetics for Instruction of the People.*

hwabaek 和白 (K): conferences or councils of Silla chiefs.

hwajŏk 火賊 (K): "fire bandits," mounted bandits carrying firearms.

Hwang Sayŏng 黃嗣永 (K): p.

Hwanghae 黃海 (K): province in Korea.

Hwangnyong (sa) 皇龍寺 (K): Hwangnyong (Buddhist) Temple.

Hwangsŏng sinmun 皇城新聞 (K): a newspaper.

hwarang 花郎 (K): Silla associations of young noblemen who functioned as an elite military body in the Silla army. Later they lost their military function.

hyang 鄉 (K): country district.

hyanggyo 鄉校 (K): country-district schools.

hyangni 鄉吏 (K): c.t., country-district clerk.

Hyech'o 慧超 (K): p.

Hyegong 惠恭 (K): Silla king.

Hyejong 惠宗 (K): Koryŏ king.

Hyo Sim 孝心 (K): p.

Hyojong 孝宗 (K): Yi king.

Hyŏkkŏse 赫居世 (K): first ruler of Silla.

hyŏn 縣 (K): prefecture.

Hyŏnjong 顯宗 (K): Koryŏ king, Yi king.

i 里 (K): village—*ri* or *ni* when preceded by name of village.

Ikeuchi Hiroshi 池內宏 (J): p.

Iki Island 壹岐 (J): p.n.

Ilchinhoe 一進會 (K): Korean society oriented toward Japan.

Inaba Iwakichi 稻葉岩吉 (J): p.

Inch'ŏn 仁川 (K): p.n. See Chemulp'o, Kyŏnggi Province.

Injo 仁祖 (K): Yi king.

Injong 仁宗 (K): Koryŏ king, Yi king.

Itō Hirobumi 伊藤博文 (J): p.

Jaisohn, Philip (K): see Sŏ Chaep'il.

Jû-chen 女眞 (C): see Jürchen.

Jürchen 女眞 (C): a Tungusic people known to the Chinese people as Jû-chen.

Ka Island 椵 (K): p.n.

kabi 家婢 (K): female household slaves.

kadong 家僮 (K): young male household slaves.

Kaegyŏng 開京 (K): p.n. See Kaesŏng.

Kaesŏng 開城 (K): p.n., Koryŏ capital, also known as Kaegyŏng and Songdo.

K'ai-yüan 開原 (C): p.n., Manchuria.

kana 假名 (J): Japanese syllabic script.

Kanazawa Shōsaburō 金澤庄三郎 (J): p.

Kang Su 强首 (K): p.

Kanghwa Island 江華 (K): p.n.

Kangwŏn 江原 (K): province of Korea.

kano 家奴 (K): male household slaves.

Kao-tsung 高宗 (C): third emperor of the T'ang Dynasty.

Karak 駕洛 (K): Pyŏn Han state. See Mimana.

Katō Kiyomasa 加藤清正 (J): p.

Kaya Mountain 伽耶 (K): p.n., South Kyŏngsang Province.

Keijō 京城 (J): Seoul.

kempei 憲兵 (J): military police.

keisatsu 警察 (J): police.

Khitan 契丹 (C): a Mongolian-speaking people known to the Chinese as Ch'i-tan.

Khublai Khan, in Chinese Hu-pi-lieh 忽必烈 (C): Yuan emperor, Hu-pi-lieh. See Shih-tsu.

Ki 奇 (K): p.,family name.

Kiaochow Bay. (C): see Chiaochou Bay.

Kida Teikichi 喜田貞吉 (J): p.

Kihwŏn 箕萱 (K): p.

kiin 其人 (K): sons of *hyangni* (country-district clerks) held at Koryŏ capital as hostages.

Kija 箕子 (K): p., also Ch'i-tzu.

Kija Chosŏn-guk (K): see Ch'i-tzu Chao-hsien-kuo.

Kil Chae 吉再 (K): p.

Kim 金 (K): Korean family name. One of the three families eligible to become kings of Silla.

Kim Chaewŏn 金載元 (K): p., also known as Kim Chewon.

Kim Chewon (K): see Kim Chaewŏn.

Kim Chongjik 金宗直 (K): p.

Kim Chuwŏn 金周元 (K): p.

Kim Hŏnch'ang 金憲昌 (K): p.

Kim Hyowŏn 金孝元 (K): p.

Kim Ilsŏng 金日成 (K): p.

Kim Inmun 金仁問 (K): p.

Kim Koengjip 金宏集 (K): p.

Kim Ku 金九 (K): p.

Kim Kyusik 金奎植 (K): p.

Kim Kuhi 金仇亥 (K): p.

Kim Okkyun 金玉均 (K): p.

Kim Po 金溥 (K): p., Silla king, Kyŏngsun.

Kim Podang 金甫堂 (K): p.

Kim Pŏmmun 金梵文 (K): p.

Kim Pusik 金富軾 (K): p.

Kim Sami 金沙彌 (K): p.

Kim Sŏngsu 金性洙 (K): p.

Kim Ujing 金佑徵 (K): p., became King Sinmu.

Kim Ŭnbu 金殷傅 (K): p.

Kim Yusin 金庾信 (K): p.

kisaeng 妓生 (K): singing girl, female entertainer.

ko 孤 (K): princely "we."

Kobu County 古阜 (K): p.n., North Chŏlla Province.

Koguryŏ 高句麗 (K): a Korean-Manchurian state (first century B.C.-668 A.D.) and the people who founded the state.

Kojong 高宗 (K): Koryŏ king, and Yi king also known as Yi T'aewang and the Kwangmu Emperor.

kol 骨 (K): bone, a Silla term that indicated blood kinship

Kolpuk 骨北 (K): Bone Northerners, Yi Dynasty party faction.

kolp'umje 骨品制 (K): Silla system of political and social ranking based on blood ties, political status and social position.

kōmin-ka 皇民化 (J): transformation into imperial subjects.

Komun Island 巨文 (K): p.n., South Chŏlla Province, also known as Port Hamilton.

Kongju 公州 (K): p.n., South Chŏlla Province.

Kongmin Wang 恭愍王 (K): Koryŏ king.

kongsinjŏn 功臣田 (K): meritorious ministers' paddy.

Kongsŏ 功西 (K): meritorious Westerners, Yi Dynasty party faction.

Kŏn'guk chunbi Wiwŏnhoe 建國準備委員會 (K): Committee for the Preparation of Korean Independence.

kongŭmjŏnsi 功蔭田柴 (K): merit paddy land and woods, conferred on those who had rendered distinguished service in the founding of Koryŏ. Later such lands were granted to officials according to their rank.

Kong'yang 恭讓 (K): Koryŏ king.

Konishi Yukinaga 小西行長 (J): p.

Koryŏ 高麗 (K): Korean state (918-1392).

Koryŏ Kongsandang 高麗共産黨 (K): Korean Communist Party.

Koryŏ-sa 高麗史 (K): l.w., *History of Koryŏ*.

Koseki chōsa hōkoku 古蹟調査報告 (J): Archeological Investigation Reports.

Kŏsŏgan 居西干 (K): the Korean title for the first king of Silla, probably meant chief.

Kowloon Peninsula (C): see Chiulung Peninsula.

Kuangchou Bay 廣州 (C): p.n.

kuk 國 (K): state or nation.

Kukcho pogam 國朝寶鑑 (K): l.w., Dynastic Mirror.

kuksa 國師 (K): instructor of the nation, on ecclesiastical rank.

Kuksa sillon 國史新論 (K): l.w., *New View of National History*.

Kuksa taegwan 國史大觀 (K): l.w., General Survey of National History.

kukt'ong 國統 (K): state abbot.

Kŭm River 錦 (K): p.n.

Kŭmgwan-guk 金官國 (K): p.n., a petty state in the Naktong River basin of the sixth century.

Kŭmhae 金海 (K): p.n., South Kyŏngsang Province.

Kŭmsŏng 金城 (K): county, Kangwŏn Province.

kun 郡 (K): county or commandery. See *chün* (C).

Kungbok 弓福 (K): p. See Chang Pogo.

Kungnaesŏng 國內城 (K): p.n., one of the capitals of Koguryŏ. Present-day T'ung-kou, Manchuria.

Kungye 弓裔 (K): p.

kunjŏn 軍田 (K): military field.

Kunsan 群山 (K): p.n., North Chŏlla Province.

kunt'ong 郡統 (K): county abbot.

Kuomintang 國民黨 (C): Chinese Nationalist Party.

Kuroda Nagamasa 黑田長政 (J): p.

Kuroita Katsumi 黑板勝美 (J): p.

kusa 驅使 (K): slaves who accompanied their masters when they rode on horseback.

kwagŏ 科擧 (K): literary examination for government posts.

kwajŏn 科田 (K): classified field.

kwajŏn-pŏp 科田法 (K): classified field law.

kwanch'alsa 觀察使 (K): c.t., governor-inspector.

Kwanggaet'o 廣開土 (K): Koguryŏ king. See Hot'ae.

Kwanghae-gun 光海君 (K): Yi king.

Kwanghwa Gate 光化 (K):

Kwangjong 光宗 (K): Koryŏ king.

Kwangju 光州 (K): p.n., South Chŏlla Province.

Kwangmu 光武 (K): reign name adopted by King Kojong in 1897.

kyesa 癸巳 (K): junior-water-serpent. Characters in the sixty-year cycle. identified in Korean history with the year 1173 and the uprising which resulted in the massacre of civil officials by military officers.

Kyoju 交州 (K): province of Koryŏ and early Yi Korea.

kyŏl 結 (K): a unit of land measure for cultivated fields. The area of the *kyŏl* has varied over the centuries from approximately 490 square feet in 1069 to roughly 10,000 square feet in the nineteenth century.

Kyŏng Taesŭng 慶大升 (K): p.

Kyŏngbok 景福 (K): a palace.

Kyŏngdŏk 景德 (K): Silla king.

Kyŏnggi 京畿 (K): capital province of Korea.

Kyŏngguk taejŏn 經國大典 (K): l.w., *Fundamental Statutes for Governing the Country.*

Kyŏnghŭng 慶興 (K): p.n., Hamgyŏng Province.

kyŏng'in 庚寅 (K): senior-metal-tiger. Characters in the sixty-year cycle, identified in Korean history with the year 1170 and the uprising of Chŏng Chungbu in that year.

Kyŏngju 慶州 (K): p.n., capital of Silla. North Kyŏngsang Province.

Kyŏngsang 慶尚 (K): province in Korea.

Kyŏngsŏng 京城 (K): Seoul.

Kyŏngsun 敬順 (K): Silla king, also known as Kim Po.

Kyŏngwŏn 慶源 (K): p.n., Hamgyŏng Province.

Later Chin 後金 (C): Manchu (Jürchen) dynasty (1616-1636), changed to Ch'ing (q.v.) in 1636.

Li Hung-chang 李鴻章 (C): p.

Li Ju-sung 李如松 (C): p.

Liang 梁 (C): Chinese dynasty (502-556 A.D.).

Liao River 遼 (C): p.n., Manchuria.

Liao-hsi 遼西 (C): p.n., Manchuria.

Liao-tung 遼東 (C): p.n., Manchuria.

Liao-yang 遼陽 (C): p.n., Manchuria.

Lin-t'un 臨屯 (C): commandery founded in Korea by the Han Dynasty Chinese.

Lo-lang 樂浪 (C): commandery founded in Korea by the Han Dynasty Chinese.

Ma Han 馬韓 (K): Han tribes in southern Korea which occupied present-day Ch'ungch'ŏng Province and Chŏlla Province in the Three Kingdoms period.

Man-chou-kuo 滿洲國 (C): Japanese puppet state in Manchuria; Manshūkoku (J).

Mangi 亡伊 (K): p.

Manmin Kongdong Hoe 萬民共同會 (K): Popular Cooperative Society.

Mangsoi 亡所伊 (K): p.

manse 萬歲 (K): ten thousand years, "long live" *banzai* (J).

Mansen chiri rekishi kenkyū hōkoku 滿鮮地理歷史研究報告 (J): *Study Reports on the Geography and History of Manchuria and Korea.*

Manshū rekishi chiri 滿洲歷史地理 (J): *Manchurian Historical Geography.* (Journal)

Manshūkoku (J): see Man-chou-kuo.

Mao Wen-lung 毛文龍 (C): p.

maripkan 麻立干 (K): Korean title for the nineteenth to the twenty-second rulers of Silla, probably meant chief.

Masan 馬山 (K): p.n., South Kyŏngsang Province.

Matsui Hitoshi 松井等 (J): p.

Meiji 明治 (J): Japanese reign 1868-1912.

Mimana 任那 (J): the Pyŏn Han area of southern Korea occupied by Japanese in the fourth century.

Min 閔 (K): the family of the consort of Yi Kojong, and the queen.

Ming 明 (C): Chinese dynasty (1368-1662). See Ta Ming.

Min-yüeh 閩越 (C): present-day Fukien Province.

Minzoku to rekishi 民族と歷史 (J): *Race and History.* (Journal)

Miryang 密陽 (K): p.n., South Kyŏngsang Province.

Mishina Akihide 三品彰英 (J): p.

Mitsubishi 三菱 (J): Japanese corporation.

Mitsui 三井 (J): Japanese corporation.

Miura Gorō 三浦梧樓 (J): p.

Miyazaki Michisaburō 宮崎道三郎 (J): p.

mok 牧 (K): department; more literally pastorate.

Mokchong 穆宗 (K): Koryŏ king.

Mokp'o 木浦 (K) p.n., South Chŏlla Province.

Mōri Yoshinari 毛利吉成 (J): p.

munhabu 門下府 (K): chancellery.

Mujinju 武珍州 (K): p.n., present-day Kwangju, South Chŏlla Province.

Mu-jung 慕容 (C): a clan of the Hsien-pi.

Mukden (C): see Feng-t'ien.

mun'gaek 門客 (K): military retainer.

Munjong 文宗 (K): Koryŏ king.

Munmu 文武 (K): Silla king.

Munsŏng 文聖 (K): Silla king.

Muromachi 室町 (J): Japanese period, 1336-1573.

Myo Ch'ŏng 妙清 (K): p.

myŏn 面 (K): township.

Myŏnghak 鳴鶴 Place 所 (K): p.n.

Myŏngjong 明宗 (K): Koryo king and Yi king.

Myŏngju 溟州 (K): p.n., Kangwŏn Province.

Naeip'o 乃而浦 (K): p.n.; present-day Chep'o, South Kyŏngsang Province.

Naemul 奈勿 (K): Silla ruler.

naisen ittai-ka 內鮮一體化 (J): unification of Japan and Korea.

Nak 洛 (K): *Nak* Party, Yi Dynasty political faction.

Naka Michiyo 那珂道世 (J): p.

Nakata Kaoru 中田薰 (J): p.

Naktang 洛黨 (K): *Nak* Party, Yi Dynasty party faction.

Naktong River 洛東 (K): p.n.

Namgyŏng 南京 (K): p.n., Seoul.

Namhae 南解 (K): second ruler of Silla.

Namin 南人 (K): Southerners, Yi Dynasty party faction.

Nan-yüeh 南越 (C): present-day Vietnam.

nisagŭm 尼師今 (K): Korean title for the third to eighteenth rulers of Silla, probably meant chief.

Noguchi 野口 (J): Japanese corporation.

Noguchi Jun 野口遵 (J): p.

nongjang 農莊 (K): farm estates.

Nongsa chiksŏl 農事直說 (K): l.w., *A Straight Explanation of Agricultural Matters.*

Nool 奴兀 Ward (K): p.n., in Sŏmch'ŏn, South Kyŏngsang Province.

Noron 老論 (K): Old Doctrine, Yi Dynasty party faction.

Nosŏ 老西 (K): Old Westerners, Yi Dynasty party faction.

Nurhachi 奴兒哈赤 (C): p.

Oda Nobunaga 織田信長 (J): p.

Okchŏ 沃沮 (K): a Korean tribe that occupied the region of modern Hamgyŏng Province in the period of the Three Kingdoms.

ŏnmun 諺文 (K): common script (for writing Korean). See *hangŭl.*

Oryeui 五禮儀 (K): l.w., *Five Ceremonies.*

Paekche 伯濟 (K): Ma Han Paekche. 百濟 (K): one of the Korean Three Kingdoms (18 B.C.-660 A.D.).

Pak 朴 (K): Korean family name. One of the three families eligible to become kings of Silla.

Pak Yŏnghyo 朴泳孝 (K): p.

P'algwanhoe 八關會 (K): Korean festival.

pangsŏng 方城 (K): Paekche area fort garrisoned by 700 to 1,200 troops.

Pao-ting-fu 保定府 (C): p.n.

P'ibuk 皮北 (K): Skin Northerners, Yi Dynasty party faction.

pobusang 褓負商 (K): swaddling-clothes carrying tradesmen, peddlers.

Pongdŏk (sa) 奉德寺 (K): Pongdŏk (Buddhist) Temple.

Pongsŏng (sa) 奉聖寺 (K): Pongsŏng (Buddhist) Temple.

Pong'ŭn (sa) 奉恩寺 (K): Pong'ŭn (Buddhist) Temple.

Pŏphŭng 法興 (K): Silla king.

Poŭn County 報恩 (K): p.n., North Ch'ungch'ŏng Province.

pu 部 (K): board.

pu 府 (K): bureau; municipality.

Pugin 北人 (K): Northerners, Yi Dynasty party faction.

pugok 部曲 (K): ward.

Pugwŏn 北原 (K): p.n., present-day Wŏnju, Kangwŏn Province.

Puin 符仁 (K): p.n., North Kyŏngsang Province.

Pujŏn River 赴戰 (K): p.n.

Puk-Chosŏn Minjujuŭi Minjok Chŏnsŏn 北朝鮮民主主義民族戰線 (K): North Korean Democratic People's Front.

Puk-Chosŏn Nodongdang 北朝鮮로동당 (K): North Korean Labor Party.

Pukkye 北界 (K): Northern March.

Puksŏn Inmin Wiwŏnhoe 北鮮人民委員會 (K): North Korean People's Committee.

Puksŏng Hoe 北星會 (K): North Star Society.

Pulguk (sa) 佛國寺 (K): Pulguk (Buddhist) Temple.

pum 品 (K): class or status.

P'unghae 豐海 (K): province of early Yi Korea, later called Hwanghae.

Punhwang (sa) 芬皇寺 (K): Punhwang (Buddhist) Temple.

punye 樊濊 (K): title of lesser chiefs of Han tribes in the Three Kingdoms period.

pubyŏng 府兵 (K): Koryŏ corps of royal guards modeled on the T'ang military system.

purak 部落 (K): hamlet.

Pusan 釜山 (K): p.n., South Kyŏngsang Province.

Pusanp'o 富山浦 (K): present-day Pusan, South Kyŏngsang Province.

Pusŏk 浮石 (K): p.n., North Kyŏngsang Province.

Puyŏ 扶餘 (K): a people of Manchuria and Northern Korea. Also Fu-yü (C).

P'yesagundan 廢四郡團 (K): Band of the Four Abolished Counties, a gang of robbers in northwestern Korea in the reign of King Yŏngjo of the Yi Dynasty.

Pyŏkchegwan 碧蹄館 (K): p.n., Kyŏnggi Province.

pyŏl-sajŏn 別賜田 (K): especially conferred paddy.

Pyŏn Han 弁韓 (K): Han tribes in southern Korea which occupied present-day South Kyŏngsang Province in the Three Kingdoms period.

P'yŏngan 平安 (K): Province in Korea.

pyŏnggyŏng 並耕 (K): joint ploughing.

pyŏngjak 並作 (K): joint work.

P'yŏngyang 平壤 (K): p.n., South P'yŏngan Province.

Rhee, Syngman (K): p. See Yi Sungman.

Sabi 泗沘 (K): p.n., Paekche capital, South Ch'ungch'ŏng Province, modern Puyŏ.

Sach'ŏn 泗川 (K): p.n., South Kyŏngsang Province.

Sach'ŏnwang (sa) 四天王寺 (K): Sach'ŏnwang (Buddhist) Temple.

sadae 事大 (K): "serve the great," i.e., to serve China.

Sa-erh-hu 薩爾滸 (C): p.n., Manchuria.

Saigō Takamori 西鄉隆盛 (J): p.

Saitō Makoto 齊藤實 (J): p.

sajŏn 賜田 (K): paddy land bestowed by the king as a mark of favor.

Sakurai Yoshiyuki 櫻井義之 (J): p.

sambyŏlch'o 三別抄 (K): irregular Koryŏ military units.

Samch'ŏk 三陟 (K): p.n., Kangwŏn Province.

samsuryang 三手糧 (K): "three hand" grain tax.

Sandang 山黨 (K): mountain party, Yi Dynasty party faction.

Sangju 尚州 (K): p.n., North Kyŏngsang Province.

sarhae 殺奚 (K): title of lesser chiefs of Han tribes in the Three Kingdoms period.

Saro 斯盧 (K): early name for Silla.

Saryang 蛇梁 (K): p.n., South Chŏlla Province.

sasimgwan 事審官 (K): c.t., inspecting officer.

saŭm 舍音 (K): land agent.

Seimu Sōkan 政務總監 (J): c.t., Civil Administrator of Korea.

Sejo 世祖 (K): Yi king.

Sejong 世宗 (K): Yi king.

Sejong sillok chiriji 世宗實錄地理志 (K): l.w., (King) *Sejong Veritable Records Gazeteer.*

Sekino Tadashi 關野貞 (J): p.

Seoul 서을 (K): capital of Korea.

Seoul Ch'ŏngnyŏn Hoe 서을靑年會 (K): Seoul Young Men's Association.

Shang 商 (C): Chinese dynasty also called Yin (c. 1600-1028 B.C.).

Shanghai 上海 (C): p.n.

Shantung Peninsula 山東 (C): p.n.

Shen-yang 瀋陽 (C): p.n., Mukden, Manchuria.

Shigaku zasshi 史學雜誌 (J): *The Journal of Historical Science.*

Shidehara Taira 幣原坦 (J): p.

Shih-tsu 世祖 (C): Yüan emperor, Khublai Khan.

Shimonoseki 下關 (J): p.n.

Shintō 神道 (J): "Way of the Gods," Japanese religion.

Shiratori Kurakichi 白鳥庫吉 (J): p.

Shu 蜀 (C): Minor Han, Chinese dynasty of the Three Kingdoms Period (221-263 A.D.)

Shu-ching 書經 (C): l.w., *Book of History.*

sigŭp 食邑 (K): emolument estates, a term of land tenure.

Silla 新羅 (K): one of the Three Kingdoms (57? B.C.-668 A.D.). Sole Korean Kingdom (668-892). Overthrown 935.

Sim Ŭigyŏm 沈義謙 (K): p.

Sinch'ang 辛昌 (K): Koryŏ king. See Ch'ang.

Sin'gan Hoe 新幹會 (K): New Foundations Society.

sinji 臣智 (K): title of paramount chiefs of Han tribes in the Three Kingdoms period.

Sinjong 神宗 (K): Koryŏ king.

Sinmu 神武 (K): Silla king. See Kim Ujing.

Sinsŏ 申西 (K): *Sin* Westerners, Yi Dynasty party faction.

Sinsŏng 新城 (K): p.n.

Sinu 新禑 (K): Koryŏ king. See U.

so 所 (K): place.

Sō 宗 (J): family name and clan on Tsushima.

Sŏ Chaep'il 徐載弼 (K): p., Philip Jaisohn.

Sobuk 小北 (K): Small Northerners, Yi Dynasty party faction.

sŏdang 書堂 (K): literary hall.

Sŏgangdan 西江團 (K): Band of the West River, a gang of robbers during the reign of King Yŏngjo of the Yi Dynasty.

Sŏhae 西海 (K): province of Koryŏ and early Yi Korea.

Sŏhak 西學 (K): Western Learning.

Sŏin 西人 (K): Westerners, Yi Dynasty party faction.

Sŏk 昔 (K): Korean family name. One of the three families eligible to become kings of Silla.

Sŏkkuram 石窟庵 (K): stone grotto on the outskirts of Kyŏngju.

Sŏmch'ŏn 陝川 (K): p.n., South Kyŏngsang Province.

Sŏndŏk 宣德 (K): Silla king.

Song Pyŏngnyak 宋秉略 (K): p.

Song Siryŏl 宋時烈 (K): p.

Songdo 松都 (K): p.n., see Kaesŏng.

sŏnggol 聖骨 (K): sage bones, a designation of members of the highest class of Silla aristocracy.

sŏk 石 (K): a unit of dry measure of grain. The volume has varied over the centuries. At the present it is approximately five bushels.

Songak 松岳 (K): Kaesŏng.

Sŏnggyun'gwan 成均館 (K): a Confucian academy.

Sŏngjin 城津 (K): p.n., North Hamgyŏng Province.

sŏngjŏn 成典 (K): Silla government offices for the repair of major Buddhist temples.

Sŏngjong 成宗 (K): Koryŏ king, also Yi king.

Sŏnjo 宣祖 (K): Yi king.

sŏri 胥吏 (K): c.t., clerk. See ajŏn.

Soron 少論 (K): Young Doctrine, Yi Dynasty party faction.

Sosŏ 少西 (K): Young Westerners, Yi Dynasty party faction.

Sōtoku 總督 (J): c.t., Governor General.

Sŏu Hakhoe 西友學會 (K): Friends of the West Study Society.

sŏwŏn 書院 (K): literary academy.

Ssangam 雙岩 (K): p.n., North Kyŏngsang Province.

Suematsu Yasukazu 末松保和 (J): p.

Sui 隋 (C): Chinese dynasty (580-618 A.D.).

sujŏk 水賊 (K): "water bandits," pirates.

Sukchong 肅宗 (K): Yi king.

Sumitomo 住友 (J): Japanese corporation.

Sunch'ŏn 順天 (K): p.n., in South Chŏlla Province.

Sung 宋 (C): Chinese dynasties: Liu Sung (420-478 A.D.), Northern Sung (960-1126), Southern Sung (1127-1279).

Sungari River (Sung-hua-chiang) 松花江 (C): p.n.,Manchuria.

Sŭngjŏn 勝詮 (K): p.

Sunjo 純祖 (K): Yi king.

Sunjong 純宗 (K): Yi king, Yi Ch'ŏk.

Suwŏn 水原 (K): p.n., Kyŏnggi Province.

Ta Ming 大明 (C): Ming state of China (1368-1662).

Tabo (t'ap) 多寶塔 (K): Many Treasures Stone Stupa of Pulguk Temple.

Taebuk 大北 (K): Great Northerners, Yi dynasty party faction.

taedaero 大對盧 (K): highest rank of Koguryŏ officials.

T'aebong 泰封 (K): a short-lived early tenth-century Korean state.

Taedong River 大同江 (K): p.n.

taedong-mi 大同米 (K): great correspondence rice, tax payable in rice.

taedong-pŏp 大同法 (K): law of great correspondence, a tax payable in rice.

Taehan Chagang Hoe 大韓自強會 (K): Great Han Self-strengthening Association.

Taehan Cheguk 大韓帝國 (K): Empire of the Great Han, Korea.

Taehan maeil sinmun 大韓每日新聞 (K): a newspaper.

Taehan Minguk 大韓民國 (K): Republic of Korea.

Taehan Minguk Imsi Chŏngbu 大韓民國臨時政府 (K): Provisional Government of the Republic of Korea.

T'aejo 太祖 (K): posthumous title of the founders of the Wang and Yi dynasties, Wang Kŏn and Yi Sŏnggye.

T'aejong 太宗 (K): Yi king.

taesahŏn 太司憲 (K): c.t., chief of the office of supervision.

Taewŏn-gun 大院君 (K): p. Also known as Yi Haŭng.

Tai-fang 帶方 (C): commandery in Korea separated from the southern part of Lo-lang Commandery (204-313).

Taika 大化 (J): Great change, a period of reform in Japan initiated in 645 A.D.

Taiping (T'ai-p'ing) 太平 (C): rebellion in China(1850-1864).

Taisei Yokusan-kai 大政翼贊會 (J): Imperial Rule Assistance Association.

T'ai-tsung 太宗 (C): Li Shih-min, second emperor of the Tang Dynasty. Abahai, posthumously known as Ch'ing T'ai-tsung.

Tak Chun'gyŏng 拓俊京 (K): p.

T'aknam 濁南 (K): Muddy Southerners, Yi Dynasty party faction.

T'akpuk 濁北 (K): Muddy Northerners, Yi Dynasty party faction.

T'aksobuk 濁小北 (K): Muddy Small Northerners, Yi Dynasty party faction.

Ta-lien 大連 (C): p.n., Dairen.

talsu 達率 (K): m.t., The commander of five hundred troops in a Paekche city.

T'ang 唐 (C): Chinese dynasty (618-906 A.D.).

Tanghyŏn 堂峴 (K): gold mine, Kangwŏn Province.

Tasan 茶山 (K): p., pen name of Chŏng Yakyong.

Terauchi Masatake 寺内正毅 (J): p.

T'ieh-ling 鐵嶺 (C): p.n., Manchuria.

Tientsin (T'ien-chin) 天津 (C): p.n.

to 道 (K): province.

To Sŏn 道詵 (K): p.

tobang 都房 (K): general chamber, a military command headquarters.

Tŏkchong 德宗 (K): p., Koryŏ king.

Tokugawa 德川 (J): p., Tokugawa Shogunate (1603-1867).

tong 洞 (K): hamlet.

Tonga ilbo 東亞日報 (K): a newspaper.

Tongbuk Kangil Yŏn'gun 東北抗日聯軍 (K): Northeast Anti-Japanese United Army.

Tonggye 東界 (K): Eastern March.

Tongguk t'onggam 東國通鑑 (K): l.w., *Complete Mirror of the Eastern Country* (Korea).

Tongguk yŏji sŭngnam 東國輿地勝覽 (K): l.w., *Survey of the Eastern Country* (Korea) *Geography*.

Tonghak 東學 (K): Eastern Learning.

Tongin 東人 (K): Easterners, Yi Dynasty party faction.

Tongmunsŏn 東文選 (K): l.w., *Anthology of Korean Literature*.

Tongmyong 東盟 (K): religious observance of the Koguryŏ people in the worship of the heavens.

to'pyŏng'ŭisasa 都評議使司 (K): supreme council of state Yi Dynasty, later called *ŭijongbu*.

Tōyō Takushoku Kaisha 東洋拓殖會社 (J): Oriental Development Company.

Toyotomi Hideyoshi 豐臣秀吉 (J): p.,

Tsu Ch'eng-hsün 祖承訓 (C): p.

Tsuboi Kumezō 坪井九馬三 (J): p.

Tsuda Sōkichi 津田左右吉 (J): p.

Tsuji Zennosuke 辻善之助 (J): p.

Tsushima 對馬 (J): p.n., islands.

Tuman River 豆滿 (K): p.n.

T'ung-chia River 佟佳 (C): p.n., Manchuria.

T'ung-chih 同治 (C): Ch'ing reign name.

Tung-i-ch'uan 東夷傳 (C): l.w., *Eastern Barbarian Section* in the *Wei-chih* (q.v.).

T'ung-kou 通溝 (C): p.n., Manchuria.

U 禑 (K): Koryŏ king. See Sinu.

Uchida Ryōhei 内田良平 (J): p.

Ugaki Issei 宇垣一成 (J): p.

ŭibyŏng 義兵 (K): "righteous troops," militia.

ŭigun 義軍 (K): "righteous army," guerrilla forces raised in the Chinese tradition to resist invaders.

ŭijongbu 議政府 (K): supreme council of state. See *to'pyŏng'ŭisasa*.

Ŭijong 毅宗 (K): Koryŏ king.

Ŭiju 義州 (K): p.n., North P'yŏngan Province.

Ŭisang 義湘 (K): p.

Ukida Hideie 宇喜多秀家 (J): p.

Ulchin 蔚珍 (K): p.n., Kangwŏn Province.

Ullung Island 鬱陵 (K): p.n.

Ulsan 蔚山 (K): p.n., South Kyŏngsang Province.

Ungch'ŏn 熊川 (K): p.n., present-day Kongju, South Chŏlla Province.

Ungjin 熊津 (K): p.n., Paekche capital, South Ch'ungch'ŏng Province, modern Kongju.

Unmun 雲門 (K): p.n., North Kyŏngsang Province.

Unsan 雲山 (K): p.n., North P'yŏngan Province.

Ŭnsan 殷山 (K): gold mine, North P'yŏngan Province.

Unyŏ 雲揚 (J): a Japanese warship.

ŭpcha 邑借 (K): title of lesser chiefs of Han tribes in the Three Kingdoms period.

Wada Ichirō 和田一郎 (J): p.

Wakō 倭寇 (J): Japanese marauders.

Wan Island 莞 (K): p.n. See Ch'ŏnghae-jin.

Wang 王 (K), (C): king, also a Chinese and Korean family name. Royal house of Koryŏ.

Wang Kŏn 王建 (K): name of Koryŏ founder, posthumous title, T'aejo.

Wang Mang 王莽 (C): Chinese emperor of Hsin (q.v.).

Wang-hsien-ch'eng 王險城 (C): the chief city of Wei-shih Chao-hsien-kuo. Present-day P'yŏngyang.

Wansan 完山 (K): p.n., present-day Chŏnju, North Chŏlla Province.

Wei 魏 (C): Chinese dynasty (220-265 A.D.); Northern Wei (Toba) (386-535 A.D.); Eastern Wei (Toba) (534-51 A.D.); Western Wei (Toba) (535-557 A.D.).

Wei-chih 魏志 (C): History of the State of Wei (q.v.).

Weihaiwei 威海衛 (C): p.n.

Wei-man 衞滿 (C): p. Also Wiman (K).

Wei-shih Chao-hsien-kuo 衞氏朝鮮國 (C): also Wisi Chosŏn-guk (K): the state founded in Korea by Wei-man.

Wen 文 (C): first emperor of the Sui Dynasty.

Wihwa Island 威化 (K): p.n.

Wiman 衞滿 (K): see Wei-man (C).

Wisi Chosŏn-guk (K): see Wei-shih Chao-hsien-kuo (C).

Wŏlsang Pavilion 月上 (K):

Wŏndang 原黨 (K): *Wŏn* Party, Yi Dynasty party faction.

Wŏnhyo 元曉 (K): p.

Wŏnjong 元宗 (K): Koryŏ king, also, the name of a Silla bandit chieftain.

Wŏnju 原州 (K): p.n., Kangwŏn Province.

Wŏnsan 元山 (K): p.n., South Hamgyŏng Province.

Wŏnsŏng 元聖 (K): Silla king.

Wu 吳 (C): Chinese dynasty of the Three Kingdoms period (222-280 A.D.).

Wu 武 (C): Chinese emperor of the Han Dynasty, also known as Han Wu-ti 漢武帝.

Wu Ch'iu-chien 毋丘儉 (C): p., Wei general.

Wu-liang-ha 兀良哈 (C): p.n., modern Chien-tao, Manchuria.

Yaksa 藥師 (K): Buddhist king of medicine.

Yamato 大和 (J): early Japanese state.

Yanai Wataru 箭内亘 (J): p.

Yang 煬 (C): second emperor of the Sui Dynasty.

yangban 兩班 (K): civil and military officials, collectively the Yi Dynasty aristocracy.

Yanggil 梁吉 (K): p.

Yanggwang 楊廣 (K): province of Koryŏ and early Yi Korea.

Yangju 楊州 (K): p.n., present-day Seoul.

yangmin 良民 (K): the good people, hence the free. Those who could enter public office and the military. This included the peasantry.

Ye 濊 (K): a Korean tribe that occupied the region of modern Kangwŏn Province in the period of the Three Kingdoms.

Yegun Namnyŏ 薉君南閭 (K): p.

Yejong 睿宗 (K): Koryŏ king.

Yen 燕 (C): Chinese state of the Warring Kingdoms period. Also a state established in Manchuria by the Hsien-pi in the fourth century A.D.

Yenching 燕京 (C): Mongol capital, modern Peking.

Yi 李 (K): family name; Yi Dynasty ruled Chosŏn (1392-1910).

Yi Chagyŏm 李資謙 (K): p.

Yi Chayŏn 李子淵 (K): p.

Yi Ch'ŏk 李坧 (K): Yi king, Sunjong.

Yi Haŭng 李昰應 (K): known as Taewŏn-gun.

Yi Illo 李仁老 (K) p.

Yi Inim 李仁任 (K): p.

Yi Kibaek 李基白 (K): p.

Yi Kwal 李适 (K): p.

Yi Kyubo 李奎報 (K): p.

Yi Pŏmsŏk 李範奭 (K): p.

Yi Pyŏngdo 李丙燾 (K): p.

Yi Sŏnggye 李成桂 (K): p., founder of Yi Dynasty. Posthumous title, T'aejo (q.v.).

Yi Sŭngman 李承晚 (K): p.,known as Syngman Rhee.

Yi Sunsin 李舜臣 (K): p.

Yi T'aewang 李太王 (K): Yi king also known as Kojong, and the Kwang-mu Emperor.

Yi Ŭibang 李義方 (K): p.

Yi Ŭimin 李義旼 (K): p.

Yi Wanyong 李完用 (K): p.

Yi Yonggu 李容九 (K): p.

Yin 殷 (C): Chinese dynasty also called Shang (c. 1600-1028 B.C.).

yin-yang 陰陽 (C): dualism in nature; yang the male, light, hot, positive elements and yin the female, dark, cold, negative elements.

yŏmno 檐魯 (K): fortified towns from which the Paekche royal clan ruled the Paekche territory.

Yŏmp'o 鹽浦 (K): p.n., present-day Ulsan, South Kyŏngsang Province.

Yŏndŭnghoe 燃燈會 (K): Korean festival.

Yongbi ŏch'ŏn'ga 龍飛御天歌 (K): l.w., Songs of Dragons Flying to Heaven.

Yŏnggil 永吉 (K): province of early Yi Korea, later called Hamgyŏng.

Yŏnghŭng (sa) 永興寺 (K): Yŏnghŭng (Buddhist) Temple.

Yŏngjo 英祖 (K): Yi king.

Yŏngmyo (sa) 靈廟寺 (K): Yŏngmyo (Buddhist) Temple.

Yŏnsan-gun 燕山君 (K): Yi king.

Yoshida Tōgo 吉田東伍 (J): p.

Yŏsu 麗水 (K): p.n., South Chŏlla Province.

Yu Chagwang 柳子光 (K): p.

Yu Sŏngnyong 柳成龍 (K): p.

Yüan 元 (C): Mongol dynasty in China (1271-1368).

Yüan Shih-k'ai 袁世凱 (C): p.n.

Yukpuk 肉北 (K): Flesh Northerners, Yi Dynasty party faction.

yugŭijŏn 六矣廛 (K): six markets.

Yun Ch'iho 尹致昊 (K): p.

Yun Im 尹任 (K): p.

Yun Kwan 尹瓘 (K): p.

Yun Wŏnhyŏng 尹元衡 (K): p.

Yunsŏ 尹西 (K): Yun Westerners, Yi Dynasty party faction.

yususgwan 留守官 (K): c.t., special resident officer.

zaibatsu 財閥 (J): cartel.

Index